Mental Health in Central and Eastern Europe

Improving Care and Reducing Stigma
— Important Cases for Global Study

World Scientific Series in Global Health Economics and Public Policy

ISSN: 2010-2089

Series Editor-in-Chief: Peter Berman *(The University of British Columbia, Canada & Harvard University, USA)*

The World Scientific Series in Global Health Economics and Public Policy, under the leadership of Professor Peter Berman, a renowned healthcare economist, public policy specialist and researcher in this field, seeks to fill this gap. It strives to publish high-quality scientific works, including monographs, edited volumes, references, handbooks, etc., which address subjects of primary scientific importance on the global scale, as related to international economic policies in healthcare, social capital and healthcare economics in different global markets, etc. The titles in this series appeal to researchers, graduate students, policy makers, practitioners and commercial businesses, dealing with healthcare economics worldwide.

Published:

Vol. 7   *Mental Health in Central and Eastern Europe: Improving Care and Reducing Stigma — Important Cases for Global Study*
edited by Richard M Scheffler, Martha Shumway and Răzvan M Chereches

Vol. 6   *Health Care Policy in East Asia: A World Scientific Reference*
edited by Teh-wei Hu

Vol. 5   *Global Health Economics: Shaping Health Policy in Low- and Middle-Income Countries*
edited by Paul Revill, Marc Suhrcke, Rodrigo Moreno-Serra and Mark Sculpher

Vol. 4   *Economics of Tobacco Control in China: From Policy Research to Practice*
edited by Teh-wei Hu

Vol. 3   *World Scientific Handbook of Global Health Economics and Public Policy*
edited by Richard M Scheffler

Vol. 2   *The Economics of Social Capital and Health: A Conceptual and Empirical Roadmap*
edited by Sherman Folland and Lorenzo Rocco

Vol. 1   *Accountability and Responsibility in Health Care: Issues in Addressing an Emerging Global Challenge*
edited by Bruce Rosen, Avi Israeli and Stephen Shortell

More information on this series can also be found at
https://www.worldscientific.com/series/wssghepp

(Continued at end of book)

World Scientific Series in Global Health Economics and Public Policy – Vol. 7

Mental Health in Central and Eastern Europe

Improving Care and Reducing Stigma
— Important Cases for Global Study

Edited by

Richard M. Scheffler
University of California, Berkeley, USA

Martha Shumway
University of California, San Francisco, USA

Răzvan M. Chereches
Babeş-Bolyai University, Romania

World Scientific

NEW JERSEY • LONDON • SINGAPORE • BEIJING • SHANGHAI • HONG KONG • TAIPEI • CHENNAI • TOKYO

Published by

World Scientific Publishing Co. Pte. Ltd.
5 Toh Tuck Link, Singapore 596224
USA office: 27 Warren Street, Suite 401-402, Hackensack, NJ 07601
UK office: 57 Shelton Street, Covent Garden, London WC2H 9HE

Library of Congress Cataloging-in-Publication Data
Names: Scheffler, Richard M., editor. | Shumway, Martha, editor. | Chereches, Răzvan M., editor.
Title: Mental health in Central and Eastern Europe : improving care and reducing stigma -- important cases for global study / Richard M Scheffler (University of California, Berkeley, USA), Martha Shumway (University of California, San Francisco, USA) and Răzvan M Chereches (Babeş-Bolyai University, Romania) Other titles: World Scientific series in global healthcare economics and public policy. 2010-2089
Description: New Jersey : World Scientific, 2019. | Series: World Scientific series in global health economics and public policy
Identifiers: LCCN 2019020008 | ISBN 9789811205637 (hc : alk. paper)
Subjects: | MESH: Mental Health Services | Mental Health | Europe, Eastern
Classification: LCC RA790.7.E9 | NLM WM 30 GA3 | DDC 362.2094--dc23
LC record available at https://lccn.loc.gov/2019020008

British Library Cataloguing-in-Publication Data
A catalogue record for this book is available from the British Library.

Copyright © 2020 by World Scientific Publishing Co. Pte. Ltd.

All rights reserved. This book, or parts thereof, may not be reproduced in any form or by any means, electronic or mechanical, including photocopying, recording or any information storage and retrieval system now known or to be invented, without written permission from the publisher.

For photocopying of material in this volume, please pay a copying fee through the Copyright Clearance Center, Inc., 222 Rosewood Drive, Danvers, MA 01923, USA. In this case permission to photocopy is not required from the publisher.

For any available supplementary material, please visit
https://www.worldscientific.com/worldscibooks/10.1142/11424#t=suppl

Desk Editors: Dr. Sree Meenakshi Sajani/Jiang Yulin

Typeset by Stallion Press
Email: enquiries@stallionpress.com

About the Editors

Richard M. Scheffler is a Distinguished Professor Emeritus of Health Economics and Public Policy at the School of Public Health and the Goldman School of Public Policy at the University of California, Berkeley, and holds the emeritus chair in healthcare markets and consumer welfare. In 2003, Scheffler served as the elected president of the International Health Economics Association. He has been a visiting professor at a number of universities, including the London School of Economics and Charles University in Prague, and at the Departments of Economics at the University of Pompeu Fabra in Barcelona and Carlos III University of Madrid, Spain. Dr. Scheffler has been a visiting scholar at the World Bank, the Rockefeller Foundation in Bellagio, and the Institute of Medicine at the National Academy of Sciences. He has been a consultant for the World Bank, WHO, and the Organisation for Economic Co-operation and Development. Scheffler has been a Fulbright Scholar at Pontificia Universidad Católica de Chile in Santiago and at Charles University. He was awarded the Chair of Excellence Award at the Carlos III University of Madrid in 2013. In 2015, Dr. Scheffler was awarded the Gold Medal at the Charles University for his long-standing and continued support of international scientific and educational collaboration. In 2016, he was awarded the Astor Visiting Lectureship at Oxford University. He earned his PhD in economics with honors from New York University.

Martha Shumway is Professor in the Department of Psychiatry at the University of California, San Francisco and is on the faculty of the department's Clinical Psychology and Clinical Services Research Training Programs. Dr. Shumway holds a doctorate in Quantitative Psychology from the University of California, Berkeley. She has worked in mental health services research for over 30 years, studying services for persons with severe mental illness and other underserved populations, with a focus on measurement and methodology. She recently completed service as Associate Statistical Editor for the *Journal of Traumatic Stress*. Her current work focuses on trauma and post-traumatic stress disorder and on disparities in acute psychiatric care and psychiatric and medical emergency services.

Răzvan M. Chereches, MD, PhD, founded the Center for Health Policy and Public Health (CHPPH) at Babeş-Bolyai University, Cluj-Napoca, Romania in 2005. He currently serves as the Executive Director of CHPPH, managing a continuously growing team. In addition to his work with CHPPH, Dr. Chereches teaches courses on Public Health Policy and Health Communication and is a member of the Faculty of Political, Administrative and Communication Sciences at Babeş-Bolyai University and has taught in the Department of Occupational and Environmental Health at the University of Iowa. In addition, each year he mentors numerous interns and students from abroad.

About the Authors

Ivana Anđelković studied Psychology at the University of Belgrade and holds a degree equivalent to Master of Science. Her interests include mental health reform and the rights of individuals with psychological disorders. Anđelković has volunteered for the biggest psychiatric hospital in Belgrade (Laza Lazarevic) and with the Association of Psychiatric Patients, Duša. As an NIH Fogarty trainee, she took part in research on factors influencing patients' access to psychiatric services, and has presented her work at several international conferences. Anđelković is currently working as Senior Child Protection Officer for the NGO Indigo and works in the Presevo Refugee Camp in Serbia, where her main duty is monitoring the conditions and well-being of refugee children.

Larisa Boderscova, MD, PhD, holds an MD from Chisinau State Medical University in Moldova as a General Practitioner with a specialization in Public Health, a PhD in Public Health, and also a Master's Degree in advocacy, social policy, and public mental health. From 2002 to 2007, Dr. Boderscova was directly involved in implementation of several projects at the governmental level as a staff of the Moldovan National Center on Health Management, namely the Stability Pact Project in Mental Health for South-Eastern Europe as National Coordinator and Country

Project Manager (2003–2007). In 2003, she became a consultant on Mental Health of the World Health Organization. Throughout her professional career, she has supported national and international civil society organizations in promotion of equal rights and opportunities for individuals with mental health problems, HIV, and other vulnerable groups, and has conducted trainings in mental health, maternal health, and adolescent health, among other topics. In 2008, Dr. Boderscova became a UNICEF staff for the early childhood development program, and has been a part of the WHO Europe team, placed in the Republic of Moldova country office, since 2009.

Jana Chihai, MD, PhD, is a psychiatrist, psychotherapist, and an Associate Professor in the Department of Psychiatry, Narcology, and Medical Psychology at the State University of Medicine and Pharmacy *Nicolae Testemitanu* in Chisinau, Moldova. She is also a Senior Mental Health Advisor at the Trimbos Institute Moldova. She received her medical degree from the Medical State University in Chisinau, Moldova in 1995 and received her specialization in Psychiatry in 1996. She also holds a PhD in Public Mental Health. After working in the psychiatric hospital and residential institution in Balti for 6 years, Dr. Chihai organized the first community mental health center in her city. She has been actively involved in mental health reform for over 10 years, working with the NGO SOMATO since 1999 and serving as the Moldovan National Coordinator and Country Project Manager for the Stability Pact in Mental Health for Children and Adolescents from 2009 to 2010. Dr. Chihai's research focus is on community-based mental health services.

Ariel Como, PhD, MD, is an Associate Professor of Psychiatry at the Tirana Medical University and is currently the Clinical Head of the Psychiatry Division at the Department of Neuroscience, Tirana University Hospital Center ("Mother Tereza"). Since November 2014, he has been the Deputy Dean for Continuing Medical Education at the Faculty of Medicine, Tirana Medical University. Dr. Como is a member of the Directors' Council of Postgraduate Schools in Neurosciences, member of the Albanian National Steering Committee on Reforming the Mental Health Sector, and a member of the working group on developing inter-sectorial strategy on Child and Adolescent Mental Health. Since 2010, Dr. Como has been the National Coordinator at the South East European Autism Network and Scientific Director of the Tirana Regional Center on Autism. He has served as a consultant to the Albanian Rehabilitation Center on Trauma and Torture, the International Organization for Migration, and other non-governmental organizations. Dr. Como received his MD in 1994 and completed his post-graduate residency in Psychiatry in 1999 at the Tirana Faculty of Medicine, with a specialization course in Child Neuropsychiatry at the University of Pavia, Italy, and a doctoral degree on "Trans-generational Transmission of Trauma" at Tirana University.

Grayson Dimick is the former Program Manager for the Nicholas C. Petris Center on Health Care Markets and Consumer Welfare at the University of California, Berkeley and a current J.D. candidate at the Georgetown University Law Center. At the Petris Center, she assisted the center's NIH Fogarty project, as well as other research on mental health and health economics. Her interest in mental health was developed by her work at Greenacre Homes and School in Sebastopol, California, a non-profit which provides residential treatment, educational and vocational training, and mental health services to boys and young men in the foster care system. Most recently, she served as a consultant to the organization, helping them navigate through changes in California legislation on mental health and foster care. Her research interests lie at the intersection of health policy and politics, particularly on issues related to access to care, women's health, mental health, and social services programs. Dimick graduated *magna cum laude* from University of California, Berkeley with a BA in Political Science and History and a minor in Public Policy.

Karolína Dobiášová, PhD, is an Assistant Professor at the Department of Public and Social Policy, Faculty of Social Sciences, Charles University in Prague. She also gives lectures on public health and health promotion at the 1st Faculty of Medicine, Charles University. She has published articles on health policy related to migrants, ethnic minorities, and other vulnerable groups; long-term care policy; and social services. Dr. Dobiášová has been a coinvestigator of several national and international projects on health policy. She has also carried out several commissioned research and policy analyses for domestic organizations in the Czech Republic, including the Ministry of the Interior, the Ministry of Health, and the Ministry of Labor and Social Affairs.

Ermelinda Durmishi is an Adviser at the Albanian Ministry of Education, Sports, and Youth and a Lecturer at the Faculty of Education, "Aleksander Moisiu" University in Durrës, Albania. She graduated with a degree in Political Science and has pursued master's studies in International Relations, Public Law, and National and Euro-Atlantic Security. Durmishi has continued her doctoral studies in Sociology and Social Sciences, with the research thesis "The Role of the State in Contemporary Society: The Welfare State at the Beginning of the 21st Century in Europe," with a case study of Albania's welfare state from 2000 to 2012. Durmishi has participated in national and international conferences, and publications as the coauthor of 2 books and multiple papers.

Ivan Duškov graduated from Charles University in Prague, Faculty of Social Sciences, with a degree in Public and Social Policy studies. He is now a PhD candidate in the same field, specializing in strategic governance and strategic management. Duškov was the director of the Section of Strategies and Policies at The Prague Institute of Planning and Development, where the "Strategic Plan of the City of Prague through 2030" was completed and approved by the Prague City Assembly in November 2016. Duškov proactively cooperates with the Centre for Social and Economic Strategies (Charles University) and headed the Strategic Project Office at the Ministry of Health. He is a coauthor of the *Strategy of Mental Health Care Reform* and of other *Ministry of Health Strategic Documents*. He chairs the Board of the National Institute of Mental Health and currently serves as director of the Institute for Language and Preparatory Studies, Charles University.

Jonila Gabrani is an Assistant Researcher and Assistant Lecturer at the University of Medicine, Faculty of Medicine, Tirana, Albania. Her primary interests are health management, the health workforce, and the performance of health services. She has been actively involved in health issues at the European Health Management Association (EHMA) where she serves as an EHMA Young Advisory Committee (YAC) member, a forum for early career professionals in health management research, practice, and Cooperation in Science and Technology (COST). Garbani served in various leadership roles including a year-long term as a Deputy Economic Director at the National Agency of Drugs and Medical Devices and Advisor at the Ministry of Health and as a 2015 Lead Albania Fellow, awarded by the Albanian-American Development Foundation as part of the White House Fellows Program which aims to become a unique and prestigious contributor to the development of future leadership in Albania. Currently, Garbani is pursuing her PhD studies at University of Basel, Faculty of Medicine and the Swiss Tropical and Public Health Institute.

Georgi Hranov holds a doctorate in medical science on neuro-psychiatric disorders and holds master's degrees in psychiatry, human medicine, and communal health and health care management. He works as a psychiatrist and psychotherapist at the University Hospital of Active Treatment in Neurology and Psychiatry, "St Naum," in Sofia, Bulgaria and in private practice. Hranov is also a Senior Assistant Professor at the Medical University in Sofia, Bulgaria. He currently is the president of Scientific Society of Neuropsychopharmacology and Neurosciences in Bulgaria, and is a consultant and lecturer for pharmaceutical companies as well as the associate editor of the *Journal of Psychiatry*. Hranov is involved in international research and clinical trials with primary interests in anxiety and mood disorders, cognitive behavioral therapy (CBT), and public health.

Cornelia Iacubovschi earned a Master's Degree in Psychology from Alecu Russo Balti State University in Balti, Republic of Moldova. She is currently a UNDP National Consultant on capacity building for national stakeholders in the implementation of the UN Convention on the Rights of Persons with Disabilities, working for the Ministry of Labor, Social Protection, and Family on the implementation of a national deinstitutionalization action plan for adults with intellectual disabilities. Iacubovschi is an advocate and volunteer coordinator at the NGO SOMATO and is a psychologist at the Community Mental Health Center.

Olga Kalašić Vidović holds a Master's degree in Institutions, Development, and Globalization from University College London in the United Kingdom and is currently a PhD candidate in Economics at Singidunum University, Serbia. Her research interests include pension system, public health care, poverty reduction, and social security policies and reforms. Currently, she is working as a Tender Manager at NIRAS International Consulting, a leading company in development consulting and managing projects in the field of governance, gender, human rights, and social security. Kalašić Vidović specializes in international economics and social welfare in global context, with analytical and advisory experience in the framework of political economy. She has also worked as a Research Associate at Faculty of Economics, Finance, and Administration Institute in Belgrade, and has been an economic and financial expert for several projects in Serbia. Kalašić Vidović is a recipient of the Open Society Institute scholarship and is a coauthor of several published papers.

Aleksandra Milićević Kalašić, PhD, MD, MSc, is a specialist in neuropsychiatry and holds a doctorate in medical science on neuropsychiatric disorders in the elderly and a master's degree in neuropsychology. She is the founder of the Department of Mental Health and Pain Treatment at the Institute of Gerontology, Palliative Care, and Home Treatment in Serbia, where she still works, improving systematical approaches for the elderly, disabled, functionally dependent people with psychiatric and neurologic disorders. She has been an Associate Professor in the Department of Social Work at Singidunum University in Serbia since 2013, and a forensic expert since 1996. She was a Professor at the Specialized Medical School in Belgrade during the period 2011–2014 and a recipient of the Fogarty fellowship from 2012–2015 at the University of California, Berkeley. Dr. Milićević-Kalašić worked as a National Counterpart for WHO Mental Health programs from 2003 to 2011. She has presented and published more than 100 articles in Serbia and abroad, and is an active member of the International Psychogeriatric Association (IPA) from 1991. She was also an associate editor of IPA bulletin (1997–2012) and a member of the panel of International Psychology Journal (2007–2013).

She has been the cochair of the OAP section of WPA since 2013. Dr. Milićević-Kalašić is involved in humanitarian work as a volunteer and a lecturer.

Raluca Sfetcu, PhD, is an Associate Professor at the Faculty of Psychology, USH Bucharest. Dr. Sfetcu's main area of interest is mental health systems, with primary focus on identifying ways of supporting the development of balanced services in low resource contexts, as well as analyzing systems' financing and the direct and indirect impact of resource allocation on systems' performance. Previously, Dr. Sfetcu had been involved as WP leader in several EC-funded international research projects in the area of health services research (e.g. REFINEMENT, CEPHOS-LINK) and is currently coordinating the research component of the all funded success project.

Maria Stoyanova, PhD, holds a master's degree in medicine and a doctorate in psychiatry. She works as a psychiatrist at the Acute Psychiatry Department at the "Professor N. Shipkovenski" Mental Health Center in Sofia, Bulgaria. Her research interests are focused on bipolar disorder, mild neurological signs, and impulsivity. Dr. Stoyanova is currently on the executive board of the Scientific Society of Neuropsychopharmacology and Neurosciences in Bulgaria and is a member of the European Academy of Neurology (EAN) Scientific Panel on Neuroepidemiology. She is also a neurologist and has defended a doctoral thesis focused on Parkinson's disease in Hannover, Germany.

Eva Tušková is a PhD student in Public and Social Policy at the Faculty of Social Sciences at the Charles University in Prague. Her doctoral thesis deals with barriers and opportunities in the health promotion policy domain in the Czech Republic. She also works as a junior researcher at the Department of Social Psychiatry at the National Institute of Mental Health in Klecany, Czech Republic, where she investigates the level of stigmatization of people with mental illness in the Czech Republic and effective anti-stigma interventions and provides support for a nation-wide anti-stigma campaign.

Marius Ungureanu, MD, is the coordinator of the Health Policy and Management Department within the Cluj School of Public Health, Babeș-Bolyai University, Cluj-Napoca, Romania. Dr. Ungureanu is actively engaged in research and teaching in the field of healthcare management and policy. His research interests are health services delivery, hospital administration, healthcare workforce, quality management, health reform, and health systems financing and reform.

About the Contributing Editors

Neal Adams, MD, MPH, is currently the Medical Director for Behavioral Health at MedZed, an innovative primary care telemedicine enterprise. In addition, he is a consultant to a number of policy and service delivery organizations working to improve the delivery of specialty mental health services. Dr. Adams has also been a practicing psychiatrist for over 35 years and continues to provide care in outpatient, inpatient, and forensic settings. He is a Distinguished Fellow of the American Psychiatric Association. He has served as the Director of Special Projects at the California Institute for Mental Health, Medical Director of the California Department of Mental Health, and President of the American College of Mental Health Administration. His book, *Treatment Planning for Person Centered Care: Shared Decision Making for Whole Health* (2013), has gained international attention.

Joan R. Bloom, PhD, is a Professor of Health Policy and Management and Chair of the Division of Health Policy and Management, School of Public Health at the University of California, Berkeley. Her areas of research are in mental health services research, interventions to improve psychosocial functioning in persons with chronic illness (including mental illness), and evaluation of natural mental health experiments. For her research in these areas, in 2006 she received the Bernard P. Fox Memorial Award for her contributions to research by the International Psycho-Oncology Association. For the past 13 years, Professor Bloom has been studying the outcomes and impacts of a major change in the financial reimbursement within the public mental health care system in the state of Colorado. In the initial NIMH funded research, "Capitating Medicaid Mental Health Services in Colorado," (Bloom, Hu, Scheffler, and Snowden) she assessed the cost and utilization of services as well as the importance of organizational structure of the community mental health care centers in adopting managed care practices following capitation. In a follow-up award by NIMH (Bloom, Hu, Wallace), they continued to follow the effects of capitation for 5 years following the implementation of capitation. This study capitalized on a natural experiment to assess both a non-profit and for-profit versions of capitation with fee for service. The major findings were published in 3 articles, one on cost and utilization, on outcomes, and on cost-effectiveness in Health Services Research; 5-year effects are being published in *Psychiatric Service*. These studies resulted in over 15 publications. She has also completed a smaller project focused on the California Public Mental Health System that focuses on the effect of required cultural competency programs on utilization of mental health services by Latinos. She is currently working on the effects of patient-centered care on the utilization of mental health services and on how to measure this concept. She is also interested in the organizational character of community mental health centers successful in implemented evidenced mental health practices and has published in this area in the *International Journal of Mental Health Economics and Policy*. As the coleader, with Professor Richard Scheffler, of the American Health Care seminar for post-doctoral scholars in Robert Wood Johnson Policy Program, Professor Bloom has invited Fogarty scholars into the seminar and has added new sessions on mental health and mental health systems for their benefit.

Howard H. Goldman, MD, PhD, is Professor of Psychiatry in the School of Medicine at the University of Maryland. Dr. Goldman received his MD from Harvard University and PhD in social policy research from Brandeis University. He is a mental health services and policy researcher, who is the author of 325 publications in the professional literature. Dr. Goldman was the editor of *Psychiatric Services* from 2004 to 2016. He served as the Senior Scientific Editor of the *Surgeon General's Report on Mental Health* for which he was awarded the Surgeon General's Medallion. In 1996, he was elected to the National Academy of Social Insurance, and in 2002, he was elected to the Institute of Medicine.

Steve Hinshaw, PhD, is a Professor of Psychology at UC Berkeley, where he was Department Chair from 2004 to 2011, and Professor and Vice Chair for Psychology in the Department of Psychiatry at UC San Francisco. He received his BA from Harvard (*summa cum laude*), and his doctorate in clinical psychology from UCLA. His work focuses on developmental psychopathology and mental illness stigma; he has received over 20 million USD in NIH funding. Hinshaw has authored over 310 articles and chapters plus 14 books, including *The Mark of Shame: Stigma of Mental Illness and an Agenda for Change* (2007), *The Triple Bind: Saving our Teenage Girls from Today's Pressures* (2009), and *Another Kind of Madness: A Journey Through the Stigma and Hope of Mental Illness* (2017). He edited *Psychological Bulletin*, the most cited journal in psychology, from 2009 to 2014, and is a fellow of the Association for Psychological Science, the American Psychological Association, and the American Association for the Advancement of Science (AAAS). He received the Distinguished Scientist Award from the Society for a Science of Clinical Psychology (2015) and the James McKeen Cattell Award (2016) from the Association for Psychological Science (2016), as well as UC Berkeley's Distinguished Teaching Award. His 24-lecture series for the Teaching Company, *Origins of the Human Mind*, was released in 2010.

Teh-Wei Hu, PhD, is a Professor Emeritus of health economics at the University of California, Berkeley. Hu's areas of expertise are the application of econometrics to heath care services research, mental health economics, and the economics of tobacco control. Hu is the author of more than 200 publications. His work on tobacco control economics has appeared in the *Journal of Health Economics*, *Health Economics*, the *American Journal of Public Health*, *Tobacco Control*, the *Journal of Public Finance*, the *National Tax Journal*, and other publications. He is the editor of the book *Tobacco Control Policy Analysis in China: Economics and Health*. Hu is also the director of PHI's Center for International Tobacco Control. He has worked at the World Bank and has been a professor of economics at Pennsylvania State University and a Fulbright visiting professor at Nankai.

Martin Potůček, PhD, is a Professor of Public and Social Policy at the Faculty of Social Sciences, Charles University in Prague, and also the guarantor of Master's and doctoral programs of Public and Social Policy. His research focuses on processes of policy formation and implementation in the Czech Republic, on the regulatory functions of the market, government and civic sector, on the European context and global dimension of policy-making, and on the problems of Czech public administration and pension reforms. As an author/coauthor and editor/coeditor, Potůček has published 86 scientific books and 7 textbooks, 90 journal articles, and about 120 research papers and policy project reports. He has been awarded the Sri Chinmoy International Honour "Lifting Up the World with a Oneness-Heart" (2003) and the NISPAcee Alena Brunovska Award (2004) for teaching excellence in public administration. He served as the Chairman of the Expert Committee on Pension Reform to the Czech Government (2013–2017) and has been an adviser to the Czech Ministers of Labour and Social Affairs (1998–2006) and to Czech Prime Ministers (2002–2004, 2014–2017).

Tea V. Rukavina, MD, PhD, is an Assistant Professor in the Department of Medical Sociology and Health Economics at the Andrija Stampar School of Public Health, School of Medicine, University of Zagreb. In 2011, she obtained her PhD in Public Health, and in 2012 received her specialization in psychiatry. Dr. Vukusic Rukavina was a project leader of the project "Picture of Mental Illness in Croatian, Czech and Slovak Print Media" (2009–2011), which was a part of the Finance and Mental Health Services Training in Czech Republic/Central Europe coordinated by the Global Center for Health & Economic Policy Research, University of

California, Berkeley. Dr. Vukusic Rukavina was the assistant coordinator from 2002–2008 of the "County Public Health Capacity Building Project—Health Counties" program that won Management Training Excellence Award in 2006 and Global Health Program of Distinction Award in 2013 from Sustainable Management Development Program, Division of Public Health Systems and Workforce Development, Centers for Disease Control and Prevention. She was the coordinator of the Motovun Summer School of Health Promotion (2002–2010) and is currently the director of the Media and Health Course, an annual course that promotes cooperation among journalists and health professionals. Her main areas of interest are management of mental health services, mental health promotion, media and health, social marketing campaigns, and qualitative methodology.

Neal Wallace, PhD, is a professor of Health System Management and Policy in the OHSU-PSU School of Public Health and the program director for the Masters in Public Health: Health Management and Policy. Dr. Wallace is a health economist whose research focuses on quantitative evaluation of large scale health and mental health policy and system interventions using state of the art observational research designs. Recent projects include evaluations of Oregon's Coordinated Care Organizations (CCOs), the Patient-Centered Primary Care Home (PCPCH) program, implementation costs of integrating primary and behavioral health care in Colorado, Oregon's 2007 behavioral health parity law, and Medicaid funding changes in California intended to reduce disparities in children's receipt of public mental health services. Dr. Wallace holds a doctorate in health services and policy analysis from the School of Public Health at the University of California Berkeley. Prior to his academic career, Dr. Wallace worked in the mental health departments of the states of Washington and New York developing and implementing innovative public mental health interventions and systems of care.

Contents

About the Editors v
About the Authors vii
About the Contributing Editors xv
List of Figures xxv
List of Tables xxvii

Chapter 1 Introduction to Central and Eastern Europe 1
    Grayson Dimick and Richard M. Scheffler
    1.1 History of Central and Eastern Europe 3
    1.2 Central and Eastern Europe Today 8
    References 12

Chapter 2 An Overview of Mental Health in Albania 15
    Ermelinda Durmishi, Jonila Gabrani, and Ariel Como
    2.1 Mental Health Status of the Albanian Population 15
    2.2 History of Mental Health Care in Albania 18
    2.3 Mental Health Policies and Legislation in Albania 21
    2.4 Organizational Structure of the Mental Health System in Albania 25

2.5	Access to the Mental Health Care System in Albania	27
2.6	Mental Health Workforce in Albania	31
2.7	Financing the Mental Health Care System in Albania	35
2.8	Quality of Care, Outcomes, and Evaluation	37
2.9	Advocacy, Stigma, and Self-Help	40
2.10	Looking Forward: Challenges and Priorities in the Albanian Mental Health System	44
References		44

Chapter 3 An Overview of Mental Health in Bulgaria   47
Georgi Hranov and Maria Stoyanova

3.1	Mental Health Status of the Bulgarian Population	47
3.2	History of Mental Health Care in Bulgaria	47
3.3	Mental Health Policies and Legislation in Bulgaria	53
3.4	Organizational Structure of the Mental Health System in Bulgaria	56
3.5	Access to the Mental Health Care System in Bulgaria	63
3.6	Mental Health Workforce in Bulgaria	63
3.7	Financing the Mental Health Care in Bulgaria	65
3.8	Advocacy, Stigma, and Self-Help	69
3.9	Looking Forward: Challenges and Priorities in the Bulgarian Mental Health Care System	73
References		74

Chapter 4 An Overview of Mental Health in the Czech Republic   77
Eva Tušková, Karolína Dobiášová, and Ivan Duškov

4.1	Mental Health Status of the Czech Population	77
4.2	History of Mental Health Care in the Czech Republic	84
4.3	Mental Health Policies and Legislation in the Czech Republic	88
4.4	Organizational Structure of the Mental Health System in the Czech Republic	90
4.5	Access to the Mental Health Care System in the Czech Republic	94
4.6	Mental Health Workforce in the Czech Republic	95

	4.7	Financing the Mental Health Care System in the Czech Republic	101
	4.8	Quality of Care, Outcomes, and Evaluation	103
	4.9	Advocacy, Stigma, and Self-Help	104
	4.10	Looking Forward: Challenges and Priorities in the Czech Republic's Mental Health Care System	106
	References		111

Chapter 5 An Overview of Mental Health in Moldova 117
Cornelia Iacubovschi, Jana Chihai, and Larisa Boderscova

	5.1	Mental Health Status of the Moldovan Population	117
	5.2	History of Mental Health Care in the Republic of Moldova	120
	5.3	Mental Health Policies and Legislation in Moldova	122
	5.4	Organizational Structure of the Mental Health System in Moldova	123
	5.5	Access to the Mental Health Care System in Moldova	126
	5.6	Mental Health Workforce in Moldova	127
	5.7	Financing the Mental Health Care System in Moldova	129
	5.8	Quality of Care, Outcomes, and Evaluation	130
	5.9	Advocacy, Stigma, and Self-Help	133
	5.10	Looking Forward: Challenges and Priorities in the Moldovan Mental Health Care System	136
	References		138

Chapter 6 An Overview of Mental Health in Romania 141
Raluca Sfetcu and Marius Ungureanu

	6.1	Mental Health Status of the Romanian Population	141
	6.2	History of Mental Health Care in Romania	145
	6.3	Mental Health Policies and Legislation in Romania	148
	6.4	Organizational Structure of the Mental Health System in Romania	154
	6.5	Access to the Mental Health Care System in Romania	159

6.6	Mental Health Workforce in Romania	160
6.7	Financing the Mental Health Care System in Romania	162
6.8	Quality of Care, Outcomes, and Evaluation	164
6.9	Advocacy, Stigma, and Self-Help	167
6.10	Looking Forward: Challenges and Priorities in the Romanian Mental Health System	170
	References	172

Chapter 7 An Overview of Mental Health in Serbia — 175
Aleksandra Milićević Kalašić, Olga Kalašić Vidović, and Ivana Anđelković

7.1	Mental Health Status of the Serbian Population	175
7.2	History of Mental Health Care in Serbia	178
7.3	Mental Health Policies and Legislation in Serbia	180
7.4	Organizational Structure of the Mental Health System in Serbia	185
7.5	Access to the Mental Health Care System in Serbia	190
7.6	Mental Health Workforce in Serbia	194
7.7	Financing the Mental Health Care System in Serbia	196
7.8	Quality of Care, Outcomes, and Evaluation	201
7.9	Advocacy, Stigma, and Self-Help	206
7.10	Looking Forward: Challenges and Priorities in the Serbian Mental Health Care System	212
	References	214

Chapter 8 The Way Forward: Improving Mental Health Systems in Central and Eastern Europe — 221
Richard M. Scheffler, Grayson Dimick, and Ivan Duškov

8.1	Overview of the Challenges Facing Central and Eastern European Countries	222
8.2	Looking Forward: Seven Areas of Action for Continued Progress	224
8.3	Conclusion	231
	References	231

Index — 233

List of Figures

Figure 2.1:	Causes of hospitalization per 100,000 inhabitants, 1993–2011.	17
Figure 2.2:	Causes of death by group diseases (per 100,000 inhabitants).	17
Figure 2.3:	Crude all ages and age-specific suicide rates (per 100,000 inhabitants).	18
Figure 2.4:	Age-standardized suicide rates (per 100,000 inhabitants).	18
Figure 2.5:	Number of post-graduates in psychiatry in Albania, 1986–2018.	33
Figure 2.6	Total expenditure on health as a percentage of gross domestic product.	36
Figure 2.7:	Public and private health expenditures as percentages of current health expenditures.	37
Figure 2.8:	Out-of-pocket expenditure as a percentage of private expenditure on health.	37
Figure 2.9:	External resources for health as a percentage of total expenditure on health.	38
Figure 2.10:	Health expenditures in Albania in Albanian Lek.	38

List of Figures

Figure 4.1:	Number of mental health first contacts in a year in outpatient settings according to ICD-10, 2000–2013.	80
Figure 4.2:	International comparison of the number of suicides per 100,000 inhabitants.	82
Figure 4.3:	Trend in number of discharged from and deceased in inpatient psychiatric facilities.	92
Figure 4.4:	Number of outpatient first contacts during 1-year period for mental disorders (F00-F99) by gender.	93
Figure 4.5:	The proportion of mental health expenditures on overall health expenditures, proportion of health expenditures on GDP, and total health expenditure (PPP) per capita—comparison of EU15 countries + USA and new EU members.	102
Figure 6.1:	Lifetime prevalence of any mental health disorder by age group.	142
Figure 6.2:	CNSMLA budget in Euros by year, 2013–2018.	153
Figure 6.3:	Psychiatric bed rates per 100,000 inhabitants, 2006–2017.	157
Figure 6.4:	Number of beds in psychiatric hospitals.	157
Figure 7.1:	Pathway of the patient through the mental health system.	190
Figure 7.2:	Profile of the insured population in Serbia.	191
Figure 7.3:	Satisfaction with state-owned and private health service according to the regions.	193
Figure 7.4:	Flow of funds in the Serbian health system.	198
Figure 7.5:	Total healthcare expenditures (in RSD) in the period 2003–2011.	199
Figure 7.6:	Healthcare expenditures (in RSD) for mental disabilities (F00-F99) in the period 2003–2011.	200
Figure 7.7:	Percentage of population which didn't satisfy their health needs due to prolonged wait times for care (Bjornberg, 2014).	203

List of Tables

Table 2.1:	Estimated DALYs ('000) by cause and age, 2012.	16
Table 2.2:	Policy, legislation, and regulation on mental health in Albania.	22
Table 2.3:	Availability of mental health facilities.	30
Table 2.4:	Mental health workforce in Albania, rate per 100,000 population.	32
Table 3.1:	Patients receiving treatment in inpatient mental health settings by diagnosis.	48
Table 4.1:	Professional staff in long-term psychiatric hospitals.	96
Table 4.2:	Professional staff in outpatient psychiatric facilities.	97
Table 5.1:	Mental health and behavior morbidity in Moldova, 2009–2013.	120
Table 5.2:	Suicides by minors in Moldova, by years.	120
Table 6.1:	International statistical classification of diseases and related health problems.	144
Table 6.2:	Mental health service use data in inpatient, outpatient, and primary care settings for 2013.	144
Table 7.1:	Number of diagnosed mental and behavioral disorders (ICD-10; F00-F99).	177

Table 7.2:	Patients treated in hospitals for mental and behavioral disorders by gender in the period 2009–2013.	177
Table 7.3:	Population signs of depression (PHQ-8), Serbia 2013.	177
Table 7.4:	Suicide rate per 100,000 residents.	178
Table 7.5:	Distribution of beds in mental health care.	187
Table 7.6:	Human resources–health professionals working in the MHS in Serbia, rate per 100,000.	194
Table 7.7:	Medical doctors by specialization in MHS in Serbia and their gender distribution.	195
Table 7.8:	Mental health care expenditures as percentage of total health care expenditures in the period 2003–2011.	200
Table 7.9:	Breakdown of expenditures in mental health care as percentage of the overall mental health care expenditures in the period 2003–2011.	201
Table 7.10:	Indicators of quality in specialist consultations services (Bjornberg, 2014).	202

CHAPTER 1

Introduction to Central and Eastern Europe

Grayson Dimick[*] and Richard M. Scheffler[†]

[*]*Georgetown University Law Center, Washington, USA*
[†]*School of Public Health and Goldman School of Public Policy, University of California, Berkeley, USA*

Since the fall of the Soviet Union in 1991, the countries of Central and Eastern Europe (CEE) have undergone profound political, economic, and social changes. As the countries' communist regimes ended, governments were faced with developing new health systems, financing these systems, and instituting reforms in the countries' existing mental health care systems. Yet, over a quarter of a century since the dissolution of the Soviet Union, the transformation of mental health systems remains incomplete. As a World Health Organization (WHO) assessment writes, "Are mental health services moving forward in Central and Eastern Europe? Of course, a quick answer is either *yes* or *no*. Or, rather, the correct answer is both *yes* and *no*" (Saraceno and Saxena, 2005).

Map of Central and Eastern Europe

In order to understand the progress, current status, and challenges of mental health care reform in CEE, this book explores the case studies of Serbia, Bulgaria, Romania, Albania, Czech Republic, and Moldova. Throughout the book, the human experiences of mental health care reform in CEE are brought to life through interviews with patients, mental health care professionals, and policymakers. These unique interviews were conducted in person by researchers on the ground in Albania, Bulgaria, Romania, Serbia and Moldova. The book itself is a product of unique, on the ground perspective, as it is the product of a 16-year National Institute of

Health/Fogarty International Center[1] grant to provide advanced, multidisciplinary research training to outstanding pre- and post-doctoral economists, psychiatrists, sociologists, clinicians, and mental health professionals from Central, Southeastern, and Eastern Europe. Participants in the program were trained in the latest research methods and issues regarding the economic and social factors that influence or drive the delivery of mental health care services. Under the mentorship of the program faculty, the authors of each chapter are graduates of this program, and provide on the ground insight to the status on mental health care in their respective countries.

Before the book delves into mental health care reform in CEE, the following chapter provides an overview of the region's history and current status, setting the political and economic context for the following case studies.

1.1 History of Central and Eastern Europe

1.1.1 *Cold War era*

While CEE was firmly entrenched behind the iron curtain during the Cold War, the region's countries did not share uniform experiences. While the Moldovan Socialist Soviet Republic was a member of the USSR, the People's Republic of Bulgaria, the Socialist Republic of Romania, and Czechoslovakia (containing the modern-day Czech Republic) were independent states who were members of the communist-aligned Warsaw Pact.[2] Although the Socialist Republic of Albania emulated Stalinist ideals, it withdrew from the Warsaw Pact in the 1960s and maintained chilled relations with the USSR until the Soviet Union's collapse.[3] Similarly, although communist, the Socialist Federal Republic (SFR) of Yugoslavia (containing modern-day Serbia) broke away from the Soviet Union in

---

[1] To learn more about the NIH Fogarty program, see www.fic.nih.gov.
[2] North Atlantic Treaty Organization. What was the Warsaw Pact? NATO. N.d. Retrieved from https://www.nato.int/cps/us/natohq/declassified_138294.htm.
[3] *Ibid.*

1948 and was non-aligned and maintained relationships with both the Western and Eastern blocs for the duration of the Cold War.[4]

The dominant health care model among CEE countries was the Semashko system. Named after Nikolai Semashko, the first people's commissar of public health of Russia after the Bolshevik Revolution, health care systems under the Semashko model were centrally planned and managed (Rechel et al., 2014, p. 92). Health care was of low priority compared to national defense, seen as a cost rather than an investment. This attitude toward health care led to Semashko systems prioritizing secondary care and inpatient treatment over primary care and outpatient treatment, and focused on curing acute conditions, rather than chronic conditions. There was little to no integration between primary and secondary care. Central planning further hindered health systems, as governments' fixed allocations of budgets, personnel, and hospital beds failed to meet the reality of local needs and resulted in suboptimal allocation of resources. The Semashko structure was particularly detrimental for the treatment of mental illness. Individuals with mental illness were treated nearly exclusively in large psychiatric hospitals, many institutionalized for decades. Mental health policy decisions were made from ideological rather than scientific considerations; and neither staff, patients, families, nor citizens were regarded as stakeholders in mental health care and policy.

Stigma surrounding mental illness was incredibly strong during the Cold War. The Russian Association of Psychiatrists supported the view that mental illness was characteristic of capitalist societies and would eventually disappear under the communist regime (Rechel et al., 2014, p. 159). Those who did not meet the expectations of socialist standards—including the disabled and the mentally ill—were seen as shameful to society, encouraging families to forget about their "faulty" relatives and abandon them to the institution (Rechel et al., 2014, p. 160). Those who were institutionalized had no legal rights or protections, and were frequently subject to inhumane treatment. While some institutions took a more humane approach, their treatment was often counterproductive and

---

[4]Office of the Historian, Bureau of Public Affairs—United States Department of State. The Breakup of Yugoslavia, 1990–1992. US State Department. N.d. Retrieved from https://history.state.gov/milestones/1989-1992/breakup-yugoslavia.

failed to meet international standards or treatment protocols (Rechel *et al.*, 2014). For the small number of individuals who were released from psychiatric hospitals, there was no possibility of reintegration into society. Mental health diagnosis excluded individuals from skilled or professional work, and Soviet psychiatry did not recognize the concept of "recovery" in mental health (Rechel *et al.*, 2014).

Another key factor that marked psychiatry during the Soviet era was the abuse of psychiatry for political purposes, beginning in the mid-1950s (Tomov *et al.*, 2007, p. 402). Studies estimate that one-third of all political prisoners in the Soviet Union in the 1970s and 1980s were locked up in psychiatric hospitals, with hospitalization presenting a means to repress and silence dissidents (Van Voren, 2009). Inside psychiatric hospitals, antipsychotic drugs were given as a punishment to those who expressed anticommunist views (Rechel *et al.*, 2014, p. 161). Government-supported psychiatrists propagated teachings that those holding political beliefs that differed from the state-sanctioned ideology were experiencing schizophrenia (Tomov *et al.*, 2007, p. 406). These practices led the World Psychiatric Association to condemn the Soviet Union in 1977, resulting in the USSR's withdrawal in 1983 (Rechel *et al.*, 2014, p. 161).

1.1.2 *The fall of communism*

After the collapse of communism 25 years ago, the countries diverged, pursuing their own paths to development, including diverging approaches to reorganization and modernization of their mental health care systems (Krupchanka and Winkler, 2016).

The fall of communism in the late 1980s and early 1990s plunged much of eastern and central Europe into chaos. The collapse of communism resulted in profound system-wide changes, as the transition to a market-based economy produced economic crises throughout the region. Eager to modernize and solve the problems of the socialist economy, the countries of CEE embraced rapid-change "shock therapy" in transitioning to a market-based economy. This approach had serious social consequences: countries faced the rapid erosion of safety nets, hyper-inflation, deepening of poverty and unemployment, devaluation of wages, and a loss of human and social capital. A rejection of state intervention in the economy produced sharp declines in industrial and agricultural output, with the region's countries seeing large decreases in industrial and agricultural output as well as GDP. As a result, the 1990s were considered a "lost decade" for economic growth in many countries of the region, as nations struggled to match their pre-1989 GDP levels.

Further fueling the chaos was widespread political and civil unrest, plunging many countries into war throughout the 1990s. Most consequential for the region was the drawn-out process of breakup and war of the SFR of Yugoslavia. The SFR Yugoslavia was a union of 8 federated entities, roughly divided along ethnic lines, which included 6 republics—Bosnia and Herzegovina, Croatia, Macedonia, Montenegro, Serbia and Slovenia—and 2 autonomous provinces within Serbia, Vojvodina and Kosovo. Throughout the 1980s, tensions began to build in Yugoslavia following the death of the country's president-for-life Josip Broz Tito, whose rule had unified the country.[5] With the decline of communism, Yugoslavia's position as a strategic buffer between Western and Eastern Europe was mitigated, and the country began to experience economic crises.[6] These conditions set the stage for rising calls for independence in some of the republics, as well as rising ethnic tensions, particularly between the ethnic Serbian majority and the ethnic Albanian and Croat minorities.

The slow disintegration of Yugoslavia began in 1991 when Croatia and Slovenia declared independence.[7] Serbian president (and *de facto* leader of Yugoslavia) Slobodan Milošević strongly opposed the dissolution of Yugoslavia, as it would divide Serbs across state-lines. This opposition cumulated in armed conflict between the Serb-controlled People's Army of Yugoslavia, local Serbs, and Croat forces and resulted in North Atlantic Treaty Organization (NATO) and UN intervention. Ultimately, the war and partition in Croatia and Bosnia and Herzegovina between 1991 and 1995 resulted in hundreds of thousands of people being wounded, dead, or missing, and the displacement of more than 2 million others (WHO Regional Office for Europe, 2008). The human toll was accompanied by billions of dollars in damage to infrastructure and industry (WHO Regional Office for Europe, 2008). Eventually, Bosnia and

---

[5] Office of the Historian, Bureau of Public Affairs—United States Department of State.
[6] *Ibid.*
[7] *Ibid.*

Herzegovina, Croatia, Slovenia, and Macedonia gained independence, leaving just Serbia and Montenegro to compose the remaining Federal Republic of Yugoslavia.[8] In the latter half of the 1990s, the simmering ethnic tensions in Kosovo escalated into full-scale war between the army of the Federal Republic of Yugoslavia (composed of Christian Serbs) and Muslim Kosovo Albanian forces. The conflict culminated in the 1999 NATO bombings of Yugoslavia following allegations of ethnic cleansing and systemic war crimes by the Yugoslav forces.[9]

The Kosovo War heavily impacted the CEE region as a whole, with over 2 million refugees fleeing Yugoslavia (Kamm, 1999). These humanitarian consequences further exacerbated the domestic unrest Albania, Bulgaria, and Romania were experiencing in the late 1990s over their own political and economic crises. Only Czechoslovakia escaped the turbulence of the 1990s relatively unscathed, experiencing a peaceful breakup (known as the "velvet divorce") between the Czech Republic and Slovakia in 1993.

The crises of the 1990s had a severe impact on population health and the health systems of CEE. The economic crises experienced during the transition to market-based economies decimated the budget for health care, impacting both the ability of the state to provide basic care as well as to implement health policy reforms. Physical destruction also weakened the capacity of health systems. For example, the 1991–1992 civil unrest in Albania destroyed almost one quarter of health centers in cities and two thirds of health posts in small villages, while the resurgence of violence in 1997 and 1998 saw the widespread looting of drugs and equipment and some destruction of district hospitals, health centers, and public health departments.[10] The turbulence of the 1990s also had a marked impact on the health of CEE's population. Poverty and the deterioration of social safety nets, as well as the violence from civil war and political unrest, all impacted health outcomes, impacting life expectancy and increasing rates of alcohol consumption.

---

[8] *Ibid.*

[9] Kosovo Conflict. Encyclopedia Britannica. 16 November 2018. Retrieved from https://www.britannica.com/event/Kosovo-conflict.

[10] Albania Reform. World Health Organization. N.d. Retrieved from https://www.who.int/mental_health/policy/en/Albania%20reform.pdf.

1.2. Central and Eastern Europe Today

Emerging from the turbulence of the 1990s, the countries of CEE have focused on economic growth, democratic engagement, and deepening ties with Western institutions and nations. Of particularly important consequence to the development of CEE has been the relationship between the European Union (EU) and the region's nations. Ties with the EU have brought crucial financial assistance. The process of working toward EU membership has prompted CEE nations to undertake significant economic, political, and legal reforms in order to bring their legislation and policies—including mental health legislation and policies—into line with international standards.

While all nations have experienced development and reform in the 21st century, progress is uneven across CEE. This section describes the current economic and political status of the case-study nations.

Membership in Regional and International Institutions

	European Union	Organization for Economic Cooperation and Development	North Atlantic Treaty Organization
Albania			Member (2009)
Bulgaria	Member (2007)		Member (2004)
Czech Republic	Member (2004)	Member (1995)	Member (1999)
Moldova			
Romania	Member (2007)		Member (2004)
Serbia			

Sources: Authors' analysis of data from "EU member countries in brief" (https://europa.eu/european-union/about-eu/countries/member-countries_en), "List of OECD Member countries—Ratification of the Convention on the OECD" (https://www.oecd.org/about/membersandpartners/list-oecd-member-countries.htm), and "Member Countries" (https://www.nato.int/cps/em/natohq/topics_52044.htm).

1.2.1 *Albania*

Albania's transition from communism has been challenging, facing issues of high unemployment, widespread corruption, dilapidated infrastructure, powerful organized crime networks, and combative political opponents (CIA, 2018a). The nation has experienced economic growth, but remains one of the poorest countries in Europe (CIA, 2018a). Albania has developed ties with the West, joining NATO in 2009 and seeking EU membership (CIA, 2018a). Albania became an official candidate for accession to the EU in June 2014; however, the EU has twice rejected full membership (European Union, 2016a). The EU has questioned the credibility of Albania's democratic values, and has warned government leaders that judicial reforms must take place before accession negotiations could begin. The EU has also raised concerns over Albania's human rights, organized crime, corruption, and public administration (Hoxhaj, 2018).

1.2.2 *Bulgaria*

Bulgaria has seen slow but steady growth and development. From 2000 to 2008, Bulgaria experienced robust growth, but was deeply impacted by the global financial crisis due to its dependency on foreign demand for its exports (CIA, 2018b). Although growth has resumed, its per capita income remains one of the lowest among EU members and austerity measures have severely impacted the country (CIA, 2018b). Bulgaria joined the EU in 2007, despite deep EU concerns regarding the nation's corruption and weak judiciary. A key effort for the EU is to reduce Bulgaria's heavy reliance on energy imports from Russia, which the EU sees as a vulnerability (CIA, 2018b). Bulgaria has also been a member of NATO since 2004 (CIA, 2018b).

1.2.3 *Czech Republic*

The Czech Republic is the most highly developed of the CEE countries. It was the first nation in the region to stabilize its economy following the collapse of the Soviet Union, and has enjoyed relative peace and stability (CIA, 2018c). Today, the Czech Republic has an upper middle income economy that boasts one of the highest GDP growth rates and lowest unemployment levels in the EU (CIA, 2018c). Due to its economic success and political stability, Czechia was the first of the selected countries to join the EU during the 2004 enlargement as well as the first to join NATO in 1999, and is the only member of the Organisation for Economic Co-operation and Development (OECD) among the case study nations (CIA, 2018c).

1.2.4 *Moldova*

Moldova's progress since the 1990s has been slow and the country is the least-developed of the selected CEE nations. Communist Party rule did not cease until 2009, with politics subsequently being dominated by a 3 party pro-EU coalition (CIA, 2018d). Moldova remains Europe's poorest economy, depending primarily on agriculture (CIA, 2018d). Its economy has been weakened by corruption and scandal; most recently, the 2015 embezzlement of 750 million USD from the Moldovan Central Bank that sparked widespread outrage (Higgins, 2015).

Moldova is actively pursuing EU membership. The country signed and ratified an Association Agreement with the EU in 2014, which fully entered into force in July 2016 after ratification by all EU member states (European Union, 2016b). This agreement moves the country closer to EU membership by deepening economic and political ties between the two parties and committing Moldova to economic, judicial, and financial reforms to meet the EU standards for policies and legislation (European Union, 2016b). However, the country's poverty has continued to present an obstacle to membership, as does the Transnistrian dispute, concerning a self-proclaimed breakaway republic backed by the Russian government (Popescu and Litra, 2012). While not a NATO member, Moldova has been a member of NATO's Partnership for Peace (PfP) program since 1994,[11] which seeks to build trust between NATO and non-member Euro–Atlantic states, particularly former Soviet states.[12]

1.2.5 *Romania*

Romania enjoyed relatively high economic development throughout the 2000s. The country's development faced major setbacks during the global financial crisis in the late 2000s, and the country has depended on IMF assistance to stabilize its economy (CIA, 2018e). Romania's macroeconomic gains have only recently started to spur creation of a middle

---

[11] North Atlantic Treaty Organization. Relations with the Republic of Moldova. NATO. 12 October 2018. Retrieved from https://www.nato.int/cps/en/natohq/topics_49727.htm.

[12] North Atlantic Treaty Organization. Partnership for Peace programme. 7 June 2017. Retrieved from https://www.nato.int/cps/en/natohq/topics_50349.htm.

class and to address the country's widespread poverty (CIA, 2018e). Corruption is rampant in Romania, and has been a large concern of the EU. The country has grown close to the West, joining NATO in 2004 and the EU in 2007 (CIA, 2018e). However, as of late 2018, fears have grown that Romania is backtracking on the democratic reforms it made since joining the EU, particularly in terms of anti-corruption (Gurzu, 2018).[13]

1.2.6 *Serbia*

In 2003, the Federal Republic of Yugoslavia became Serbia and Montenegro. In 2006, Montenegro seceded from the union (CIA, 2018f). Tensions between Serbia and the province of Kosovo have continued since the 1990s. In 2008, Kosovo declared its independence from Serbia, an action Serbia refuses to recognize (CIA, 2018f). International recognition of Kosovo independence is mixed, with 115 UN member states as of 2018 recognizing it as an independent nation (Bytyci, 2018). However, 23 of 28 EU member nations recognize Kosovo (Bytyci, 2018), and the EU has worked to create talks between Serbia and Kosovo, leading to the normalization of relations in 2013 with the Brussels Agreement (CIA, 2018f).

Economically, Serbia remains in transition—the economy is largely dominated by market forces, but the state sector remains significant in certain areas. International sanctions, civil war, and the destruction from NATO bombing in the 1990s significantly delayed Serbian growth—in 2015, Serbia's GDP was 27.5% lower than where it was in 1989 (CIA, 2018f). Today, high unemployment and stagnant household incomes are ongoing political and economic problems for the country (CIA, 2018f). Serbia is pursuing EU membership, and has been a candidate for membership since 2012; formal accession negotiations were opened in 2014 and the country is currently targeting membership in 2025 (CIA, 2018f). The nation has been a member of NATO PfP program since 2006 (CIA, 2018f).

---

[13] European Commission. *Report from the Commission to the European Parliament and the Council: On Progress in Romania Under the Cooperation and Verification Mechanism*. Strasbourg: European Commission, 13 November 2018. Retrieved from https://ec.europa.eu/info/sites/info/files/progress-report-romania-2018-com-2018-com-2018-851_en.pdf.

References

Bytyci, F. (2018) Serbia must accept Kosovo independence to join EU: German foreign minister. Reuters. 14 February 2018. Retrieved from https://www.reuters.com/article/us-kosovo-germany-serbia/serbia-must-accept-kosovo-independence-to-join-eu-german-foreign-minister-idUSKCN1FY329.

Central Intelligence Agency (2018a) Albania. CIA World Factbook. Retrieved from https://www.cia.gov/library/publications/the-world-factbook/geos/print_al.html.

Central Intelligence Agency (2018b) Bulgaria. CIA World Factbook. Retrieved from https://www.cia.gov/library/PUBLICATIONS/the-world-factbook/geos/bu.html.

Central Intelligence Agency (2018c) Czechia. CIA World Factbook. Retrieved from https://www.cia.gov/library/publications/the-world-factbook/geos/ez.html.

Central Intelligence Agency (2018d) Moldova. CIA World Factbook. Retrieved from https://www.cia.gov/library/PUBLICATIONS/the-world-factbook/geos/md.html.

Central Intelligence Agency (2018e) Romania. CIA World Factbook. Retrieved from https://www.cia.gov/library/PUBLICATIONS/the-world-factbook/geos/ro.html.

Central Intelligence Agency (2018f) Serbia. CIA World Factbook. Retrieved from https://www.cia.gov/library/publications/the-world-factbook/geos/ri.html.

European Union (2016a) Albania and the EU. European External Action Service. Retrieved from https://eeas.europa.eu/delegations/albania_en/6953/Albania%20and%20the%20EU.

European Union (2016b) The Republic of Moldova and the EU. European External Action Service. 12 May 2016. Retrieved from https://eeas.europa.eu/delegations/moldova_en/1538/The%20Republic%20of%20Moldova%20and%20the%20EU.

Gurzu, A. (2018) Brussels slams Romania on corruption as EU presidency nears. Politico. 13 November 2018. Retrieved from https://www.politico.eu/article/brussels-slams-romanias-anti-corruption-efforts-as-eu-presidency-nears/.

Higgins, A. (2015) Moldova, Hunting for Missing Millions, Finds Only Ash. The New York Times. Retrieved from https://www.nytimes.com/2015/06/05/world/europe/moldova-bank-theft.html.

Hoxhaj, A. (2018) EU accession talks on the horizon? Assessing Albania's priorities for the next year. London School of Economics—European Politics and Policy Blog. Retrieved from http://blogs.lse.ac.uk/europpblog/2018/08/14/eu-accession-talks-on-the-horizon-assessing-albanias-priorities-for-the-next-year/.

Kamm, H. (1999) Yugoslav Refugee Crisis Europe's Worst Since 40's. The New York Times. 24 July 1999. Retrieved from https://www.nytimes.com/1992/07/24/world/yugoslav-refugee-crisis-europe-s-worst-since-40-s.html.

Krupchanka, D. and Winkler, P. (2016) State of mental healthcare systems in Eastern Europe: Do we really understand what is going on? *BJPsych International* **13** (4), 96–99.

Popescu, N. and Litra, L. (2012) *Transnistria: A Bottom-Up Solution*. (European Council on Foreign Relations, London) Retrieved from https://www.ecfr.eu/page/-/ECFR63_TRANSNISTRIA_BRIEF_AW.pdf.

Rechel, B., Richardson, E. and McKee, M. (eds.) (2014) *Trends in Health Systems in the Former Soviet Countries*. (World Health Organization and European Observatory on Health Systems and Policies, Copenhagen) Retrieved from http://www.euro.who.int/__data/assets/pdf_file/0019/261271/Trends-in-health-systems-in-the-former-Soviet-countries.pdf.

Saraceno, B. and Saxena, S. (2005) Mental health services in Central and Eastern Europe: Current state and continuing concerns. *Epidemiology and Psychiatric Sciences* **14** (1), 44–48.

Tomov, T., Van Voren, R., Keukens, R. and Puras, D. (2007) Mental Health Policy in Former Eastern Bloc Countries. In: Knapp, M. *et al.* (eds.) *Mental Health Policy and Practice across Europe: The Future Direction of Mental Health Care*. (Open University Press/ World Health Organization).

Van Voren, R. (2009) Political abuse of psychiatry—An historical overview. *Schizophrenia Bulletin* **36** (1), 33–35.

WHO Regional Office for Europe (2008) *Approaching Mental Health Care Reform Regionally: The Mental Health Project for South-eastern Europe*. (World Health Organization, Sarajevo) p. 17.

CHAPTER 2

An Overview of Mental Health in Albania

Ermelinda Durmishi[*], Jonila Gabrani[†], and Ariel Como[‡]

[*]*The Faculty of Education, Aleksandër Moisiu University, Durrës, Albania*

[†]*Faculty of Medicine, University of Medicine, Tirana, Albania*

[‡]*Psychiatry Division, Department of Neuroscience, Tirana University Hospital Center, University of Medicine, Tirana, Albania*

2.1 Mental Health Status of the Albanian Population

Although mental health is a public health priority, the system still has gaps—this is especially true in terms of data reporting and health statistics. Based on available national data, mental disorders are ranked as the 10th most common cause for hospitalization at a rate of 180 cases per 100,000 inhabitants. The incidence of mental disorders, as measured by hospitalizations, has increased by about 40% over the past 20 years; in 2011, the rate increased to 180.2 cases.

2.1.1 *Morbidity and mortality*

The metric of Disability Adjusted Life Years (DALYs) can help to provide an estimate of the impact of mental and behavioral disorders by both age and diagnosis. As seen in Table 2.1, those between the age of 30 and

Key Country Statistics

Region: Southeastern Europe
Government system: parliamentary republic
Area: 28,748 square kilometers
Population: 3,038,594
Capital: Tirana
Gender ratio: 0.98 males to females
Ethnic groups:
- Albanian 82.6%
- Greek 0.9%
- Other 1% (including Vlach, Roma, Macedonian, Montenegrin, and Egyptian)
- Unspecified 15.5%

Literacy rate: 97.6%
Population under age 18: 30%
Population above age 65: 11%
Average life expectancy: 75.7 years for males and 81.2 years for females
Suicide rates: 5.93 per 100,000 inhabitants
Economy: upper middle income economy
GDP annual growth rate: 2.8%
GDP per capita: 11,300 USD (PPP)
Unemployment rate: 17.3%
Youth unemployment rate: 30.2%
Average net salary:
Population below poverty line: 14.3%
Health expenditure as percentage of GDP: 5.9% of GDP

Source: CIA World Factbook (2016).

Table 2.1: Estimated DALYs ('000) by cause and age, 2012.

Mental and behavioral disorders	All ages	0–4	5–14	15–29	30–59	60–69	70+
	107.1	0.2	8.5	32.3	52.7	7.7	5.7
1 Unipolar depressive disorders	41.6	0.0	3.7	10.8	20.4	3.7	3.0
2 Bipolar disorder	5.7	—	0.0	1.6	3.6	0.3	0.2
3 Schizophrenia	7.1	—	0.0	1.3	4.7	0.7	0.5
4 Alcohol use disorders	19.3	0.0	0.2	6.4	11.1	1.2	0.5
5 Drug use disorders	6.5	—	0.2	3.6	2.5	0.1	0.1
6 Anxiety disorders	18.1	0.0	1.6	5.8	8.2	1.4	1.0
7 Eating disorders	0.7	—	0.0	0.3	0.3	0.0	0.0
8 Pervasive developmental disorders	3.4	0.2	0.6	1.0	1.3	0.2	0.2
9 Childhood behavioral disorders	2.8	0.0	1.7	1.1	0.0	—	—
10 Idiopathic intellectual disability	1.1	0.0	0.3	0.4	0.4	0.0	0.0
11 Other mental and behavioral disorders	0.8	0.0	0.1	0.1	0.2	0.1	0.2

Source: WHO (2012a).

50 years suffered the greatest impact with 52.7 DALYs per 100,000 inhabitants. In terms of diagnoses, unipolar depressive disorders appear to have the highest impact at 41.6 DALYs per 100,000 inhabitants. Alcohol and substance use disorders are the next highest group followed by anxiety disorders. The lowest rate observed is associated with eating disorders (WHO, 2012a).

Based on national data from the Albanian Ministry of Health (MoH), mental disorders as a cause of death have decreased in Albania from

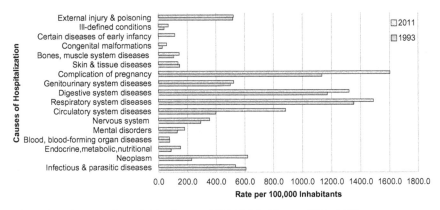

Figure 2.1: Causes of hospitalization per 100,000 inhabitants, 1993–2011.
Source: Albanian Ministry of Health (2011).

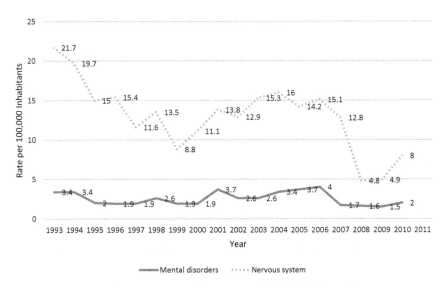

Figure 2.2: Causes of death by group diseases (per 100,000 inhabitants).
Source: MoH (2010).

3.4 cases per year in 1993 to 2 cases per year in 2010 (Figures 2.1 and 2.2) (MoH, 2010). This can be attributed, at least in part, to developments in mental health policy that have led to improved services, an increase in the number of mental health specialists, and better access to early intervention in the treatment of mental health conditions.

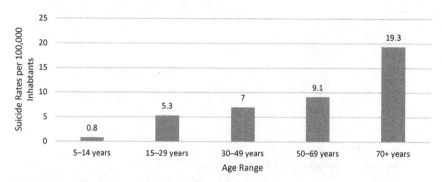

Figure 2.3: Crude all ages and age-specific suicide rates (per 100,000 inhabitants). *Source:* WHO (2012b).

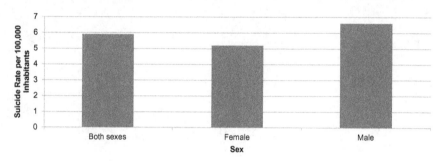

Figure 2.4: Age-standardized suicide rates (per 100,000 inhabitants). *Source:* WHO (2012b).

WHO data from 2012 estimates that the age-adjusted suicide rate in Albania was 5.7 per 100,000 inhabitants; the rate for women was 5.3 and for men 6.2. Significant differences exist amongst various age groups, with the highest number of suicides being seen in the age group over 70 years, which account for 19.3% of all suicides; the lowest rate is the age group 5–14, accounting for 0.8% of all suicides (Figures 2.3 and 2.4) (WHO, 2012b).

2.2 History of Mental Health Care in Albania

2.2.1 *Early and communist-era systems*

Before 1912, most Albanians received medical care in the form of traditional folk medicine in the absence of doctors and a more structured health care system. However, in 1912 Albania proclaimed its independence from the Ottoman Empire, and the creation a national health system was a component of the new government's agenda. Thus, following independence, there was effort to develop an adequate health care system; however, after the fall of the government and the start of World War I, there was effectively no further development of a health care system in Albania. Finally, in 1920, a new government, established by the Lushnja Congress, created the General Department of Health, which functioned until 1944.[1]

One of the most important periods of health care development in Albania was during the reign of King Zogu (1925–1939), who established a public and private health system and built several hospitals. The government organized community health services, performed by local doctors in each municipality, as there were not enough clinics or hospitals to provide adequate care. The treatment of the poor—the majority of the Albanian population at this time was poor and rural—was free, generally performed by municipal doctors.

Following World War II, the communist regime came to power and the Semashko public health system was established. During this time, mental health care in Albania was mostly provided by centralized, biologically oriented, and symptom-focused services (WHO-MoH, 2005). Inpatient services dominated the health system, both in terms of treatment and allocation of resources (Demi and Voko, 2014).

The Semashko system was organized as follows:

- A primary health care system, that included an increased number of community-based primary care centers based on population, as well as clinics in urban and rural areas;
- A tertiary health care system, including general hospitals and psychiatric facilities;
- Pharmacies, in both urban and rural areas;
- Maternal and child consulting services;
- Medical laboratories, radiology centers, and health service structures. (Agron, Elvana, Albana, 2011).

---

[1] MoH WEB-SITE, http://www.shendetesia.gov.al/al/ministria/historiku, Retrieved 1 September 2015.

In 1948, a psychiatric department was founded in Tirana, with 32 beds, increasing to a capacity of 53 beds by 1953. In 1956, the Psychiatric Clinic with 100 beds was established at the Faculty of Medicine in Tirana. In 1978, the Neuro-Psychiatric University Hospital in Tirana had 100 beds for neurology and 100 beds for psychiatry. In 1980, a Department of Child and Adolescent Psychiatry was created in response to the unique mental health treatment needs of youth.[2]

2.2.2 *Modern psychiatric system*

Following the collapse of the communist government, modern psychiatry in Albania has been established over the last 2 decades. Since 1993, there have been efforts to establish a system based upon the respect of human rights and focused on the needs of individuals and their families.[3] These reform efforts were guided by the Balanced Community Mental Health System of Care and focused mainly on the operation of Community Mental Health Centers in Tirana and other cities. Some of the changes included adoption of a new Mental Health Act, as well as increased attention on reducing institutional care, the establishment of forensic psychiatry practice, and the inclusion of non-medical professionals (e.g. psychologists, social workers, occupational therapists, etc.) as part of the mental health workforce, along with providing continuing education for practitioners.

Today, the health care system in Albania is primarily a public system in which the state provides the majority of services, including health promotion and disease prevention as well as diagnosis and treatment, including care for mental disorders. The public health care system is financed by the national budget and administrated by the Ministry of Health, but there is not a separate budget for mental health.[4]

---

[2] QSUT WEB-SITE, http://www.qsut.gov.al/index.php/sherbimet-mjekesore/sherbimi-psikiatrise/, Retrieved 1 September 2015.

[3] QSUT WEB-SITE, http://www.qsut.gov.al/index.php/sherbimet-mjekesore/sherbimi-psikiatrise/, Retrieved 5 September 2015.

[4] MoH WEB-SITE, http://www.shendetesia.gov.al/al/ministria/organizimi-i-sistemit-shendetesor, Retrieved 5 September 2015.

2.3 Mental Health Policies and Legislation in Albania

In Albania, mental health is considered to be a general health issue; accordingly, it is regulated not only by mental health law, but also by general health legislation addressing Health Care, Public Health, Health and Social Compulsory Insurance, and Inclusion and Accessibility of Persons with Disabilities laws, among other categories.

The first Albanian law specific to mental health was Law 8092, adopted in March 1996 (see Table 2.2 for full list of mental health legislation since 1996 in Albania). This legislation defined access to mental health care and protected service users' and family members' rights, along with addressing issues of guardianship for people with mental disease. Removal or restriction of a mentally ill individual's legal right to make autonomous decisions can be proposed by a psychiatric-legal commission. The decision is made by a court in accordance with the provisions of the Albanian Civil Procedure Code. If necessary, the court will appoint a legal guardian. In addition, the law addressed voluntary and involuntary treatment and mechanisms to oversee involuntary admission and treatment practices, as well as issues of law enforcement and other judicial considerations for individuals with mental illness (WHO, 2006). More substantial reform occurred in 2000, when the Ministry of Health established the Steering Committee on Mental Health and drafted the first policy documents on mental health, including the *Strategic Document on the Development of Mental Health in Children and Adolescents Albania*. The *Policy for the Development of Mental Health Services in Albania*[5] was approved in 2003, and in May 2005 the *Action Plan for the Development of Mental Health Services in Albania, 2005–2010* was adopted.

---

[5]The first policy document of *mental health care services* was based on 2 main objectives:
 (a) *Deinstitutionalization by reducing the number of beds in psychiatric inpatient services*;
 (b) *Decentralization of mental health services by developing community-based mental health services.*

Table 2.2: Policy, legislation, and regulation on mental health in Albania.

	Policy and legislation on mental health in Albania	
Legislation	Mental Health	Law No. 8092, dated 21 March 1996 "On Mental Health" Law No. 44/2012 "On Mental Health" Law No. 61/2013 "On certain amendments to Law No. 44/2012 "On Mental Health"
	Dedicated general health	Law No. 10107, dated 30 March 2009 "On health care in the Republic of Albania" Law No. 10138 dated 11 May 2009 "On public health" Law No. 10 383, dated 24 February 2011 "On Health Care compulsory insurance in the Republic of Albania", etc. Law No. 7703, dated 11 May 1993 "On Social Insurance in the Republic of Albania", amended with the Law No. 104/2014, dated on 31 July 2014 Law No. 93/2014 "On inclusion and accessibility of persons with disabilities" Albanian Charter of Patient Rights Law No. 7895, dated 27 January 1995 "Penal Code of Albania Republic" Law No. 7815, dated 20 April 1994 "On Drugs"
Policy	Strategic documents and action plans	Strategic Document on the Development of Mental Health in Children and Adolescents Albania, March 2002 The Policy and the Operational Plan for Mental Health Services Development in Albania, 2003 Action Plan for the Development of Mental Health Services in Albania 2005–2010 The Action Plan Development of Mental Health Services in Albania 2013–2022
	Regulations	Regulation of Mental Health Services, 2013 (reviewed and improved the Regulation of 2007) Standards of Physical Limitation in Mental Health Services Specialized with beds, 2013 Roles, Responsibilities and Basic Competences Mental Health of Professionals, 2013 Manual for Mental Health file use, 2013 Order of the Minister of Health No. 95 dated 16 February 2009 "On basic package of services in primary health care"

Source: MoH (2015).

The focus of this Action Plan included:

- The creation of a Mental Health Department within the Ministry of Health;

- The creation of professionals and infrastructure to support the development of community services in priority areas;
- Deinstitutionalization of long-term inpatients and a shift to community-based services;
- Increased access to care, created by having mental health professionals train family doctors in the diagnosis and treatment of major mental health disorders;
- The promotion of mental health activities thought the development of a national plan for mental health;
- Additional reform of existing mental health legislation (Demi and Voko, 2014).

In 2007, the MoH developed the Regulation of Mental Health Services. This policy document provided rules for the organization and operation of mental health services in the country based on prior mental health laws. The Regulation covers key areas of mental health services in the country, such as organization, human resources, duties and responsibilities, and other issues related to ethics and professional practice, orienting service providers and policymakers toward the demands, functions, and development of mental health services at all levels of health care.[6] In 2009, the MoH introduced mental health services as a package of services for primary health care services MoH, 2009). In 2012, new mental health laws were adopted to better protect the rights of persons with mental disorders consistent with international standards in order to further promote mental health system reform. These new laws helped establish a National Mental Health Committee as an advisor to the Minister of Health and the Ombudsman. There is still a need for additional legislation to address treatment and services for victims of physical violence, psychological trauma, as well as people with mental disorders who have engaged in criminal behavior (*DITA Journal*, 2012).

A new Action Plan for the Development of Mental Health Services, looking forward from 2013–2020, proposed additional mental health regulations to address issues such as deinstitutionalization, a deeper coverage of Albania with services and professionals for mental health;

---

[6] *Regulation of Mental Health Services*, Ministry of Health, April 2013.

A Policymaker's Perspective

Would you say things have changed in the mental health system in the past 25 years?

The mental health system has had positive, radical changes since 1996, the year the first Law on Mental Health was adopted. Mental health services before 2000 were centralized, biologically oriented, and concentrated on symptoms. Developments in the past 15 years have imposed new approaches on mental health through the implementation of strategic key tasks: deinstitutionalization, by reducing the number of psychiatric beds and the establishment/strengthening of mental health community services; and decentralization, through the expansion and enrichment of the existing network of services closer to the community. The establishment of mental health community services (Community Center of Mental Health, supported houses, day centers, etc.) was a significant step of the reform, allowing those with mental health problems to live independently and be integrated into the community. The community approach and delivery of multidisciplinary mental health care is a key element upon which a more integrated system of mental health services should be established.

Positive achievements are also seen in terms of budgetary and financial issues, where the percentage of the budget allocation for mental health within the total health budget has increased progressively. There have also been budget reallocations from hospital services to community services. In terms of human resources, besides the professional improvement of the specialists, new types of mental health specialists have been introduced as part of multidisciplinary teams, improving the quality of care.

Are there upcoming reforms in the mental health system?

We are in constant reform. Although progress has been made in small steps, mental health reform is stable and guided by 2 key objectives: deinstitutionalization and decentralization of mental health services.

What are the main setbacks in implementation of reforms?

Any changes regarding the improvement of policies, regulation, and services has a cost, and due to the world economic crisis, Albania has been experiencing budget restrictions, which creates obstacles in the reform progress. Another obstacle is the lack of psychiatrists, who can't cover all Albanian regions because of their limited number.

defined roles, responsibilities, and basic competencies of mental health professionals; and the creation of a manual for Mental Health records (see Table 2.2).

In summary, over the past 10 years, numerous developments in the Albanian mental health care system have been realized by advancing legislation, policies, and regulations. These achievements include but are not limited to the following:

- Establishment of the Mental Health Department in the Ministry of Health;
- Implementation of the Law on Mental Health and regulatory documents;
- Creation of 8 community mental health centers;
- Establishment of Psychosocial and Mental Health Services in the majority of Regional Health Directorates;
- Establishment of 11 new residential care centers;
- Establishment of a psychiatric inpatient service for children and adolescents at the Clinic of Psychiatry, University Hospital Center in Tirana;
- Inclusion of a separate chapter for "Mental Health" in the basic package of services in primary health care;
- An increased number of human resources and trainings;
- An increase in the mental health budget, from 3.6% of the total health budget in 2006 to 4.1% in 2010;
- Creation of a new system of monitoring and data collection (MoH, 2013a).

2.4 Organizational Structure of the Mental Health System in Albania

The health system in Albania is primarily a public system. Since 1995, health care services are provided by the state and are financed by the Health Insurance Fund and state budget.[7] The National Health Insurance Fund allocates and administers health care contributions and state budget

---

[7] Law 7870 dated 13 October 1994, *On health insurance in the Republic of Albania*, Article 5.

allocations. Between 2003 and 2015, the health insurance budget increased by about 13%: Employee and taxpayer contributions have decreased from 53% of the total budget in 2003 to 33.5% in 2015; meanwhile, the state budget allocations have increased (Ministry of Finance, 2015). The private sector covers mostly pharmaceutical services, dental services, and some clinical specialties which are primarily concentrated in Tirana. In the field of mental health care, there are non-public psychotherapy services available.[8]

The administrative structure of the health sector in Albania is part of the Ministry of Health. The principal institutions/bodies responsible for mental health services include the following:

- **At the National level:** The National Mental Health Committee, an advisory body to the Minister of Health, and the Department of Mental Health and Addictionology within the Ministry of Health;
- **At the Regional level:** Psychosocial and Health Services in Regional Mental Health Departments.

Following the passage of a legislation in 2012, there has been an effort to develop an integrated system of mental health services overseen by the 2013 *Regulation of Mental Health Services* law.[9] The basic organization of the system includes two parts: primary health care services (PHCS) and specialized mental health services.

2.4.1 *Primary health care services*

PHCS staff provide the first level of mental health care intervention as part of their provision of general health care. This aspect of the system involves care based on clinical protocols (MoH, 2009), which includes identification, referral, and follow-up for patients with mental health disorders. Primary care is responsible for management of common mental problems, e.g. depression, anxiety, alcohol and drugs disorders, sleep

---

[8] MoH WEB-SITE, http://www.shendetesia.gov.al/al/ministria/organizimi-i-sistemit-shendetesor.
[9] Law 44/2012, "*On Mental Health*", Article 10, paragraph 2.

problems, chronic tiredness and unexplained somatic complaints, etc.; more serious psychotic disorders are referred for specialized services. PHCS also promotes community education about mental health problems, works with the families of patients, and refers patients to the Community Mental Health Centers.

2.4.2 Specialized mental health services

Specialized care is limited to four geographic areas: Tirana, Elbasan, Shkodra, and Vlora, in total covering about half of the Albanian population. This includes 2 psychiatric hospitals (Elbasan and Vlora), psychiatric wards located within general hospitals (Tirana and Shkodra), 9 community mental health centers (CMHCs), 11 supportive houses, 2 day centers, and the National Center for Child Development and Rehabilitation (MoH, 2013b).

Based on the *Regulation of Mental Health Services*, specialized services include the following:

- Outpatient mental health care, involving specialized ambulatory services and mental health community services such as multidisciplinary teams, day care centers, supported housing, and recreational centers;
- Inpatient mental health services in the 4 inpatient facilities in Albania, in spite of the decline in the number of beds during last 13 years is noteworthy;
- Specialized psychiatric inpatient service for children and adolescents in Tirana.

2.5 Access to the Mental Health Care System in Albania

The model of health insurance scheme in the Republic of Albania is a mixed model (Bismarck and Beveridge) that is based on mandatory and voluntary contributions, as well as on funding from the state budget. The employed population pays health insurance, while state budget funds (which come from general taxation), cover the retired and vulnerable population. The single-payer, Compulsory Health Insurance Fund manages the scheme in accordance with national health care policies.

A Policymaker's Perspective

Would you say things have changed in the mental health system in the past 25 years?
Things have changed for the better. Quality of services has increased, including a much wider range of services and better access due to deinstitutionalization and decentralization processes. New facilities for inpatient care have been constructed and the old ones rehabilitated. More outreach services through community mental health centers are available in main cities. The number of mental health professionals has increased substantially, and specialized child psychiatrists have become available recently. Financial support to the mental health system has increased moderately in the last 25 years but could still improve. Anti-stigma campaigns in media, schools, and other health institutions have also made possible a more open-minded attitude of the general population toward mental illness as well as toward mental health services and professionals. Nevertheless, much work needs to be done in all these areas of mental health.

Could you describe one or more particular events which, in your opinion, is representative for how the mental health system works in your country?
I will describe 1 positive case of reform and 1 more negative case.

Case 1: *Positive*—The CMHC in Korca district started to function in 2007 and offered community mental health services to an important area of the country previously receiving inpatient services from the psychiatric hospital in Elbasan. Previously, the quality of services was very low and many patients from the Korca area were institutionalized for decades in Elbasan. The staff of the CMHC was selected through a competition call from the local Directory of Public Health and the WHO mental health program, which financed the rehabilitation of a public building to be used as a CMHC. Staff were trained intensively by the WHO mental health program. Since then, all evaluations conducted by the MoH, WHO, and other independent bodies identify a sense of ownership for the process of care and treatment of mental health issues among staff. Evaluations also have found a substantial reduction of inpatient treatment in Elbasan for the inhabitants of the Korca CMHC catchment area, anti-stigma campaign

(Continued)

(Continued)
initiatives, and the highest rate of outreach services compared with all other CMHCs in the country.

Case 2: *Negative*—The Psychiatric Hospital in Elbasan is the largest inpatient treatment facility in the country. The hospital has been perceived as a horrible place where all the most severe cases were sent and admission to that hospital in many cases resulted in many years of institutionalization. Unfortunately, this perception is not far from the truth. The physical structure of the hospital, the shortage of staff, the fact that almost half of the residents in that hospital are individuals with learning disabilities created many difficulties in reforming this institution. However, reforms have been initiated: 1 CMHC and 2 supported accommodation facilities were opened in the catchment area of Elbasan, reducing the number of residents in the hospital by 22 individuals. The beds that were freed from these processes were symbolically destroyed to give the message of deinstitutionalization to the whole community. However, this reform gave the hospital management the leading role and all funds for the system went through them. In my opinion, this created a situation of underfunding of community services and "helped" the activation of a larger number of beds than before reform interventions were started. These developments were influenced, according to my opinion, from a clear lack of insight for the need to change among management and staff, which fueled a huge resistance to the reform process.

The inclusion of health services in the compulsory insurance packages of services is based on the following criteria:

- **Medical:** the level at which the service affects the improvement of life quality, avoids the further deterioration of health, and increases life expectancy;
- **Economical:** the report of cost effectiveness of services and availability of financial resources of the Fund;
- **Social:** patient's ability to pay, availability of services, and number of benefiters in relation to the population.

Table 2.3: Availability of mental health facilities.

	Total no. of facilities/beds	Rate per 100,000 population
Mental health outpatient facilities	20	0.63
Day treatment facilities	3	0.09
Psychiatric beds in general hospitals	130	4.10
Community residential facilities	9	0.28
Beds/places in community residential facilities	99	3.12
Mental hospitals	2	0.06
Beds in mental hospitals	250	16.41

Source: WHO (2011).

Insurance programs in Albania must include the following benefits: visits, medical examinations, and treatment in public/private primary health care centers and public/private hospitals, as well as drugs, medical products, and treatments by contracted providers of health services. For example, for primary care, 7 services are included in the services package: emergency care, children's health care, adult health care, women's health and reproductive health, geriatric care, health promotion, and health education.

The availability of mental health facilities per 100,000 is summarized in Table 2.3.

Mental health care services—including outpatient, inpatient, and rehabilitation—are not provided in all areas of Albania; a significant number of people must travel long distances to obtain care. In contrast, the availability of primary health care is much greater. Community-based mental health care services and inpatient care are currently available in only 4 out of 12 districts, translating to about half of the population without mental health services readily available.

The Action Plan 2013–2020 establishes government objectives related to improving access to mental health. These specifically include:

- The creation of 12 district catchment areas including 34 cities;
- Availability of psychiatric beds only in district hospitals;
- Establishment of CHMCs in 20 cities, including day centers, community-based teams and supportive housing;

- Improved distribution of psychiatric inpatient beds in regional hospitals.

2.6 Mental Health Workforce in Albania

It is projected that by 2035 there will be a global shortage of almost 13 million health care workers; today, that figure stands at a shortage of 7.2 million. A recent WHO report argues that these workforce shortages could impact the health of billions of people around the world (WHO, 2013). Albania too is experiencing these shortages, and they are especially acute in the field of mental health.

The health care workforce in Albania is quite young; the average age is less than 45. There are also significant differences based on gender: nurses, midwives, pharmacists, and dentists are predominantly female, while physicians are mostly male. Both males and females are well represented among general practitioners (GPs), although the younger cohort of GPs has a higher proportion of men than women. These patterns were inherited from the communist-era socialist policies (Ryan and Poster, 1989).

According to the WHO statistics (WHO, 2014a), during the period 2006–2013, there were on average 115 physicians and 399 nurses and midwives per 100,000 inhabitants in Albania. This included 50 general practitioners per 100,000, as well as 33 dentists and 43 pharmacists (IPH, 2014). About 40% of all physicians are family practitioners; this number has remained fairly stable except for a small increase over the last 5 years. Obstetricians/gynecologists are the next largest group, making up 6% of the total number of physicians, followed by surgeons and pediatricians. In contrast, there are relatively few specialists, including psychiatrists (WHO and MoH, 2006). The mental health workforce in Albania per 100,000 population is summarized in Table 2.4.

There is a total of 13.5 mental health workers per 100,000 inhabitants; this includes a total of 397 professionals providing inpatient psychiatric care and 108 providing outpatient services (WHO, 2014a). Virtually, all the psychosocial staff and about three-quarters of psychiatrists work in community outpatient facilities, while nurses predominately work in inpatient settings, with 45% in mental hospitals and 33% in community-based

Table 2.4: Mental health workforce in Albania, rate per 100,000 population.

	Health professionals working in the mental health sector (rate per 100,000)
Psychiatrists	1.32
Other medical doctors	0.16
Other mental health workers	3.14
Nurses	6.66
Psychologists	1.00
Social workers	0.78
Occupational therapists	0.44
Total	13.50

Source: WHO (2014a).

psychiatric inpatient units. In addition, the distribution of human resources between urban and rural areas is disproportionate; the availability of psychiatrists and nurses is about one-third higher in or near Tirana than in the rest of the country (WHO–MoH, 2006). Almost all the psychiatrists (90%) worked in government-administered mental health facilities. In terms of staffing in mental health facilities, there was 1 psychiatrist per 10 beds in community-based psychiatric inpatient units, in comparison to 1 psychiatrist per 50 beds in mental hospitals. As for nurses, there was 1 nurse for every 3 beds in community-based psychiatric inpatient units, in comparison to 1 for every 6 beds in mental hospitals.

In Albania, the responsibility for medical education rests with the Ministry of Education, while responsibility for licensing, employing, and planning for the health care workforce lies with the Ministry of Health. Postgraduate education in psychiatry started in 1960 as a curriculum provided by the Faculty of Medicine at the University of Tirana. Education in psychiatry has seen a recent transformation since the mid-1990s in order to meet international standards. From 1975–1992, psychiatric clinics located at the "Mother Tereza" University hospital center prepared psychiatrist specialists with a 1-year academic program. However, in 1994, a new program for postgraduate studies in general psychiatry was established, with training growing from 1–4 years. Today, the University of Medicine offers 2 postgraduate training programs: 1 for specialists in child and adolescent psychiatry and 1 for psychiatrists primarily treating

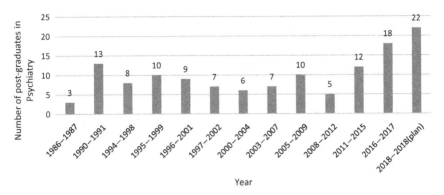

Figure 2.5: Number of post-graduates in psychiatry in Albania, 1986–2018.
Source: Faculty of Medicine (2018).

adults. While the curriculum offers satisfactory training in biological psychiatry, it is difficult to train young residents properly in the psychosocial aspects of practice, as there are few supervisors with sufficient experience and knowledge in this area.[10] An additional limitation is posed by that fact that over the past 29 years, the number of post-graduate trainees in psychiatry has declined (see Figure 2.5). Until 2015, a number of post-graduate health programs was approved at central level by Ministry of Health and Ministry of Education based on prevalence of diseases and priority areas. Beginning in 2015, with the new Law of Higher Education (no. 80/2015), universities have the autonomy to assess and create a number of programs at all levels of education, based on their capacities and needs. As Figure 2.5 shows, in 2016–2017, the first year of implementation of the higher education law, the number of post-graduates in psychiatry increased for the first time, and is projected to continue to increase.

There is limited ongoing education in mental health for professionals. Inservice training and continuing education about the rational use of psychiatric medicines is offered to both psychiatrists and other physicians, as well as training on psychosocial interventions in mental health. These trainings are provided by the University of Medicine, Faculty of Social Sciences, and other public and private institutions and organizations

---

[10] QSUT WEB-SITE, http://www.qsut.gov.al/index.php/sherbimet-mjekesore/sherbimi-psikiatrise/, retrieved 5 September 2015.

A Mental Health Care Provider's Perspective

Interview with Dr. Valentina Asanbella, Psychiatrist, Mental Health Care Center

Would you say things have changed in the last 25 years?
There have been changes in last 25 years. Today, community mental health care centers are closer to patients and offer diversified services; meanwhile, hospital service has improved significantly, and hospitals are more efficient in providing assistance to patients who are going through acute episodes of mental disorders.

Would you say there is a need for any other types of services in the mental health system?
There are different needs, but 1 of the immediate needs has to do with human resources, specifically the development and increase of the number of specialists to accommodate the increased flow and geographic reach that CMHCs cover. There's also a need in terms of infrastructure. There is an immediate need is for transportation vehicles (ambulances, transportation cars) for rapid service delivery. There is a lack of residential day care centers offering psychotherapy, occupational therapy, etc. to support families and patients.

What is the main flaw of the current mental health care system?
There is a lack of functionality in the current mental health care system, which is reflected by the poor implementation of policies. Another problem that is affecting the proper functioning of the system is the lack of funds for the development of infrastructure and human resources.

Do you have any additional comments or insights on the provision of mental health services in your country?
Solutions can be accomplished through a better allocation of the state budget toward mental health, but also with the assistance of foreign donations.

licenced to provide training on health issues. However, there is no ongoing training on child/adolescent mental health issues (WHO, 2006). There is also limited engagement of mental health care professionals in this research field. Based upon a survey of citations in PubMed,[11] only about 2% of Albanian health publications over the past 5 years have focused on mental health. These published articles were mainly epidemiological studies based on community or treatment populations; however, some articles addressed mental health service research, policies, and programs analysis as well as pharmacological studies. In the last 5 years, less than 20% of Albanian mental health professionals were involved in mental health research as an investigator or coinvestigator.

2.7 Financing the Mental Health Care System in Albania

The World Health Organization's 2000 report entitled *Health Systems: Improving Performance* (WHO, 2000) identified financing as 1 of the 4 essential functions of a health system. Financing the health system consists of 4 specific subfunctions including: (1) revenue collection, (2) pooling of funds, (3) purchasing of services, and (4) policies to define and ration benefit—most commonly through patient cost-sharing obligations. In addition, there are 3 dimensions of coverage: breadth, scope, and depth (Gotsadze and Gaál, 2010).

In 2013, Albania spent roughly 6% of its GDP on health care, out of which 48.4% came from government and 51.6% from private funds. Health care expenditures as a percentage of GDP have decreased in the last decade, from 6.5% in 2002 to 5.9% in 2013 (see Figure 2.6) (WHO, 2014b). Albania spends a substantially lower percentage of GDP on health care than other countries with comparable income levels (WB, 2015).

The Albanian government faces ongoing challenges in its effort to enhance revenue and the pooling of health care resources, as well as in its efforts to expand insurance coverage and reduce reliance on payroll taxes. There has been some success: the total health expenditure per capita was 298 USD in 2002 and rose to 539 USD in 2013. However, governmental health expenditure per capita has been always under 50% of total health expenditure, and has dipped as low as 35% (in 2002) (WHO, 2014b).

In Albania, private expenditures on health consist mainly of "out-of-pocket expenditure," whereas "private prepaid insurance plans" are still in

---

[11] www.ncbi.nlm.nih.gov/PubMed, retrieved 1 September 2015.

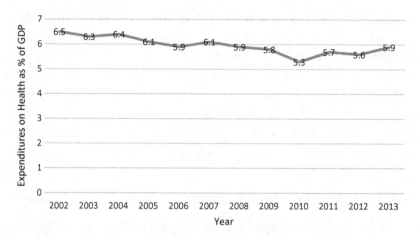

Figure 2.6: Total expenditure on health as a percentage of gross domestic product.
Source: WHO (2014b).

the early stage of development (Figure 2.7).[12] Out-of-pocket expenditures are among the highest in the region, accounting about 62.4% of total expenditures on health (Figure 2.8).

The majority of health expenditures in Albania occur in primary care followed by secondary care; public health and administration have the lowest percentage of expenditure as depicted in Figure 2.10.

The government provides the bulk of funding for the treatment of severe mental disorders. There is no inpatient/outpatient budget breakdown, and in the 2014 *Mental Health Atlas Country Profile*, there was no estimate of per capita expenditures for mental health. This shows the funding for mental health services in Albania is low—it is only 3% of all governmental health care expenditures; of that 3%, 97% is typically directed towards mental hospitals.

---

[12] In many industrialized countries, a complete list of health expenditure data is available from national health accounts (NHAs) that collect expenditure information based on an internationally standardized protocol, the system of health accounts. In the case of Albania, a NHA has not yet been established.

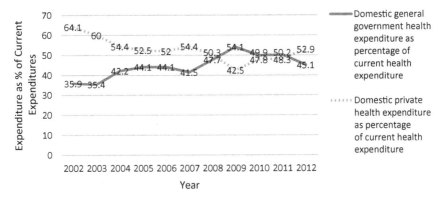

Figure 2.7: Public and private health expenditures as percentages of current health expenditures.
Source: WHO (2014b).

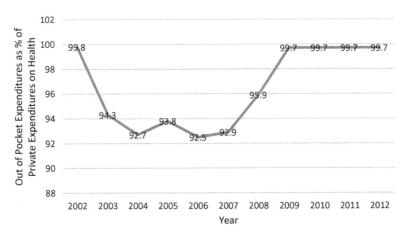

Figure 2.8: Out-of-pocket expenditure as a percentage of private expenditure on health.
Source: WHO (2014b).

2.8 Quality of Care, Outcomes, and Evaluation

Every initiative taken to improve quality and outcomes in health systems has as its starting point some understanding of what is meant by "quality." Without this understanding, it would be impossible to design the interventions and measures used to improve results. According to the WHO

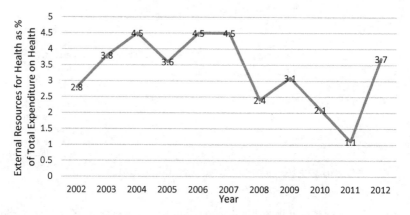

Figure 2.9: External resources for health as a percentage of total expenditure on health.
Source: WHO, Global Health Estimates (2014).

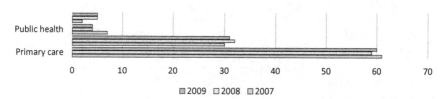

Figure 2.10: Health expenditures in Albania in Albanian Lek.
Note: As of September 2018, the currency rate was 1 USD to 108 Albanian Lek.
Source: MoH (2010).

definition regarding quality of care, which uses 6 dimensions of quality (WHO, 2006); care should be:

- **Effective:** evidence-based care results in improved health outcomes for individuals and communities;
- **Efficient:** care maximizes resource use and avoids waste;
- **Accessible:** care is timely, nearby, and in a setting where skills and resources are appropriate to medical need;
- **Patient-centered:** care takes into account the preferences and aspirations of individual service users and the cultures of their communities;

- **Equitable:** care does not vary in quality because of personal characteristics such as gender, race, ethnicity, geographical location, or socioeconomic status;
- **Safe:** care minimizes risks and harm to service users.

In Albania, the National Center for Quality, Safety and Accreditation of Health Institutions (NCQSA-HI) is the most important organization addressing concerns about quality and safety. The Center supports the Ministry of Health in the implementation of the national long-term health strategy and promotes Continuous Quality Improvement (CQI), hospital accreditation, and patient safety.

There have been efforts in Albania to assess patient satisfaction, including both medical and non-medical aspects of hospital care, as well as the quality of care in Albanian health care services. One study, "Assessing the Quality of University Hospitals," reported a high level of dissatisfaction among patients receiving hospital care. The primary sources of dissatisfaction included long waits and complaints about poor staff attitudes. For example, 43.8% of respondents were unhappy with how they were treated by nurses. In addition, a considerable number of patients did not know how to go about making a complaint. Other reasons for dissatisfaction included problems with obtaining prescribed medication and substandard conditions in the facilities (Hoxha, Sarolli, Petrela and Gabrani, 2007).

The WHO and the Albanian Ministry of Health (MoH) assessed the strengths and weaknesses of the Mental Health system in Albania in 2014. This assessment included a survey which was conducted to identify concerns and inform efforts to improve care. The study evaluated inpatient and community-based services, and included virtually all of the inpatient services, 10 out 11 supported-living residences, and 70% of Community Centers.

The findings from inpatient setting surveys can be summarized as follows:

- Geographic access was poor;
- There was a lack of available written information for patients;
- Infrastructure and emergency provisions were inadequate;
- Patient privacy was lacking;

- Procedures for evaluating and reviewing the legal status of service users were not available;
- Information for service users about their legal rights was insufficient;
- Care planning was absent or limited;
- Specific protocols or procedures on behavior management and excessive use of tranquilizers was limited;
- Psychological support was poor;
- Access and treatment in regional general hospitals were problematic;
- Family involvement was inadequate.

The problems associated with outpatient mental health services included:

- A lack of funds for health promotion and awareness and little advocacy;
- More than half of the population lacked coverage;
- Facilities were poorly maintained;
- A need for more CMHCs with better distribution to improve accessibility;
- The need for additional resources for community care teams to provide services;
- The need for staff to be better trained in psychological/psychotherapeutic interventions and working with families;
- The need for more integrated documentation;
- Improved follow-up for medication administration;
- A shortage of rehabilitation and recovery services;
- A need for better access to emergency medications in CMHCs;
- That care plans are inadequate;
- Patients and family members need to be more involved in treatment planning medication administration (Demi and Voko, 2014).

2.9 Advocacy, Stigma, and Self-Help

2.9.1 *Prevalence of stigma*

In Albania, stigmatization of those with mental illness is a very significant problem. Media representation of mental health issues has not changed

An Overview of Mental Health in Albania 41

significantly over the past 25 years, and while there is no clear data, the general perception is that stigma remains prevalent among health professionals as well as in the general population. At the same time, there seems to be a low level of awareness about stigma and its negative impacts.

In 2008, A National Study on Public Attitudes Towards Mental Health in Albania was conducted by the WHO. This study revealed the following:

- 3 in 4 people acknowledged that mental health problems can affect anyone and people with mental health problems should have the same rights as all the others. However, an equally high number of interviewees stated that the community should be better protected from people with mental health problems and that people with mental health problems are often dangerous;
- 9 in 10 people agreed there is prejudice against people with mental health problems;
- Only 4 in 10 people stated that they are not bothered by public opinion and are willing to be open about mental illness within their families;
- 9 in 10 people believed that people with mental health problems should not be employed in occupations such as doctors, nurses, or teachers;
- More than 1 in 2 respondents believed that people with mental health problems should not have voting rights;
- More than 1 in 3 people believed that people who have had past mental health problems should not marry;
- 1 in 4 respondents believed that a pregnant woman who in the past has suffered from mental health problems should have an abortion (WHO, 2009).

2.9.2 *Efforts to reduce stigma and increase protection and reform*

Article 8 of Law 44/2012 addresses the need for protection from discrimination, torture, inhumane acts, and degrading treatment for people with mental disorders; in addition, discrimination against people with physical, sensory, intellectual, and mental disabilities is prohibited by the

Constitution and discrimination in employment, education, transportation, access to health care, and the provision of other state services is outlawed. Despite this, widespread poverty, unregulated working conditions, and poor medical care are still significant problems for many persons with disabilities in Albania.[13] For example, the 2011 Census revealed that 24% of people with any form of disability (of which mental illness is included) had never attended school.

As noted earlier, Albania's primary mental health policy and legislation is embodied in *Law 44/2012 "On Mental Health"*; of which *Article 4 stipulates the need for protection and promotion of mental health by fighting discrimination and stigma.*[14] The most recent Action Plan for Mental Health, 2013–2020 also establishes the need to help mental health professionals to fight stigma and discrimination in their professional practice as a priority. Additionally, the Plan calls for the promotion of positive attitudes about mental health problems to stimulate demand and increase access to services, as well as to promote the inclusion of those with mental illness into society (MOH, 2013a).

Over the past 2 decades, advocacy initiatives in mental health have paralleled the emergence of mental health-focused Non-governmental Organizations (NGOs). These organizations include participation by service users, families, civil libertarians, politicians, health providers, psychologists, psychiatrists, and other professional groups. There was a substantial increase in the number of NGOs following the crisis in Kosovo in 2000; however, despite their effectiveness, many if not most of these NGOs lost funding from their international sources over time. Today, only 3–4 out of more than 20 original organizations are still operating. In addition to NGOs, there are a range of stakeholders that support advocacy among general health and mental health professionals and work toward improving quality and respect for individual rights, along with policymakers and planners who focus on improving mental health policy and legislation. There are also initiatives aimed toward engaging the

---

[13] Albanian Human Rights Report: 2013, http://www.state.gov/documents/organization/220457.pdf. Retrieved 1 September 2015.

[14] Law no.44, 2012: *On Mental Health, Article 4.*

A Patient's Perspective

B, a 45-year-old with Schizophrenia, hospitalized 4 times since 2012

Prior to developing a mental illness, did you know of or hear about any people suffering from a mental condition?
I had not heard about nor had noticed people suffering from mental illness. Generally, I was not interested and I did not give mental illness any attention.

What did the whole experience of being a patient in a psychiatric facility mean to you?
At the beginning, I was hospitalized involuntarily and I thought that it was the wrong action, but over time I accepted the situation and that the treatment was needed. I have been convinced regarding taking treatment. I initially did not use it and this led me to have an episode with behavior change.

Was group therapy available and did you participate in any sessions during your last episode of care?
We did not have group therapy; it is not practiced. I think that our treatment [medication] is the only therapy.

Could you describe the accommodation at the psychiatric hospital?
Given actual conditions, the staff tries very hard to keep them in good condition with cleaning and washing. Initially, I was isolated alone in a room, because I was involuntarily hospitalized; afterwards, I moved in a double room.

Was mental health care affordable to you?
Hospitalization and treatment in hospital are free. While monthly treatment is not reimbursed 100%, it is certainly affordable, at least for our family.

---

general population in raising awareness, increasing knowledge, and changing attitudes about mental illness (WHO, 2003).

Stigma and negative attitudes about mental illness are persistent and prevalent in Albania. There is real concern that many people avoid seeking needed help because of the impact of stigma, and these attitudes taint the entire field of mental health at all levels of government, service delivery, and the general public. Clearly, there is much to be done to improve this situation.

2.10 Looking Forward: Challenges and Priorities in the Albanian Mental Health System

There is a real need to raise awareness, increase understanding, and articulate strategies for advancing and integrating mental health as part of the national health agenda in Albania. This is not unlike the challenges seen in other countries around the world, and it is highly similar to the challenges shared by other Central and Eastern European countries.

Priorities for development and improvement in the mental health care system in Albania include the need for the following:

- An integrated system of mental health services;
- Better training and increased numbers of mental health professionals;
- Promotion of a positive mental health plan;
- Medical infrastructure improvement.

Challenges to overcome include the following:

- The lack of adequate funding and resources—especially for community mental health services;
- High levels of stigma in policy as well as in the service delivery system;
- The need to enhance workforce and educational resources;
- The lack of funding for research;
- Inadequate statistics and mental health information. (MoH, 2013a).

References

Agron, B., Elvana, H. and Albana, A. (2011) *Health insurance in Albania.* http://www.isksh.com.al/images/stories/publikimet/botimet/sigurimi%20shendetesor%20ne%20shqiperi.pdf.

Demi, N. and Voko, K. (2014) *Report on the survey on the mental health system in Albania.* Study of needs assessment of mental health services in Albania carried out by the Ministry of Health of the Republic of Albania and World Bank Organization, Office—Albania.

DITA Journal (2012) *On the new law of Mental Health.* http://www.gazetadita.al/mbi-ligjin-e-ri-per-shendetin-mendor/. Retrieved on 3 September 2015.

Gotsadze, G. and Gaál, P. (2010) Coverage Decisions: Benefit Entitlements and Patient Cost Sharing. In: Kutzin, J., Cashin, C. and Jakab, M. (eds.) *Implementing Health Financing Reform: Lessons from Countries in Transition* (World Health Organization, Copenhagen).

Hoxha, A., Sarolli, Y., Petrela, E. and Gabrani, J. C. (2007) Quality Assessment of University Hospital Center, Tirana. National Library, Tirana. ISBN 99927-36-7-1.

IPH (2014) *National Health Report. Health status of Albanian population.*

Ministry of Finance (2015). Budget over years, http://www.financa.gov.al/al/raportime/buxheti/buxheti-ne-vite. Retrieved on 1 September 2015.

MoH (2009) Order of the Minister of Health no. 558, dated 26.10.2009 "On Registration, Patient Identification with Health Institutions on the Implementation of the Referral System.

MoH (2010) Causes of Death by group Diseases (per 100,000 thousand inhabitants). http://www.shendetesia.gov.al/al/publikime/statistika/dokumenta-statistikore-mbi-shendetesine. Retrieved on 8 September 2015.

MoH (2013a) *The Action Plan development of Mental Health services in Albania 2013–2020.*

MoH (2013b) *Regulation of Mental Health Services.*

Ryan, J. A. and Poster, E. C. (1989) The assaulted nurse: Short-term and long-term responses. *Archives of Psychiatric Nursing* **3** (6), 323–331.

WB (2015) ALBANIA World Bank Group Partnership Program Snapshot. https://www.worldbank.org/content/dam/Worldbank/document/eca/Albania-Snapshot.pdf.

WHO (2000) *World health report 2000. Health systems: Improving performance.* WHO Library Cataloguing in Publication Data, ISBN 92 4 156198 X, ISSN 1020–3311.

WHO (2003) *Advocacy for Mental Health.* Mental Health Policy and services Guidance Package, WHO Library Cataloguing-in-Publication Data, ISBN 92 4 154590 9.

WHO (2006) *Quality of Care: A process for making strategic choices in health systems,* WHO Library Cataloguing-in-Publication Data, ISBN 92 4 156324 9, ISBN 978 92 4 156324 6.

WHO (2009) *National study on public attitudes towards mental health—2009,* World Health Organization.

WHO (2011) Mental Health Atlas. Department of Mental Health and Substance Abuse.

WHO (2012a) DALYs (thousands) by cause. http://www.who.int/healthinfo/global_burden_disease/estimates/en/index2.html. Retrieved on 3 September 2015.

WHO (2012b) Suicide rates. Data by country (per 100,000 thousand inhabitants). http://apps.who.int/gho/data/node.main.MHSUICIDE?lang=en. Retrieved on 5 April 2016.

WHO (2013) *The Action Plan development of Mental Health services in Albania 2013–2020.*

WHO (2014a) Mental health Atlas Country profile. http://www.who.int/mental_health/evidence/atlas/profiles-2014/alb.pdf. Retrieved on 8 September 2015.

WHO (2014b) Albania statistics summary (2002–present). http://apps.who.int/gho/data/node.country.country-ALB. Retrieved on 4 September 2015.

WHO-MoH (2005) *Policy Document on the Development of Mental Health Services in Albania.* The National Steering Committee for Mental Health.

WHO-MoH (2006) *A Report of the Assessment of the Mental Health System in Albania using the World Health Organization—Assessment Instrument for Mental Health Systems (WHO-AIMS)*, http://www.who.int/mental_health/albania_who_aims_report1a.pdf. Retrieved on 5 September 2015.

CHAPTER 3

An Overview of Mental Health in Bulgaria

Georgi Hranov[*,†] and Maria Stoyanova[‡]

[*]*University Hospital of Active Treatment in Neurology and Psychiatry, "St Naum," Sofia, Bulgaria*

[†]*Medical University, Sofia, Bulgaria*

[‡]*Acute Psychiatry Department, "Prof. N. Shipkovenski" Mental Health Center, Sofia, Bulgaria*

3.1 Mental Health Status of the Bulgarian Population

In recent years, there have been national efforts to introduce an integrated Medical Information System. While currently available data is not specific to the mental health system, there are some data that can be utilized to help better understand the prevalence and burden of the mental illness in Bulgaria. Table 3.1 characterizes patients receiving treatment in inpatient mental health settings by diagnosis.

3.2 History of Mental Health Care in Bulgaria

3.2.1 *Mental health care before World War II*

In the Middle Ages, care for the mentally ill in Bulgaria was provided primarily by relatives, monasteries, and churches (Milenkov, 1966). Later,

Key Country Statistics

Region: Southeast Europe
Government system: parliamentary republic
Area: 110,879 square kilometers
Population: 7,144,653
Capital: Sofia
Gender ratio: 0.95 males to females
Ethnic groups:
- Bulgarian 76.9%
- Turkish 8%
- Roma 4.4%
- Other 0.7% (including Russian, Armenian, and Vlach)
- Unspecified and Unknown 10%

Literacy rate: 98.4%
Population under the age 18: 18.4%
Population above the age 60: 17%
Average life expectancy: 71.2 years for males and 78.0 years for females
Suicide rates: 0.0123% per 100,000 residents
Economy: upper middle income economy
GDP annual growth rate: 3%
GDP per capita: 19,4200 USD (PPP)
Unemployment rate: 10.1%
Youth unemployment rate: 23.8%
Average net salary: around 325 EUR
Poverty:
Total health expenditure as percentage of GDP: 8.4%

Source: CIA World Factbook (2016).

Table 3.1: Patients receiving treatment in inpatient mental health settings by diagnosis.

ICD-10 Diagnoses	2012 Patient	2012 per 100,000 pop.	2013 Patient	2013 per 100,000 pop.
Total	144,310	1,981.0	144,203	1,990.2
Mental and behavioral disorders	135,390	1,858.6	135,314	1,867.5
Dementia	2,549	35.0	2,492	34.4
Delirium, not induced by alcohol and other psychoactive substances	542	7.4	510	7.0
Mental and behavioral disorders due to use of alcohol	12,119	166.4	11,193	154.5
Mental and behavioral disorders due to use of other psychoactive substance	996	13.7	1,299	17.9
Mental and behavioral disorders due to use of opioids	837	11.5	1,140	15.7
Schizophrenia, schizotypal and delusional disorders	35,358	485.4	35,605	491.4
Mood [affective] disorders	25,609	351.6	25,030	345.4
Neurotic, stress-related and somatoform disorders	13,970	191.8	14,029	193.6
Mental retardation	31,375	430.7	31,184	430.4
All other classes of diseases	8,920	122.4	8,889	122.7
Epilepsy	8,917	122.4	8,880	122.6

during the Ottoman rule, the mentally ill were placed in the so-called "imarets" (shelters) (Golovina, 1895). The conditions were often quite primitive to the point of being inhumane; while chains and bars were used, no one with a mental illness was burned at the stake, as was common in earlier periods (Bradel, 1885; Danadziev, 1914; Temkov *et al.*, 1953/1954; Tzafarov, 1970; Kirov, 1970).

In 1881, the Bulgarian Exarchate (Orthodox Church) ceded 5 monasteries in order to create hospitals and asylums for the mentally ill (Milev *et al.*, 1982; Moskov, 1902; Milenkoc, 2013). In 1883, the first psychiatric ward in Varna was opened (Temkov *et al.*, 1953/1954; Milev *et al.*, 1982; Petrovski, 2001); later, it was moved to the Peter and Paul Monastery. In the same year, the first rules for treatment of mentally ill people were created (Petrovski, 2001). Planning for the hospital structure in Bulgaria identified the need for 4 main wards: internal diseases, surgery, infectious diseases, and psychiatric disorders (Milenkov, 2008/2009). In 1887, an independent psychiatric ward was established at the Aleksandrovska Hospital (Milenkov, 2005). Later, the ward was upgraded to a Neuropsychiatric Clinic (Milenkov, 2013).

During the following years, many psychiatric wards, as well as asylums for mentally ill people, were founded in different cities; most of them were harsh environments that were operated like a prison (Milenkov, 2013; Donchev, 2006).The Rules from 1904 stated that the mentally ill should be placed under surveillance of the State performed by a National Health Directorate (Temkov *et al.*, 1968; Milenkov *et al.*, 1969). In 1922, the first Nervous and Mental Diseases Department within the Medical Faculty in Sofia was established (Milenkov, 1978). In 1936, at the Psychiatric Hospital in Lovech, insulin coma therapy was introduced and in 1942 electroconvulsive therapy (ECT) became available (Milenkov, 2013). Until 1944, there were also 3 private psychiatric clinics in Sofia, which were subsequently nationalized (Milenkov, 2013).

3.2.2 Mental health care under the communist regime, 1945–1989

Health care, and in particular psychiatric care, was free for the whole population during the Communist rule and was coordinated by a sector of the Ministry of Health (MoH) and Social Services. The psychiatric health care network was composed of psychiatric hospitals for acute and long-term treatment, psychiatric hospitals exclusively for long-term treatment, independent psychiatric clinics as well as clinics affiliated with psychiatric hospitals, psychiatric consultation at district general hospitals and psychiatric wards within general hospitals (Donchev, 2006).

In 1944, the overall number of inpatient psychiatric beds in Bulgaria was 1,135 (Milenkov, 2013). After 1951, a unified national system of mental health care was created. Thirteen regional psychiatric dispensaries (separate outpatient structures created by the communist regime for a specific area of health care, in this case, psychiatry) were opened[1] and the overall number of psychiatric beds increased gradually to 7,300 in 1980. The number of clinics and other treatment facilities also increased from 18 in 1944 to 532 in 1980 (Milenkov, 2013). Outpatient services were provided by the clinics, and regional psychiatrists and nurses provided scheduled visits to patients in their homes. The dispensaries also provided supervision and social support. There were also social care establishments for children and youth with mental illness, as well as for adults with persistent mental health problems (Donchev, 2006).

Efforts to eliminate limitations of patients' rights and make treatment more humane were made during the second half of the 20th century. Chlorpromazine was introduced to Bulgarian psychiatry in 1955 in Karlukovo and in the 1960s ECT using muscle relaxation and general anesthesia (Donchev, 2006) became available. Removing the bars on hospital windows and serving food with spoons and forks on porcelain instead of metal plates are but a few examples of the improvements made in the care environment. In addition, patients were provided with opportunities to draw, garden, socialize, and access various modes of occupational and cultural therapy. Censorship of mail ceased and patients could freely choose their own clothing (Milenkov, 2013).[2] Psychiatric associations in

---

[1] Within each of the dispensaries prophylactic treatment unit for basic psychiatric outpatient care, department for children and youth, forensic psychiatric office, speech therapy office, physiotherapy section, clinical laboratory, sector for outpatient occupational therapy, and statistics were included. Every single dispensary served roughly 500,000–600,000 people. The area served by the dispensary was divided into regions.

[2] Healthcare 2014, National Statistical Institute, National Center of Public Health and Analyses, Sofia, 2015.

the Soviet Union, Czechoslovakia, and Bulgaria had announced their withdrawal from the WPA, charging the body was a political tool of the West following moves to expel the Soviet Union for political abuse of psychiatry. Following corrections in the policy, Bulgaria's membership was restored (McCagg and Siegelbaum, 1989; Donchev, 2006).[3]

3.2.3 *Mental health care under democracy (1989–present)*

One of the major developments in the Bulgarian mental health care system following the fall of Communism and Soviet influence has been the trend toward deinstitutionalization. As a result of health reform after 1989, when the communist regime in Bulgaria was overthrown, the number of inpatient beds was drastically reduced. By 2012, there were approximately half as many beds.[4] While the number of psychiatric hospitals and dispensaries did not change, there was a reduction in the number of hospitalized patients, as well as their average lengths of stay.

Although the Bulgarian government has adopted a large number of strategies and policies regarding mental health care over the past 15 years (including the United Nations' Convention on the Rights of Persons with Disabilities), real deinstitutionalization is beginning to be realized only recently. Despite having a national deinstitutionalization strategy, few people with mental disabilities have left the institutions. Bulgaria is still spending much more money on psychiatric institutions instead of funding community-based services.[5]

---

[3] My home, My choice in Bulgaria. The rights to community living for people with mental disabilities in 2014. Mental Disability Advocacy Center, 2014.

[4] Report for the results from the audit of the activity connected with National program "Assistants of the disabled people" in the Ministry of Labour and Social Policy, Social assistance agency, National employment agency for the period from 01 January 2005 to 31 December 2007, Bulgarian National Audit Office, 2009.

[5] In 2012, 71% of the governmental funding for disability services was spent on institutions, whereas only 29% went to community-based services. In 2012, the Ministry of Social and Labor Policy spent 7,200,440,000 million EUR for institutional care approximately for people with mental retardation, 7,482,000 million for people with mental disabilities, and 5,980,000 million for people with dementia (see Footnote 3). Additionally, 4,500,000 million EUR were spent on institutions for children with mental retardation.

Recently, the Bulgarian government has developed new forms of personal assistance for people with disabilities; however, its real impact on the ability of mentally disabled people to live more independently remains unclear. The existing day services are insufficient in number and unevenly distributed over the country; as a result, people with disabilities in some regions do not have real access to these important community supports. The majority of people with mental disabilities in Bulgaria reside mostly in a range of social care institutions, including homes for adults and children with mental retardation, homes for adults with psychosocial disabilities, homes for adults with dementia, and homes for children in need of medical and social services. These institutions are funded by the MoH, the Ministry of Labor and Social Policy, and the Ministry of Finance.[6]

Bulgarian community-based services include family-type residential centers, transitional homes, and supported living arrangements. However, in reality, these community-based services function more often as institutions and there is limited capacity compared to the need or demand for care.[7] The "National Strategy for Long-term Care" and the "Action Plan for Implementation of the United Nations Convention on the Rights of Persons with Disabilities" have been developed in order to further advance efforts at deinstitutionalization; however, implementation is very slow and the actual creation of a community-based psychiatric network has not yet been realized.

The report of the National Financial Audit Office and the annual report on the activities of the Social Assistance Agency for the period 2006–2009 show that only 67 people have left the institutions (see Footnotes 4 and 6). In the following years, in accordance with the adopted plan *Vision For The Deinstitutionalization of People With Intellectual Disabilities, Mental Health Problems and Dementia 2010–2011*, another 4,441 people should have left the institutions; in reality less than 2,000 people live in community-based services. According to the third evaluation report in 2013, based on the implementation of the National Strategy "Vision for Deinstitutionalization of the children in Bulgaria" the number of children in Bulgaria living in institutions has decreased from 4,755 to 3,592 and 2 homes for medical and social care for children were closed.

[6] Report of the activity of the Social assistance agency for 2008, Ministry of Labour and Social Policy.

[7] *Ibid.*

3.3 Mental Health Policies and Legislation in Bulgaria

Legislation related to psychiatric care in Bulgaria encompasses multiple laws, policies, and regulations; the Health Act, the Law for Healthcare Institutions, the Health Insurances Act, the Law on Integration of Disabled People, the Social Assistance Act, and finally the National Mental Health Policy along with an action plan for its implementation are the key documents. Additionally, the Medical Standard in Psychiatry, the Law for Individuals and Families, the Family Code, the Anti-discrimination Act, and the Regulation on the Conditions and Order for Implementation of Medical Activities Related to the Treatment of Persons with Mental Disorders also address legal issues related to mental health care.

The focus of each of these key pieces of law and policy, and their relevance to mental health care, are detailed as follows:

- *The Health Act*[8] establishes public health as a national priority and guarantees the equal treatment of service users and promotes quality and affordable health care, and services for special populations including individuals with physical disabilities and mental disorders.[9] The government participates in financing services under the Health Act and the MoH is responsible for the management of the National Health System, which includes supervision of inpatient psychiatric care and access to services regardless of insurance. The State, the municipalities, and the non-governmental organizations (NGOs) are also involved in the organization of all activities related to providing mental health services; municipalities are specifically responsible for providing psychosocial rehabilitation and financial support.
- *The Health Insurance Act*[10] states that all inpatient psychiatric services are financed by the state or municipality budgets and that all Bulgarian citizens have the right to cost-free psychiatric care.

---

[8] Law on Integration of Disabled People, State Gazette, Vol. 40, 2014.

[9] According to the Health Act the fundamental principles governing the treatment of people with mental illness include respecting patient's rights, reducing institutionalism, building a network of hospitals for mental health care, as well as assuring parity in psychiatric care and compliance with humanitarian principles and norms.

[10] Social Assistance Act, State Gazette, Vol. 66, 2013e.

- *The Law on Integration of Disabled People*[11] in Bulgaria guarantees equality to people with disabilities, community integration, social support for people with disabilities and their families, and integration in the labor market. The national policy for integration of people with disabilities is the responsibility of the National Council for People with Disabilities. The responsible body for its implementation is the Agency for People with Disabilities.[12]
- According to *the Social Assistance Act*,[13] all Bulgarian citizens who are unable to meet their basic daily needs are provided resources and assistance to promote their capacity for independent living. Unemployed mentally ill people are not required to participate in employment programs in order to receive social assistance. The Agency for Social Assistance was established for implementation of the Social Assistance Act; social services are provided by specialized institutions and in the community. Disabled people may apply for a "social inclusion monthly allowance;" the amount of services and supports received is based on the type and extent of the disability.
- *The Medical Standard in Psychiatry*[14] defines the principles of treatment and services for people with mental disorders. It specifies the requirements for outpatient and inpatient psychiatric facilities as well as the activities and duties of medical staff at all levels. There are specific guidelines for the treatment of acute psychotic disorders, affective disorders, delusional disorders and dementia. The Standard provides criteria for care in ambulatory settings and also establishes standards and regulations for child and adolescent psychiatry.

---

[11] Directive No. 24 from 7 July 2004 for accepting medical standard "Psychiatry," State Gazette, Vol. 49, 2012.

[12] The Agency for People with Disabilities is responsible for creation and maintenance of information database of people with disabilities for activities related to education, medical, and social rehabilitation and integration, development of programs and projects for people with disabilities and maintains a database of specialized enterprises and exerts control over the granting of assistive devices.

[13] Mental Health Policy (MPH) of the Republic of Bulgaria (year 2004–2012), Ministry of Health.

[14] National Action Plan for Implementation of the Mental Health Policy of the Republic Bulgaria 2006–2012, Ministry of Health.

- The primary objective of the *National Mental Health Policy*[15] is to improve the mental health of the population and to integrate mental health care services into the public health care system. The policy's priorities include deinstitutionalization, the protection of human rights of mental health care consumers, assurance of quality services, the integration of users in the process of treatment and rehabilitation, creating evidence-based mental health care facilities, along with the prevention, promotion, and destigmatization of mental disorders. In order to achieve these objectives, the Mental Health Policy has several long- and short-term aims. The long-term aim is to engage politicians and civil society in addressing mental health problems and needs, assuring adequate funding needed for program improvements, as well as integrating and coordinating the efforts of different institutions and agencies. The short-term aims of the Policy focus on the development of an action plan that includes assessment of existing activities and the creation of programs for prevention and early intervention, as well as the introduction of programs for psychosocial interventions in the community along with the integration of mental health care services.
- *The National Action Plan for Implementation of Mental Health Policy*[16] of the Republic of Bulgaria identifies activities similar to those already mentioned in the National Mental Health Policy.
- *The Healthcare Institutions Act*[17] identifies access for persons with mental disorders to social support in mental health centers and other health care institutions as well as the criteria for admission. In accordance with the law, mental health centers must be located based on some determination of the population's needs.
- *Law for Individuals and Family*[18] identifies 2 essential criteria for determining the capacity of individuals: 18 years of age and the ability to acquire rights and obligations through their actions. Adults with mental illness who cannot care for themselves can be placed under guardianship and declared formally incapacitated; this requires deter-

---

[15] Medical-Treatment Facilities Act, State Gazette, Vol. 20, 2013.
[16] Law for individuals and family, State Gazette, Vol. 120, 2002.
[17] Family Code, State Gazette, Vol. 68, 2013г.
[18] Anti-discrimination Act, State Gazette, Vol. 68, 2013.

mination by a forensic specialist and court review. According to Bulgarian law, people under full guardianship are not allowed to enter into contracts and are not allowed to work in particular professions such as military service.
- *The Family Code*[19] governs relations based on marriage, kinship and adoption, guardianship and trusteeship; the Code also addresses the protection of the rights and interests of those placed under guardianship.
- *The Anti-Discrimination Act*[20] is the primary legislation to address disability-based discrimination. It regulates various protections related to labor rights, access to training, promotions, and harassment.
- *The Regulation on the Conditions and Order for Implementation of Medical Activities Related to the Treatment of Persons with Mental Disorders*[21] identifies which health care facilities are allowed to provide medical services and specifies the criteria for psychotherapy, diagnostic testing, electroconvulsive therapy, etc. The regulation also provides guidelines for the use of psychotherapy, care programs, and case management.

3.4 Organizational Structure of the Mental Health System in Bulgaria

3.4.1 *Overview of the medical system*

The National Assembly (NA) plays an important role in the development of national health policy. It approves not only the national budget but also the budget of the National Health Insurance Fund (NHIF). There is a Parliamentary Commission on Health that has legislative authority; the

---

[19] Directive No. 1 from 11 January 2007 for the conditions and rules for conducting medical activities connected with the treatment of the persons with mental disorders, State Gazette, Vol. 22, 2007.

[20] Treating and heath facilities report on 31.12, National Center of Public Health and Analyses, 2014.

[21] Bulletin "Beds fund and activity of the treatment facilities," National Center of Public Health and Analyses, 2014.

Commission also reviews pressing health-related issues put forward by its members as well as issues brought to its attention by other members of the NA, the Minister of Health or the Director of the NHIF. Proposals to this Commission can be submitted by individual professionals, professional associations and NGOs.

The MoH is the branch of the government responsible for the overall organization and functioning of the health system. The MoH is also responsible for planning and ensuring an adequate workforce for the health system, advancing medical science, as well as collecting and maintaining data on the health status of the population and the national health accounts. The Ministry oversees a range of activities related to protection of the public's health including:

- National health strategy;
- National health report;
- Emergency care;
- Transfusion hematology;
- Psychiatric care;
- Medical and social care for children under 3 years of age;
- Transplantation services;
- Health information;
- Development and control of health interventions medical expertise;
- Medical professional training;
- Medical research.

The Supreme Medical Council (SMC) is an advisory body to the MoH. The SMC gives advice to the NHS on a wide range of topics including health-related legislation, budgets, annual report of the Minister, early admission quota for students and post-graduate students in health care, as well as issues related to medical ethics. Executive Agencies (e.g. pharmaceuticals, transplantation, etc.) and National Centers (e.g. public health, communicable diseases, health information, protection of public health) are subordinate to and funded by the MoH.

At the district level, health policy is organized and implemented by the 28 Regional Health Offices (RHO). The tasks of these Offices include:

- The collection, registration, handling, storage, analysis, and provision of health information;
- Oversight for the registration and quality of health care providers;
- Implementation of information technology in health;
- Organization of action plans for natural disasters and accidents;
- Coordination of activities regarding the implementation of national and regional health programs;
- Research into the demand for human resources in health care.

The Bulgarian health system is an insurance-based system with both compulsory and voluntary health insurance. All Bulgarian citizens are required to enroll in the health insurance program and pay 8% of their monthly salaries as premiums. Payment is divided such that the employer pays 60% and the employee pays 40%. The NHIF is the largest of the insurance programs and it dominates the market leaving only a small share to voluntary health insurance companies.[22]

The insurance system covers diagnostic, treatment, and rehabilitation services as well as medications for insured individuals; this includes outpatient mental health care. The state is the sole owner of all university hospitals and national centers; this includes specialized hospitals dedicated to the treatment of cardiovascular disease and oncology as well as physical therapy and rehabilitation. In addition, there are centers for emergency medical care and psychiatric hospitals, along with centers for transfusion hematology and dialysis. At the level of the district hospitals, the state is the majority shareholder and can exert substantial political influence.[23]

The National Center for Drug Addictions was founded in 1994 and its primary responsibility is coordination and provision of substance abuse treatment and related services, as well as supporting education and research on the problems of addiction and contributes to national anti-drug initiatives. This includes preparing data for policy development and legislation as well as maintaining a national register for addiction treatment facilities along with a patient registry.

---

[22] Reports, Financial Supervision Commission, 2013.
[23] Health act, State Gazette, Vol. 108, 2000.

The private sector is responsible for all primary medical and dental care, pharmacy services, and most of the specialized outpatient care as well as some hospital treatment. Health care providers are independent business entities and comprise:

- Outpatient care providers (single and group, primary and specialized medical and dental practices, medical and dental centers, diagnostic laboratories);
- Inpatient care providers (specialized and multiprofile hospitals, for active or long-term treatment and rehabilitation);
- Emergency care centers;
- Mental health centers;
- Centers for comprehensive cancer treatment;
- Centers for dermatology and sexually transmitted diseases;
- Homes for medico–social care, hospices;
- Dialysis center;
- Cell/tissue banks.

As the health care system has become less centralized, the municipalities have become the owners of a considerable share of health care facilities (including some mental health centers). Local health care offices organize health care within the municipalities under the responsibility of the RHO. In some cities, Public Health Councils function as advisory bodies to the Mayor's office.

Irrespective of the form of ownership, all health care providers must be registered in accordance to the Medical Treatment Facilities Act as well as the Trade Law or Cooperation Law. All health care providers, except emergency care centers, can contract with the NHIF. However, contracts for mental health care providers are very limited; for example, no psychotherapy is included.

There are 4 medical universities in the following cities in Bulgaria: Sofia, Plovdiv, Varna, and Pleven. In addition, there are medical faculties at Sofia University and at Trakia University in Stara Zagora. These universities train masters of medicine, dentistry, pharmacy, public health, health management, and bachelors of nursing, midwifery and health management (Dimova *et al.*, 2012).

Other regulators of heath care providers include the professional organizations of physicians (including several organizations of psychiatrists and psychologists as well as nurses working in mental health). There are 4 professional medical organizations established by law: The Bulgarian Medical Association, The Bulgarian Dental Association, The Bulgarian Pharmaceutical Association, and The Bulgarian Association of Professionals in Health Care (i.e. nurses). Membership in these associations is mandatory. They represent the rights and interests of their respective professions and members. Examples of their activities include providing comments and statements on draft legislation, participation in drafting Good Medical Practice Guidelines for each specialty, as well as consideration of ethical issues.

3.4.2 *Inpatient care*

Mental health care is provided both in outpatient and inpatient settings. Ambulatory services are provided by general practitioners (GPs), by individual and group psychiatric practices, and by psychiatrists' offices in diagnostic consulting centers and medical centers. Unfortunately, these facilities are unevenly distributed across the country and care concentrated predominantly in the 3 largest cities (Sofia, Plovdiv, and Varna). Inpatient care is provided by specialized psychiatric hospitals and psychiatric wards in general hospitals, as well as by the mental health centers (former dispensaries for psychiatric diseases).[24] Generally, mental health centers have more patients than specialized psychiatric hospitals—these facilities, mostly provide long-term care for persons with persistent problems. The shortest inpatient stays occur in multispecialty hospitals (including university hospitals), which can provide more comprehensive and integrated treatment.[25]

---

[24] In March 2013, there were 316 medical facilities with a total of 46,804 beds in Bulgaria. This included 12 psychiatric hospitals with 2,413 beds, 12 mental health centers with 1,480 beds accounting for 3,893 out of a total of 4,792 psychiatric beds in the country.

[25] Regulation for implementation of the national education act, State Gazette, Vol. 43, 2014.

A Mental Health Care Provider's Perspective

What are, in your opinion, the particularities of the mental health care system in your country?
The system's main problem is the lack of communication between different services and during different stages of treatment. After the patient is discharged the treatment is started all over again. There is no general paradigm for continuation of the treatment, therapeutic dosage, continuation to the maintenance treatment. There are no standards—or more accurately, there are standards, but nobody sticks to them. A good improvement would be to have electronic patient history.

What are, in your opinion, the particularities of the patients in the mental health care system?
The patient is not eager to seek help from a psychiatrist during the first episodes of the disease, perceiving this as shame. There are many stigmas surrounding mental illness; not only for the patient, but also for the healthy people as well, including the hospitals, the medical staff, and the family. Everything connected with dealing with mental illness and the shame of mental illness is on the back of the relatives of the patients. They often run out of resources and quit helping the patients, because the social benefits are not enough even for treatment alone.

Would you say things have changed in the past 25 years?
A good change is the availability of more drugs and new drugs on the market; the other positive change is reduction of the hospital beds. However, there has been no increasing number of the community services in the last 25 years. I think this is due to a lack of vision. In addition, there is lack of a systematic use of the well-established, good clinical practices from all over the world.

Do you have any additional comments or insights about the provision of mental health services in your country?
There is still fear of the authorities by the mentally ill. There is a tendency for the authorities to hide mental health problems, because it discredits the government. In addition, the lack of the government taking small steps to reform the system leads to big consequences and problems in the future—by which I mean now, because lack of the reforms in the past 25 years or more have consequences we're seeing today.

3.4.3 Emergency services

Emergency psychiatric services are also provided by mental health centers; in addition, state psychiatric hospitals, psychiatric wards at multispeciality hospitals and emergency care centers can provide emergency care. Emergency care is available to anyone who presents for care, but there is no established network for ambulances with mental health professionals or designated mobile teams. In emergency care, a patient is assessed and either hospitalized for inpatient care, referred to a different specialty (e.g. neurology), or referred for outpatient care.

3.4.4 Outpatient care

Mental health centers provide outpatient and inpatient care, as well as preventative treatment and some social services. They offer programs for the identification of people with mental disorders and for early diagnosis, continuous treatment, and mental health promotion. The centers include community care units which provide counseling, home care, psychosocial rehabilitation and inpatient care for active treatment of acutely ill mental patients is also offered.

3.4.5 Treatment and medication

In Bulgaria, most internationally recognized treatments are available including ECT and transcranial magnetic stimulation (TMS). Psychosurgery exists as an option, but it is uncommon and limited to several cases per year. Nearly all psychotropic medications available in Europe and the United States of America are available without restrictions on prescription irrespective of the provider's medical specialty. Prescriptions for drugs with a high potential for abuse or dependence are closely regulated. Medications are partially reimbursed (usually at 50%) from NHIF, with the exception of anti-psychotics which are fully reimbursed.[26]

---

[26] Policies and practices for mental health in Europe, WHO Europe.

School Mental Health is a national program that provides support to only a limited network of schools. They provide a set of services and educational activities including sensitization and support to teachers on issues related to the emotional well-being of children as well as initiatives addressing the school environment, along with counseling programs for children with problems.[27]

3.5 Access to the Mental Health Care System in Bulgaria

There are gaps in the services available in Bulgaria. While there are several NGOs focused on helping people with mental disabilities by providing legal as well as psychological help, their funding is neither stable nor sufficient. There is little in the way of occupational mental health and home care is nearly non-existent. For people without NHIF enrollment, mental health care is often limited with the exception of treatment for affective and psychotic disorders.

3.6 Mental Health Workforce in Bulgaria

Over the past 25 years, the total number of physicians in Bulgaria has remained almost the same; there were 28,497 doctors in 1990 and 28,937 in 2013. In comparison with other European countries, there are 386 physicians per 100,000 population in Bulgaria and 346 physicians per 100,000 in the European Union.[28] However, the migration of doctors and nurses has become a serious challenge to the Bulgarian health workforce over the past several years;[29] as a result the number of medical specialists, i.e. nurses, lab technicians, medical assistants, etc., has decreased significantly from 88,387 in 1990 to 48,463 in 2013.

---

[27] News, Bulgarian Medical Association, Saturday, 22 February 2014.
[28] Short statistical report, Healthcare 2014, National Center of Public Health and Analyses, 2014.
[29] According to the Bulgarian Medical Association, approximately 80% of the newly graduated physicians would like to leave the country. Every year for the period between 2009 and 2012, approximately 500 Bulgarian physicians migrated to another country.

Although the total number of physicians has remained the same, the number of physicians working in psychiatric institutions has reduced from 693 in 1990 to 555 in 2013.[30] The number of psychiatrists per 100,000 population in Bulgaria is 8.7. According to the WHO, the number of psychiatrists in the EU15 is 12.9; in countries joining the EU since 2004 it is 8.9; in countries in south-eastern Europe there are 8 psychiatrists per 100,000. The median rate of psychiatrists per 100, 000 in the 41 countries that provided information in this survey of the WHO is 9. There is also concern about the aging of the medical workforce in Bulgaria. Approximately 50% of practicing physicians are between 46 and 60 years of age and additional 20% are above the age of 60 years.[31]

The proportion of medical school training hours for physicians dedicated to psychiatry in Bulgaria is 1.5%, i.e. 75 hours; this time is more focused on theory than practice. Post-graduate training in psychiatry lasts 4 years.[32] The curriculum consists of basic and clinical psychiatry, child and adolescent psychiatry, emergency psychiatry, drug addiction, geriatric psychiatry, forensic psychiatry, liaison psychiatry, community-based psychiatry, general medicine, neuroimaging, and neurology. Following completion of the training, a national board exam covering all topics in psychiatry is required. There are virtually no specially trained psychiatric nurses in Bulgaria; the term psychiatric nurse simply refers to a nurse working in any psychiatric department without consideration of training or expertise. There are 15.5 Bulgarian nurses per 100,000 population working in mental health. The proportion of undergraduate training hours dedicated to mental health training for nurses in Bulgaria is 3.3%, i.e. 165 training hours.[33]

---

[30] Report of the results from the audit of the activity connected with National program "Assistants of the disabled people" in the Ministry of Labour and Social Policy, Social assistance agency, National employment agency for the period from 01 January 2005 to 31 December 2007, Bulgarian National Audit Office, 2009.

[31] Analysis development and realization of the human resources in the health care, Confederation of independent trade unions in Bulgaria, 2013.

[32] Short statistical report, Healthcare 2014, National Center of Public Health and Analyses, 2014.

[33] *Ibid.*

There has also been an increase in the number of recognized professionals; clinical psychology became recognized in 1995[34] and in 2001, the regulations for the specialty of clinical psychology were published by the MoH.[35] Currently, Clinical Psychologists are required to have 3-years of additional training following the attainment of a master's degree in psychology.[36] In Bulgaria, the number of psychologists working in mental health care in 1992 was 62 and 77 in 1998 or 0.8 per 100,000 population; however, many are practicing privately, often without proper training.[37] In 1992 there were 30 social workers in Bulgaria, and in 1998 there were 29 or a rate of 0.36 per 100,000 population. The number of occupational therapists in Bulgaria is unknown;[38] all activities in the field of occupational therapy are part of the social care system.[39]

3.7 Financing the Mental Health Care in Bulgaria

Bulgaria has a mixed public–private health care financing system. Health care is financed from compulsory health insurance contributions, taxes, out-of-pocket payments, voluntary health insurance premiums, corporate payments, donations, and external funding. The total health expenditure as a percentage of GDP is 4.2%.[40] The structure of total health expenditure has been changing over time, especially after the introduction of the health insurance system. Private expenditure on health as a percentage of total health expenditure has increased due to the reduction in public financing, the increase in the number of private health care entities (which did not

---

[34] Directive No. 1 from 22 January 2015 for gaining specialty in the healthcare system, State Gazette, Vol. 7, 2015.

[35] Mental Health Atlas 2011—Department of Mental Health and Substance Abuse, World Health Organization.

[36] Healthcare 2014: condition, problems, solutions, challenges, Bulgarian Industrial Association.

[37] Short statistical report, Healthcare 2014, National Center of Public Health and Analyses, 2014.

[38] Law for the budget of the national social security for 2014, State Gazette, Vol. 1, 2014.

[39] Short statistical report, Healthcare 2014, National Center of Public Health and Analyses, 2014.

[40] Law for the budget of the NHIF, State Gazette, Vol. 98, 2014.

A Mental Health Care Provider's Perspective

What are, in your opinion, the particularities of the mental health care system in your country?

The system is not well organized and the financing of the system is very limited.

Salaries are too low. Everything is based on the personal qualities of individual workers, and workers are not motivated by the system itself. We should expect much more from the quality of care. I think that the time for an examination (20 minutes) that the health insurance fund pays for is too short a time for doing a good job and to give patients the attention they need.

In addition, the financing of the inpatient care is too limited regarding medication, which leads to limited supply in hospital pharmacies. There is a limitation on which forms of disease are financed—there is no medical reason that medication for paranoid schizophrenia is reimbursed but not to reimburse for other forms of schizophrenia or for other disorders.

Would you say things have changed in the past 25 years?

I think that the only difference is in the development of the new drugs—we have better medication now. This is not connected with the development of democracy or the reforms in the health sector—this is only connected with the pharmaceutical industry. I think the lack of reform is connected with the levels of corruption in the government and the choice of incompetent policymakers not involved with the mental health system.

What is the main flaw of the current mental health system? How would you change it?

I think that the government must recruit more people with medical education, rather than only those with administration qualities, in order to change the system.

Would you say there is a need for any other types of services in the mental health system?

We need better social services for the patients—more day centers and better vocational services for unemployed ones not needing inpatient care. There were better vocational services in the past, but now there's nearly nothing available. The mentally ill are just kept aside in hospitals as to not to bother society, but they can—and prefer to—be useful and have better social integration.

exist during the communist regime), and the increases in health care costs which require more out-of-pocket spending. Although out-of-pocket payments account for the largest source of revenue, public sources prevail over private sources.

Public funding for health care is a patchwork; as a share of total health expenditures this support has gradually decreased from officially 100% in 1989–1990 to 54% in 2012 (Dimova, 2012). The principle purchaser of health services is the NHIF. As of 2005, all inpatient care, with some exceptions, for example inpatient mental health services, some dispensary services and HIV inpatient treatment, is covered by the NHIF. Medical care provided by health care establishments, both public and private, is paid for by the NHIF according to contracted prices. Municipalities can also use local tax revenues to finance health services, while transfers from the central budget to municipalities for health make up about one-quarter of the overall amount of tax revenue allocated to health care.

The Social Health Insurance (SHI) contribution is 8% of monthly income, paid by the insured individuals, their employers or the state. The overall budget of NHIF is comprised of 65% from SHI and 35% from national budget.[41] A large proportion of the expenses of MoH were redirected for payment from NHIF, and in 2013 the budget of MoH was reduced significantly to 184 million EUR.[42] A major problem of health care financing is the low rate of collection of SHI due to a combination of avoidance (around 1 million non-exempt persons do not pay for health insurance), unemployment, and poor collection mechanisms. For outpatient services, NHIF makes per capita payment to mental health care providers irrespective of diagnosis; inpatient services provided by the national centers for emergency care, state psychiatric hospitals, and health and social care institutions for children are funded by the MoH (Dimova, 2012).

Beyond the package covered by the NHIF, all citizens are free to purchase different voluntary insurance packages, however, less than 3% of the population purchased some form of voluntary health insurance (VHI) in 2010. Private expenditure on health in Bulgaria includes out-of-pocket payments, voluntary health insurance payments, payments by non-profit

---

[41] Law for the budget of the NHIF, State Gazette, Vol. 98, 2014.
[42] *Ibid.*

institutions, and commercial organizations. User fees exist for visits to physicians, dentists, laboratories, and hospitals and apply to all patients with few exceptions; children, pregnant women, chronically disabled patients, unemployed persons, people with low incomes, and patients with mental health disorders are not required to pay.

The primary source of revenue for the health system is these out-of-pocket payments, which include direct payments, cost-sharing, and VHI premiums. Together, they accounted for more than 96% of all private health expenditures in 2007 and more than 86% in 2008 (Dimova, 2012). VHI provides only a small amount of coverage; it is available in the form of a community-rated premium (flat premium) or a risk-rated premium (differentiated premium). Another small contribution to the total of private expenditures comes from corporate payments, donations, and external funds. The private share is likely to be underestimated and reported amounts do not include informal payments connected with traditionally high level of corruption in Bulgaria's health care system.

The second largest source of revenue is SHI contributions. These contributions are shared between the employee and employer, or paid individually by the self-employed or unemployed. For individuals receiving compensation for disability due to illness, pregnancy, childbirth or maternity leave, the contributions are paid only by the employer. Single entrepreneurs, individuals who have established limited liability companies, partners in trade companies, freelance practitioners, and unemployed individuals not entitled to social support are personally responsible for paying the full contribution. For 2014, the lowest base for insurance premium is 210 EUR and the highest possible is 1,200 EUR (Lambreva, 2014). For some categories of insured individuals, for example, children, pensioners, low-income groups contributions are 8% of the minimal insurance income paid by the state.

In 2013, per patient payments for a psychiatric care were very low; for example, the average payment for care in a state hospital is 15.8 EUR per day stay, 1 EUR per day for drugs, and 1.2 EUR per day for food.[43]

---

[43] Report for the results from the audit of the activity connected with National program "Assistants of the disabled people" in the Ministry of Labour and Social Policy, Social assistance agency, National employment agency for the period from 01 January 2005 to 31 December 2007, Bulgarian National Audit Office, 2009.

In 2014, NHIF had a budget of 88 million EUR for primary outpatient services, 35.8 million EUR for specialized medico-diagnostic services, and only half a million Euros for ambulatory follow-up of patients with psychiatric and other disorders.[44] In 2014, the total budget for state mental health hospitals was slightly more than 12 million EUR.

Most physicians and other health personnel working in health institutions funded by the MoH are salaried; however, starting salaries specified in the Collective Labor Agreement for health care are lower than those paid in the commercial public and private hospitals' outpatient care establishments. For inpatient care, physician payments are determined by the institution, be it private or public. Doctors working in state and municipal hospitals can also receive additional performance-related bonuses determined by the financial status of the hospital; in public hospitals, additional remuneration is typically nominal or entirely lacking. In private hospitals, performance-related bonuses contribute substantially to health personnel incomes.

Health personnel reimbursement differs from one professional group to another in terms of remuneration methods and rates. Doctors' reimbursement methods depend on whether they work in primary, specialized, or hospital care. Nurses and other health workers such as physiotherapists, laboratory assistants, dental auxiliaries, and assistant pharmacists typically receive a fixed monthly salary; however, in some instances can also receive performance-related bonuses. As a result, compensation can be highly variable.

3.8 Advocacy, Stigma, and Self-Help

Despite the availability of effective treatments, people with mental health problems or disabilities still face many problems in Bulgarian society, including social isolation and exclusion, stigmatization, discrimination, as well as threats to their autonomy, human rights, and personal dignity. A survey among the relatives of patients with psychiatric disorders has revealed that approximately 70% of these relatives believe that society is intolerant of people with mental illness and that one-third of the patients

---

[44] NGO program in Bulgaria under the European Economic Area Mechanism.

are isolated and suffer discrimination. Only 5.1% of the interviewees believe that their relative would be hired if an employer was aware of their illness. In a survey among randomly selected respondents, approximately 70% believed that psychiatric patients have mandatory registration requirements, and 35%–50% of the respondents believe that psychiatric patients are not supposed to have families and children, to study, or to work. Half of the respondents reported they believe that mentally ill people must be placed in institutions because they are potentially dangerous to society (Lambreva, 2014).

The rights of patients are protected by the Ethics Committees within each treatment setting as well as by the Law. Bulgaria does not have government directives requiring representation of service users on committees and groups responsible for planning, implementing, and evaluating mental health services; nor are they involved in organizations responsible for anti-stigma, mental health promotion and mental disorder prevention. Moreover, the Bulgarian government does not provide dedicated funding for associations of service users to promote their participation in advocacy, legal representation and the protection of service users' rights. All patients have the right to complain about the quality and organization of medical services as well as identify instances of suspected fraud or corruption. Concerns about fraud and corruption can be reported on the web sites of each official institution. Accreditation requires that health care providers establish procedures for collecting and responding to patient complaints. Furthermore, citizens frequently use the media as mediators in cases of patient rights' violation. However, engaging the media is probably not an effective strategy for advocacy and system change as the media also perpetuates stigma about the dangerousness and problematic behavior of mentally ill people.

Several governmental agencies and NGOs are involved in the protection of human rights in general and in particular for individuals with mental illness. These governmental agencies include the Ministry of External Affairs, the Commission for Protection of Personal Data, the Commission for Protection Against Discrimination, the National Bureau for Legal Help, the Bulgarian Ombudsman, the Agency for People With Disabilities as part of the Ministry of Labor and Social Affairs, the National Council For Mental Health and the Consultative Councils which

A Patient's Perspective

What is the first thing you can think of when referring to "mental disorder?"
The mentally ill person is different from normal people. When people look at me, they say to themselves "she is mad, she is not normal."

Before suffering from a mental disorder yourself, have you known or heard of others suffering from mental disorders? Could you tell us some words about this?
No. I am 50 years old, and I learned what depression was when I was 20 and experienced it in a very acute form.

Do you discuss mental health issues in your family or community?
No. I thought in the past people were born like this.

Do you believe that psychiatry is effective in addressing, improving, and treating mental health issues?
Yes, the hospital is helping a lot. They have a kind attitude toward the mentally ill. The medications are helping. I'm not ashamed that I'm here; my neighbors know where I am.

What was your own experience as a patient in a mental health facility? How would you describe it?
I'm pleased with my experience. They helped me a lot. I would describe it as them entering into your mind and trying to help you, to analyze you.

Has your knowledge and understanding of psychiatry changed over time? What about your knowledge and understanding of psychology?
I cannot differentiate between psychiatry and psychology. I understand that there are patients that are worse than me. I understand that I cannot calm myself.

Could you describe a particular moment that illustrates your interactions with the medical personnel?
The doctors are very nice. Sometimes the nurses are rude. Once when I was trembling, I looked for help, and the nurse said, "We know that you are

(Continued)

(Continued)

> trembling and that you cannot walk well, this is nothing new, go to bed." The nurses don't want to ask for a doctor.
>
> **Could you describe the accommodation conditions in the psychiatry hospital?**
> There are 3 beds in the room; I was with a girl that acted strange because she was very ill. The room was smelly because of her, but they cleaned it several times per day. There is a restroom inside and it is clean. I have a shower every evening.
>
> **Do you think that mental health services are financially available?**
> Yes, it is affordable for me; I'm not paying anything.

are part of municipal government. In Bulgaria, national or regional bodies perform regular inspections of mental health facilities, review involuntary admissions and discharge procedures, review restriction of rights, as well as instances where physical restraints have been used. However, while these groups receive complaints and conduct investigations they do not have the ability to impose sanctions in response to human rights violations.

On the side of NGOs, the Bulgarian Helsinki Committee is one of the most active NGOs involved in monitoring and protecting the rights of mentally ill people; the Committee has an agreement with the MoH for regular monitoring. The Union of the Disabled in Bulgaria is another NGO actively involved in defending and representing disabled people in a range of settings. Recently a self-help group for relatives of patients with different psychiatric disorders as part of the project "Open minds" supported by a NGO Program in Bulgaria under the European Economic Area Financial Mechanism was established.[45] However, there are few self-help groups for individuals and families challenged with bipolar disorder, gambling disorder, and alcohol, as well as other substance abuse.

---

[45] NGO program in Bulgaria under the European Economic Area Mechanism.

3.9 Looking Forward: Challenges and Priorities in the Bulgarian Mental Health Care System

In conclusion, though mental health is considered to be a priority area in national health policy, it is not realized in actual implementation or practice. This is reflected in the continued imbalance of resource allocations between inpatient and outpatient mental health care, and the slow pace of reform compared with changes in other sectors of the health system in Bulgaria. The very small allocations for capital improvements, the maldistribution of services, the low salaries for professionals, and the limits on covered services all contribute to high levels of dissatisfaction in the system and further stigmatization of patients and providers. In addition, neither mental health care providers nor patients perceive improvements in the quality of care.

Additionally, reductions in the availability of psychiatric beds and occupational/rehabilitative services are unevenly distributed over the different regions of the country. In the past several years, funding to support the mental health centers' programs has been reduced and this has negatively impacted the centers' efforts at outreach mental health promotion and early diagnosis of people with mental disorders, as well as the provision of ongoing treatment and supportive services.

These problems have a real impact on patients and their families. For example, due to the lack of anesthesiologists in psychiatric settings, electro-convulsive therapy is offered only in university hospitals. There is also a problem with the availability of some generic drugs (e.g. lithium); many believe that the limited profit for pharmaceutical companies and high taxes contribute significantly to these shortages. Other barriers to the needed care include delays in payment, long wait times for the delivery of medications to pharmacies, and the lack of coverage from NHIF for many diagnoses other than affective and psychotic disorders. The lack of adequate insurance payments for psychotherapy is also problematic.

The split of responsibilities for mental health care between MoH and NHIF causes regulatory problems that are manifest in lack of access and underfinancing of the mental health system. For example, payment for outpatients by NHIF is lower for psychiatrists when compared with other specialists, and payment by the MoH for monthly ambulatory visits is low. This too contributes to the lack of a well-developed connected network of psychiatric services within the community or other mechanisms to provide the care or adequate support to relatives for time and expenses. As a result, patients are largely left required to provide such care. The existing day services are insufficient in number and unevenly distributed so people with disabilities in some regions do not have real access; moreover, collaboration between day care centers, protected homes, and hospitals providing mental health services is lacking.

That being said, there have been some positive changes in the past several years and reason for hope that the situation can improve. Recently, several projects have tried to improve the quality of life for mental health patients and their relatives and new NGOs are established to address these needs. In addition, legislation is changing and adopting new standards, leading to the development and implementation of national programs and strategies. These changes promise that much needed change and improvements can be achieved in the years to come.

References

Analysis development and realization of the human resources in the health care, Confederation of independent trade unions in Bulgaria, 2013.

Bradel, Y. (1885) To the question about the right organization, looking and care for the mentally ill in Bulgaria. *Health* **1** (16), 125–127; **1** (17), 133–134.

Bulgaria — A Country Overview, Angloinfo. Available at: https://www.angloinfo.com/how-to/bulgaria/moving/country-file/country-overview.

Bulgaria Demographics Profile 2014, Index Mundi. Available at: https://www.indexmundi.com/bulgaria/

Bulgaria: life expectancy, World health rankings. Available at: https://www.indexmundi.com/bulgaria/

Bulgaria — Literacy rate, Index Mundi. Available at: https://www.indexmundi.com/bulgaria/

Bulgaria Sex ratio, Index Mundi. Available at: https://www.indexmundi.com/bulgaria/

Danadziev, S. (1914) Arrangement of the institutions for mentally ill abroad and in the country. *BIAD* **3** (4 and 5).

Dimova, A., Rohova, M., Moutafova, E., Atanasova, E., Koeva, S., Panteli, D. and van Ginneken, E. (2012) Health Systems in Transition, Vol. 14 No. 3.

Donchev, P. (2006) Forensic psychiatry manual. Dr. Ivan Bogorov, Sofia. ISBN 9789543160310, pages 320.

Golovina, A. (1895) Care of the mentally ill and the arrangement of the psychiatric hospitals. *Medical digest* **I**, 36–37; **II**, 235–257, **III**, 385–425.

Kirov, K. (1970) Historical notes for the psychiatric hospital in Karlukovo. *Neurology, Psychiatry and Neurosurgery* **IX** (2),190–196.

Lambreva, D. (2014) Public attitudes toward mental health (Medical University, Sofia).

List of countries by suicide rate, Wikipedia. Available at: https://en.wikipedia.org/wiki/List_of_countries_by_suicide_rate.

List of European countries by average wage, Wikipedia. Available at: https://en.wikipedia.org/wiki/List_of_countries_by_average_wage.

McCagg, W. O. and Siegelbaum, L. (eds.) (1989) *The Disabled in the Soviet Union: Past and Present, Theory and Practice* (University of Pittsburgh Press, Pennsylvania) p. 270.

Milenkov, K. (1966) The fight for humanistic attitude toward mentally ill. B: Pages from the history of the medicine in the country, Sofia, 65–69.

Milenkov, K. (1978) Short historical review of the care for the mentally ill in Bulgaria. СборнAsclepius, Vol. V, 83–88.

Milenkov, K. (2008/2009) History of the Bulgarian psychiatry. Unpublished notes. National archive, Sofia.

Milenkov K. (2013) Psychiatry. In: *History of the Medical Science in Bulgaria*. Georgiev M., Mitev V. (Eds.), Sofia, Prof. Marin Drinov Publishing House, ISBN 9789543225613, p. 472.

Milenkov, K., Ignev, G., Kisiov, G. and Kolchev, K. (1969) About psychiatric facilities with open doors in the country. *Neurology and psychiatry* **4**, 288–293.

Milenkov, S. (2005) Informed consent from suicidal patients. *Receptor* **2**, 59–63.

Milev, V., Tzafarov, K. and Milenkov, K. (1982) Development of the psychiatric care in Bulgaria. *Bulletin SINPN* **10** (1), 5–15.

Moskov, N. (1902) Mentally ill in the country. Advances in medicine: 22–31.

National Statistical Institute (2011). Census. Available at: https://www.nsi.bg/census2011/PDOCS2/Census2011final_en.pdf.

Petrovski, I. (2001) Contemporary Bulgarian Healthcare from 1887 Till Now, Vol. 1, DNK.

Policies and practices for mental health in Europe, WHO Europe. Available at: http://www.euro.who.int/__data/assets/pdf_file/0006/96450/E91732.pdf.

Population Ageing and Development 2012, United Nations, 2012. Available at: https://www.unfpa.org/resources/population-ageing-and-development-2012.

Population Bulgaria 2014, Country Economy. Available at: https://countryeconomy.com/demography/population/bulgaria.

Public health statistics, Bulgaria 2014, Annual, Sofia, 2014. Available at: http://www.mh.government.bg/en/ministry/commissions/national-council-prices-and-reimbursement-medicinal-products/.

Shipkovenska, Y. and Predov, N. (1981) Bulgarian monastery for psychiatric help. XXVI International congress for the history of medicine—1978, Vol. IV, Sofia, 36–37.

Temkov, I., Ivanov, V. and Hristozov, H. (1953/1954) Development of the Bulgarian psychiatric science. Works of SRPI, Vol. I, 3–36, Sofia.

Temkov, I., Milenkov, K. and Popov, N. (1968) Neurology, Psychiatry and Neurosurgery, Vol. 5, 375–384.

The World Bank data. Available at: https://data.worldbank.org/country/bulgaria

Tzafarov, K. (1970) Documents about the first steps in the organization of the psychiatric care in Bulgaria after our freedom from the Ottoman yoke. *Neurology, Psychiatry and Neurosurgery* **IX** (3), 259–260.

Youth unemployment in Bulgaria, Institute for Market Economics, 2014. Available at: https://bednostbg.info/var/docs/reports/Youth_Unemployment_IME.pdf.

CHAPTER 4

An Overview of Mental Health in the Czech Republic

Eva Tušková[*], Karolína Dobiášová[†], and Ivan Duškov[‡]

[*]Department of Social Psychiatry, National Institute of Mental Health, Klecany, Czech Republic

[†]Department of Public and Social Policy, Faculty of Social Sciences, Charles University in Prague, Prague, Czech Republic

[‡]Institute for Language and Preparatory Studies, Charles University, Prague, Czech Republic

4.1 Mental Health Status of the Czech Population

In the Czech Republic (CR), the 10th revision of the International Statistical Classification of Diseases and Related Health Problems (ICD-10) is used for the classification of the mental health disorders. The ICD-10 chapter on mental health disorders also includes disorders that are diagnosed as being due to psychoactive substance use. In the CR, the substance use and related disorders are perceived as closely connected to other mental health disorders and are treated within the mental health care system.

Key Country Statistics	
Region: Central Europe	**Population above the age of 65:** more than 17%
Government system: parliamentary republic	**Average life expectancy:** 75.5 for males and 81.8 years for females
Area: 78,867 square kilometers	
Population: 10,644,842	**Suicide rate:** 12.7 per 100,000 residents
Capital: Prague	**Economy:** upper middle income economy
Gender ratio: 0.97 male to female	**GDP annual growth rate:** 2%
Ethnic groups:	**GDP per capita:** 32,100 USD (PPP)
• Czech 64.3%	**Unemployment rate:** 6.5%
• Moravian 5%	**Youth unemployment rate:** 15.9%
• Slovak 1.4%	**Total health expenditure as percentage of GDP:** 7%
• Other 1.8%	
• Unspecified 27.5%	**Population below poverty line:** 8.6%
Literacy rate: 99%	
Population under the age of 15: 15%	*Source*: CIA World Factbook (2016).

4.1.1 Mental health status measurements—Main approaches and data sources

Routine statistics provide the best available approximation of the mental health status of the Czech population. Data collection and management is provided by the Institute of Health Information and Statistics (IHIS-CR), which publishes yearbooks entitled *Psychiatric Care* and *Hospitalizations*. It is also possible to create data tables via the online Data Presentation System (DPS) on the Institute's webpages.[1] Routine statistics are based on treatment prevalence; because of gaps in access to treatment, along with a high level of stigmatization of mental illness in the CR (as detailed in one of the following sections), available data may significantly underestimate the true prevalence of mental disorders.

The last comprehensive health survey, which covered the overall true mental health morbidity of the population, *Czech National Probability Survey of Mental Health and Comorbidity* (CNPS), was conducted in 1999 by the Prague Psychiatric Center in partnership with the World Health Organization (WHO). Using the Composite International Diagnostic Interview (CIDI)/ICD-10 instrument, the survey was based on face-to-face interviews across the nation. The survey findings are summarized by Dzúrová *et al.* (2000). Some data on true prevalence are also provided in

---

[1] www.uzis.cz.

the report by Gustavsson et al. (2011). The CR also participates in the European Health Interview Survey (EHIS), where basic questions related to healthy lifestyle, vitality, risk behavior, and other health related issues are investigated. Additional data on youth risk behavior is regularly monitored by cross-national Health Behavior In School-Aged Children (HBSC) survey, assessing health-related risk behavior, along with the European School Survey Project on Alcohol and Other Drugs (ESPAD) survey.

4.1.2 Treated mental health morbidity

Altogether, 603,205 patients in the CR were treated in outpatient psychiatric facilities for mental health in 2013; this involved 2,896,558 service encounters. The most common mental disorders were not of a psychotic nature; these patients account for 40% of "first contacts" in a year. Individuals diagnosed with affective disorders were 19% and organic disorders were 11%. The overall number of patients in outpatient care rises year by year, as demonstrated in Figure 4.1. In general, women were more frequently treated for affective, neurotic, organic disorders, and schizophrenia, as well as much more frequently for eating disorders. Men were more frequently treated for sexual disorders, and disorders due to psychoactive substance use and developmental disorders. In 2013, young people represented less than 10% of identified mental health patients. They were treated mainly for developmental disorders and mental retardation (IHIS CR, 2014b).

Based on data from 2012, collected on a routine basis by IHIS-CR, almost 50% of individuals requiring inpatient psychiatric care were diagnosed as follows: schizophrenia (19%), neurotic disorders (16%), and disorders due to alcohol use (16%). Men were more frequently hospitalized for substance-related disorders and women for neurotic disorders. Patients aged 0–14 years represented 4.4% of all hospitalized patients and, as noted above, were usually treated for developmental disorders. The average length of stay for inpatient care reached 63.4 days, but there was a significant difference between the psychiatric departments of general hospitals (18.8 days) and at specialty psychiatric hospitals (83.8 days); inpatient treatment for sexual disorders[2] was an average of 377 days (IHIS CR, 2013a).

---

[2]F64-F66 according to ICD 10 (gender identity disorders, disorders of sexual preference and psychological and behavioral disorders associated with sexual development and orientation).

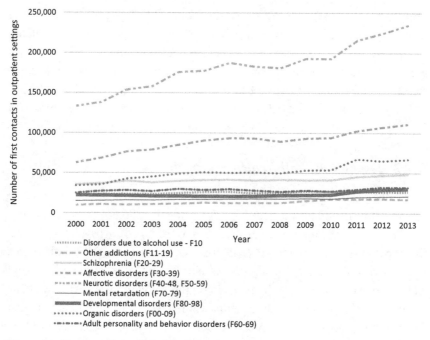

Figure 4.1: Number of mental health first contacts in a year in outpatient settings according to ICD-10, 2000–2013.

Source: Authors' analysis of Yearbooks on outpatient psychiatric care by IHIS-CR, available at http://www.uzis.cz/category/tematicke-rady/zdravotnicka-statistika/psychiatrie-obecne.

4.1.3 True prevalence of mental disorders in the Czech Republic

Very little is known about the true prevalence of mental disorders in the CR. The most reliable data is from a study that is now more than 15 years old. Conducted between 1998 and 1999, the study found that approximately 27% of respondents reported at least one episode of psychiatric disorders in their lifetime. The highest lifetime prevalence included neurotic, stress-related, and somatoform disorders (18.4%), mental and behavioral disorders due to psychoactive substance use (13%) and mood disorders, especially depression (13%). Women were twice as likely as men to have neurotic and affective disorders and men twice as likely as women to suffer from substance use disorders; this pattern is similar to what is seen in the treatment prevalence data. The highest rate prevalence during a year was in the group of women aged 40–49, and overall, women had a higher 12-month prevalence (23.2%) than men (17.9%). For men, the highest annual prevalence rates of mental illness were observed amongst those aged 18–29 years. Increased rates were also observed among people who were unemployed as well as unmarried men and women from big urban areas and those living alone (Dzúrová et al., 2000).

Mental disorders represent a significant societal burden; in 2008, 24.5% of all DALYs (Disability Adjusted Life-Years) in the CR and 26.6% of all DALYs in the EU[3] were attributed to mental disorders. In the CR, mental disorders accounted for about 33,000 cases of incapacity for work in 2012; the average length of the incapacity was 93 days. This places the duration of incapacity due to mental disorders third right after incapacity due to cancer and pregnancy (IHIS CR, 2013b). According to Janoušková et al. (2014), mental disorders were the second highest cause of receiving disability pensions in 2011, accounting for 16%–17% of all disability pensions. Psychotic, mood, and anxiety disorders are the most frequent causes of disability due to mental health problems.

Looking at prevalence and impact of the impact of mental disorders, we find the following in the CR:

Suicides: The lowest number of suicides in recent history in the CR was reported in 2007 (13.3 per 100,000), but since then, the number has been increasing. In 2012, the rate of suicides was 15.7 per 100,000. Men have a 2–3 times higher probability of successful suicide than women, while women are 3 times more likely to have para-suicidal behavior than men (Ministry of Health, 2014). Figure 4.2 compares suicide rates in CR to those in other European countries; here, CR has a relatively low number of suicides in comparison to the new European Union (EU) member states and a comparatively high number of suicides when compared to EU members of longer tenure. In 2011, the OECD (2014b) compared the number of inpatient suicides and suicides after discharge from psychiatric

---

[3] Mental health DALYs in the old EU member states ranged from 25.6% in Portugal to 35.6% in Spain and in the new EU member states from 19.9% in Romania till 27.5% in Slovenia (WHO, 2011).

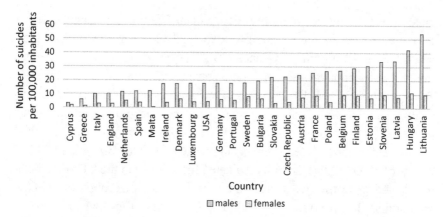

Figure 4.2: International comparison of the number of suicides per 100,000 inhabitants.
Source: Authors' analysis of WHO Mental health atlas 2011—country profiles, available at http://www.who.int/mental_health/evidence/atlas/profiles/en/#C.

inpatient facilities committed by patients diagnosed with schizophrenia or bipolar disorder across Europe. CR and Italy had the lowest rate of inpatient suicides (0.0 per 100 patients) while the highest was found in Slovenia (0.25 per 100). However, in the CR 0.14 suicides per 100 patients occur after discharge; this rate is about 10 times higher than in general population.

Depression and depressive symptomatology: According to EHIS (Daňková, 2011) 3.9% of the Czech population reported that they experienced depression in the preceding 12 months (64% of these individuals reporting depression reported that they were diagnosed with depression); this was above the European average of 3.1%. Women reported depression more frequently (5.4%) than men (2.3%), while the highest prevalence was observed in the group of women over 75 years (8.8%).

Anxiety disorders: According to EHIS, chronic anxiety was reported by 2.6% of women and 1.2% of men, while the highest prevalence was reported by 7.7% women aged 75 years and older (IHIS CR, 2011a).

Eating disorders: The majority of patients receiving outpatient care for the treatment of eating disorders are women (approximately 90%) and older than 20 years (approximately 60%). The trend in both the number of hospitalizations and the number of patients is decreasing. Patients are hospitalized mainly for anorexia nervosa (62%) (IHIS CR, 2010, 2011b, 2012, 2013c).

Substance-related disorders: Alcohol, tobacco, and drugs consumption is substantial in the CR and represents a significant risk for the mental health of the population in general, and in particular youth and young adults. The most frequently used illicit drugs in the CR were marijuana and hashish. In 2012, a survey conducted by Czech National Monitoring Centre for Drugs and Addiction found that 28% of respondents aged 15–64 years reported experience with those drugs (NMS, 2013). The ESPAD study found that 42.3% of 16 year olds reported at least 1 experience with marijuana and hashish. This was the highest prevalence in Europe (NMS, 2011) and has been a stable statistic since 2003. In 2009, CR had an average per capita consumption of 16.6 liters of pure alcohol compared to the average of 12.5 liters in the EU (Anderson et al., 2012. Drinking by Czech adolescents is a particular concern; in 2011, 60% of 16-year olds were regular consumers of alcohol and 54% of them reported binge drinking (5 or more glasses of alcohol) at least once in the preceding month in comparison with 39% of their European peers (NMS, 2011).

Approximately 30% of the adult Czech population smoke tobacco. Tobacco products are easily accessible for Czech youngsters and this is reflected in the data on tobacco use. The highest proportion of smokers is in the group 15–24 years; approximately 45% of 15–24 year olds smoke (Ministry of Health, 2014). In 2011, 28% of 16 year olds were smoking. This is of higher prevalence than observed in Bulgaria, Croatia, France, Latvia, Monaco, and Slovakia; however this shows a trend toward lower rates over time.

In 2013, the data suggest that there was a slight decrease in the number of patients who sought services related to psychoactive substance use. The majority of cases concerned alcohol use (61% of patients); this compares to 9% of patients treated for methamphetamine use, 8.5% treated for opiate use, and 8.6% treated for multiple drug use. Individuals between the ages of 40 and 64 comprised 54% of alcohol users, and men represented 64% of all the patients. Men predominate in all groups of substance use, except for sedatives and hypnotics where women represented 58% of all users (IHIS CR, 2014c). Approximately two-thirds of inpatient admissions in 2012 attributed to psychoactive substance use were caused by alcohol use; men represented 68% of all such patients. The concurrent use of more than one drug accounted for 19.5% of all the hospitalizations (IHIS CR, 2013d).

4.2 History of Mental Health Care in the Czech Republic

4.2.1 *General context*

Since the "Velvet Revolution" in 1989,[4] governmental health policy has been largely focused on the problems of health services provision and funding. The system relies on the public health insurance model, where negotiations between government, health care insurers, and health care providers play a crucial role. From a political point of view, health policy is one of the main sources of conflicts in government. This has contributed to a high level of turnover among the Czech ministers of health.[5] Moreover, health promotion and health protection are rather marginalized in the political discourse, as is the field of mental health care. As detailed below, the history of mental health policy is characterized by repeated attempts at reform by mental health care professionals; however, implementation of recommended reforms often suffers from the inattention of policymakers.

The CR's social security system provides financial support and services in response to a range of social needs. The system consists of a social insurance system, a non-contributory social benefit system, and a system of social services along with unemployment policy. The social insurance system covers benefits related to old age, disability, death of breadwinner (covered by pension insurance), sickness and childbirth (covered by sickness insurance). The social benefit system includes both the

---

[4]"Velvet Revolution" is a term used to describe the peaceful transition of Czechoslovakia from former communist rule to a democratic government.
[5]From 1989 through 2017, 23 ministers were in the office, which is the highest number in comparison with other departments of government.

state social support system (which provides family supports) and the material assistance system (provides those with insufficient income assistance for living, housing, and extraordinary circumstances).[6]

4.2.2 Mental health care before World War II: 1790–1939

The history of state-provided mental health care dates back to the Austro–Hungarian Empire and the foundation of the first general hospital in Prague in 1790. The hospital also included the first inpatient department for the care of the mentally ill (often referred to as the "madhouse"), but care was largely long term and custodial. Between 1860 and 1910, another 8 large psychiatric inpatient facilities were established during a time when there was a reduction in stigma toward people with mental illness (Scheffler and Potůček, 2008). During the existence of the Czechoslovak Republic from 1918 to 1939, psychiatric research flourished, treatment became more effective, and the number of psychiatric inpatient facilities continued to grow as did the number of professionals (Scheffler and Potůček, 2008). However, during World War II universities were closed, and many psychiatrists went into exile or were sent to concentration camps. Many patients were deported. Even though psychiatric hospitals had only limited resources during this period, they continued to provide care and conduct research (Scheffler and Potůček, 2008).

4.2.3 Mental health care under communist regime: 1945–1990

After World War II, the Semashko model of health care system was introduced in the Czech territory. This meant that health care was nationalized and governed through a hierarchical centralized system of national committees. The entire system was financed by taxes. During this time, there were specialized psychiatric hospitals, psychiatric departments of general

---

[6]Ministry of Labor and Social Affairs. "Assistance in Material Need." https://www.mpsv.cz/en/1608.

hospitals, and outpatient facilities to provide services. The number of departments in general hospitals and outpatient facilities increased, and during this period medical aspects of mental illness were given greater attention than social concerns (Scheffler and Potůček, 2008).

4.2.4 Mental health care under democratic government: 1991–Today

After the Velvet Revolution, Czechoslovakia split into 2 independent states: creating the CR and Slovakia. Both countries adopted the then current basic international human rights documents. The CR endorsed the *Charter of Fundamental Rights and Freedoms*.[7] In the early 1990s, CR switched to the health insurance system which included compulsory health insurance and partial liberalization of policies related to the ownership of health care facilities. The transformation of the Czech health system focused mainly the methods of funding and financing of health care services, while public health and health promotion were relatively neglected.

In 1992, an informal work group was designated to create the *Framework of Psychiatry*. In 2002, the new *Framework of Psychiatry* was accepted by the Scientific Council of the Czech Ministry of Health. The Framework proposed a system in which acute mental health care would be provided predominantly in departments of general hospitals, the overall number of inpatient beds would be reduced and home and community care services would be further developed (Koncepce oboru psychiatrie, 2007). While the number of beds may have gradually decreased, other objectives identified by the Framework have not been addressed, as the Framework lacked a specific implementation plan (Raboch and Wenigová, 2012). Therefore, in 2004, the Ministry of Health appointed an Implementation Committee tasked with proposing specific methods and processes for Framework implementation.

---

[7] In terms of mental health care, the most relevant articles are those about freedom and equality, dignity, rights, and protection of health for everyone, as well as protection against torture and inhumane or humiliating treatment.

In 2005, several members of the Committee published a document entitled *Mental Health Care Policy—Roads to Implementation*. This policy paper proposed:

- Diversification of services provided in psychiatric hospitals (in order to maintain the capacity and staff of the hospitals while lowering the number of hospitalized patients);
- Closing of selected departments in psychiatric hospitals;
- Closing of selected psychiatric hospitals (Center for mental health care development 2005).

This plan, however, was not implemented, and in 2006 the Minister of Health dissolved the Committee. Another attempt at system reform occurred in 2007 when the Psychiatric Society published *The National Psychiatric Program*, which was created in collaboration with the regional WHO office. This initiative sought to incorporate recommendations from the WHO *Action Plan for Europe* (2005) and the EU Commission's 2005 *Green Paper*. The Society's work established general goals and tasks, but failed to tackle the question of who would be responsible for implementation of proposed reforms.[8]

Finally, in 2008, the Psychiatric Society appointed a new "Commission for the Revision of the Framework of Psychiatry;" building on the earlier *Framework of Psychiatry*. This initiative advocated for strengthening of community-based mental health care. Unfortunately, the revised framework did not identify strategies for change and did not specify a timeline for implementation (Koncepce oboru psychiatrie, 2008).

Despite the several attempts at system reform described above, community care is still not well developed in the CR (see the section below regarding organization of care). The Czech system for mental health service delivery remains, for the most part, organized around institutional care. Deinstitutionalization of mental health care is one of the main objectives of the recent mental health care reform, initiated by the Ministry of Health in 2012 detailed in the section that follows.

In the CR, patients may gain access to psychiatric care (i.e. inpatient, outpatient, and community care facilities) via several entry points—by

---

[8] *Národní psychiatrický program* (2007).

referral from a general practitioner (GP), a specialist (mainly neurologists), emergency medical services, or an inpatient medical facility. People may also seek services directly from mental health providers (i.e. without any referral as detailed above). According to Raboch and Wenigová (2012), a survey of inpatient throughput in 7 facilities providing acute care, revealed that 34% of patients were referred to the hospital by an outpatient psychiatrist, 12% were referred by a GP, and 20% approached the system directly without a referral. Reliable data on how GPs serve as an entry to outpatient psychiatric care are not available.

4.3 Mental Health Policies and Legislation in the Czech Republic

There is currently no unifying and binding mental health law in the CR (the *Framework of Psychiatry* is merely guidelines); this is the same circumstance in about 10 other European countries. Instead, in the CR, the legal framework of providing care to patients with mental health problems can be found in several acts; in particular, the Act on Healthcare Services specifies the terms and conditions for providing services along with the Act on Specific Health Services and other laws.

In the past, there was no clear consensus among professionals about the value or importance of creating a standalone Mental Health Act. A large number of people expressed concern that a standalone act for mental health would cause even greater stigmatization of both psychiatry as a medical field and its patients. However, experience from abroad (France, Poland, etc.) demonstrates that those concerns were unwarranted. Nowadays, there appears to be a consensus among key stakeholders that the benefits of Mental Health Act would outweigh its negatives. In addition to such a law's ability to specifically address the treatment of mentally ill patients, such an Act would also serve to strengthen and protect their human rights.

However, the need for a Mental Health Act remains debatable. According to Professor Genevra Richardson,[9] a special law would be

---

[9] Genevra Richardson is a professor of Law at King's College London. In her research, she deals with the relationship between law and medicine, particularly law and psychiatry.

discriminatory. She believes that while a mental health law in the CR could offer some advantages, it is highly complex and there are very few real safeguards for patients. While a mental health law could enable the introduction of meaningful safeguards they must be properly implemented. However, concern remains that such a law would create a form of legal discrimination against people with mental disorders. At the same time others believe that people with mental disorders are particularly vulnerable and they need to be protected from the consequences of those disorders. That is the argument that a lot of clinicians in the UK would use.[10] Passage of a Mental Health Act could advance the implementation of the Strategy for Reform of Psychiatric Care (Ministry of Health, 2013). Another key advantage of having a standalone Act would be a clear articulation of the responsibilities of individual ministries and other collaborating institutions.

4.3.1 *International perspectives in mental health policy*

Promotion of mental health, along with prevention and treatment of mental health disorders, is increasingly a global as well as a European priority. This can be seen in the various resolutions recently adopted by World Health Assembly and Regional Office of WHO for Europe.[11] One of the most important international initiatives in this respect derived from the European Ministerial Conference on Mental Health held in Helsinki in January 2005. The Conference's recommendations called for a shift away from care provided in large isolated institutions to services provided by a broad spectrum of community-based services.

The CR is bound by several documents (e.g. laws) defining conditions of care provided to disabled persons; in some instances, the special

---

She was a book review editor of Public Law for many years and currently is on the editorial board of the *Journal of Mental Health Law* and the *Journal of Forensic Psychiatry*. She was invited to chair the Expert Committee on the Reform of Mental Health Legislation in 1998.

[10] Kondratova & Janouskova. *Genevra Richardson and Gareth Owen about Mental Health Legislation*. Interview with Genevra Richardson and Gareth Owen. Not published yet.

[11] For example, the resolution of the World Health Assembly WHA65.4 on the global burden of mental disorders.

needs of patients suffering from mental illness are also considered. In January 2005, the CR made a commitment to implementation of the recommendations coming from the Helsinki conference through the European Mental Health Action Plan. In 2008, the original Helsinki Declaration was succeeded by the European Pact for Mental Health and Wellbeing. In 2009, the CR ratified the UN Convention on the Rights of Persons with Disabilities and this became part of the Czech legal system in February 2010. The European Mental Health Action Plan was adopted by member states in September 2013; a primary objective is the closure of large institutions and the development of community-oriented services provided by multidisciplinary teams. Unfortunately, despite the above-mentioned international recommendations adopted by Czech ministers, and the support and bilateral cooperation of the WHO Regional Office for Europe, significant changes in mental health care in line with these principles have not yet been implemented in the CR. The Strategy for Reform of Psychiatric Care, adopted by Ministry of Health in 2013, provides a promising opportunity to effect much needed change.

4.4 Organizational Structure of the Mental Health System in the Czech Republic

4.4.1 *Administrative framework of mental health care*

Mental health care operates within the wider health care framework. There are numerous entities at different levels of government that are involved in the planning, finance, administration, and provision of mental health services in the CR. The legislative role belongs to Parliament; the Ministry of Health and Ministry of Labor and Social Affairs focus on policy.[12] The Ministry of Health may also influence the functioning of the system through public notices and regulations, through the management of sev-

---

[12] Ministries play a role of moderators in the process of formulation of a new governmental law. However, a law might be submitted for consideration into Parliament also by a deputy, group of deputies, Senate (as a whole), and regional governments.

eral psychiatric hospitals (by appointing hospitals' directors, investing) and the influence that it exercises on the health insurance system via the annual negotiations about reimbursements as well as through its nominees to the insurance companies' boards. The Ministry of Labor and Social Affairs plays a role mainly in direct financing of the NGOs providing social care. The Government Councils for the Human Rights and for People with Disabilities monitor the protection of human rights and freedoms grounded in the Constitution. The Public Defender of Rights protects citizens against the possibly illegal behavior of government agencies and inspects institutions, including psychiatric hospitals, where individuals' rights may be restricted. County offices manage some of the general hospitals, support NGOs, and form plans for the development of health and social services. Health insurance companies also have a major role in the system. They participate in the above-mentioned negotiations and enter into contracts with service providers. Professional organizations work as advisory and expert bodies for the Ministry of Health and have a major role in the medical education. The participation of users' organizations on the mental health care system is not formally institutionalized in the CR.

4.4.2 Overview of how mental health care services are provided

The majority of mental health care in the CR is provided as outpatient services by a number of professionals in a range of settings including GPs, diagnostic and advisory centers for children and adolescents, centers for family and human relationships, as well as adult, child, and geriatric psychiatry. Other services include specialists in the treatment of drug and alcohol related problems, centers for opioid substitution therapy, eating disorders specialists, sexologists and clinical psychologists, inpatient facilities (psychiatric hospitals and psychiatric departments of general or university hospitals), and community services.

There are 21 psychiatric hospitals that provide acute care, subacute care, and rehabilitation; 18 are for adults and 3 are dedicated to providing care to children. Although 30 general hospitals also have psychiatric

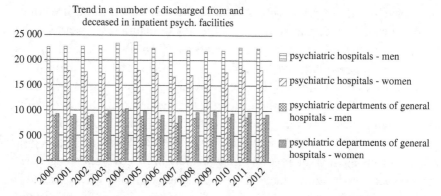

Figure 4.3: Trend in number of discharged from and deceased in inpatient psychiatric facilities.

Notes: This chart represents the best available number describing what is happening in inpatient care. It is the number of hospitalizations, counted as a number of terminated hospitalizations per year, and not a number of unique patients, meaning one patient can be counted several times per year.
Source: Authors according to *IHIS-CR* yearbooks on psychiatric care, available at https://www.uzis.cz/category/tematicke-rady/zdravotnicka-statistika/psychiatrie-obecne.

departments that provide acute care, the majority of care takes place in the specialized psychiatric hospitals (88% of beds in 2012) (IHIS CR, 2013a).

The CR has a long tradition of large psychiatric hospitals; the average number of beds per psychiatric hospital is 502, which is the highest average in the EU (WHO, 2011). Psychiatric hospitals are unevenly distributed across the country and may have responsibility for large catchment areas. Since 2008, there are almost 400 fewer beds in psychiatric hospitals and there has been a reduction of 136 beds in psychiatric departments of general hospitals (IHIS CR, 2013a). However, the number of patients in psychiatric hospitals slightly increased in recent years (2007–2012) as the average length of stay decreased, and men represent a majority of those patients as illustrated in Figure 4.3. The average length of stay continuously decreases (IHIS CR, 2013a).

In 2013, there were on average 1,600 registered adult patients for each GP in the CR and this accounted for a total of 7,200 annual visits per GP. In other words, 1 registered patient was provided with an average 4.5 examinations per year; preventive examinations represented 6.5% of the total number of examinations (IHIS CR, 2014d).

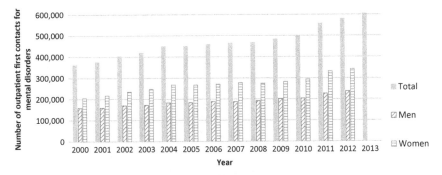

Figure 4.4: Number of outpatient first contacts during 1-year period for mental disorders (F00-F99) by gender.
Source: Authors' analysis, according to *IHIS-CR* (http://www.uzis.cz/katalog/zdravotnicka-statistika/psychiatricka-pece) and updated 2013 data.

Based on the number of patients served and the number of encounters, outpatient psychiatric services are the foundation of the mental health service delivery system; outpatient specialists also provide long-term care (Raboch and Wenigová, 2012). The overall number of outpatient psychiatric facilities is increasing, as is the number of outpatient physician posts per 100,000 inhabitants (6.8 per 100,000 in 2004, 7.5 in 2012) and the number of patients (see Figure 4.4).

Community services focused on mental health are not fully developed in the CR. As of 2016, only 5 of 14 districts have community mental health centers, with 4 of the 5 established in 2016. In addition, there are 21 day clinics across the country, and approximately half of them are associated with an inpatient facility. Most of these clinics were founded before 1999. There is also 1 mobile case management team for emergency interventions in Prague. Other services across the country include 3 case management centers available on a 24/7 basis that include a psychiatrist (Pěč, 2012). The need for more community-based health–social care is partially addressed by NGOs, but, this cannot be described as a systematic coordination of health and social care. According to the Association for Community Services,[13] there were 37 such organizations registered in March 2015 in all of CR.

---

[13] www.askoz.cz.

4.5 Access to the Mental Health Care System in the Czech Republic

The right to health care is enshrined in the CR Constitution, which states: *"Everyone has the right to health protection. Citizens are entitled under public insurance to free medical care and medical aids under the conditions provided for by law."*[14] All Czech citizens, all permanent residents, and a few other groups (e.g. asylum seekers, all EU citizens residing in the CR on a long-term basis) are entitled to health care which is provided on the basis of mandatory public health insurance. All other residents, such as self-employed persons, all children through age 18, parents and partners of non-EU migrants (if they are not EU citizens or do not have permanent residence permits), as well as students not covered by international agreements and other individuals,[15] must purchase commercial health insurance. However, this does not cover the same amount of care as the public health insurance; for example, treatment in psychiatric hospitals is not covered by the commercial insurance (Hnilicová and Dobiášová, 2011).

Despite the legal entitlement to healthcare, psychiatric patients often face significant barriers in seeking access to mental health care services. The distribution of inpatient psychiatric facilities in the CR is very uneven across the regions, and the Czech mental health system is also challenged by a lack of specialized outpatient care (e.g. in the fields of child psychiatry,[16] sexual disorders, addiction treatment, etc.) as well as a lack of emergency field services. The shortage of clinical psychologists, coupled with an insufficient network of psychiatric services and social care in most rural regions, results in the greater use of biological therapies (e.g. medications) as compared to bio–psycho–social approaches (Raboch and Wenigová, 2012). The copayment for mental health services in general is 15.3 % in the CR, and is one of the lowest rates among European

---

[14]*Charter of Fundamental Rights and Freedoms. Constitutional Act No.2/1993 Coll. Amended by constitutional act Nr. 162/1998 Coll*, Article 13.

[15]The total number of all these migrants is estimated to be 100,000–120,000 persons, which represents about one-quarter of the overall number of migrants in the Czech Republic (Hnilicová and Dobiášová, 2011).

[16]For example, total number of child psychiatrists in the CR is only 70 (ÚZIS, 2014), but according to the Czech Psychiatric Society there is a need for about 200 specialists.

OECD countries (OECD, 2014a).[17] However low, these costs may still be a barrier and negatively impact real access to care for vulnerable groups, such as homeless people, the Roma population, unemployed, immigrants, elderly, etc.

4.6 Mental Health Workforce in the Czech Republic

According to current legislation (Council Directive 1993), the following groupings of professional staff in Czech mental health care system include (Scheffler and Potůček, 2008):

- Psychiatrists (including general psychiatry as well as child and geriatric specialists);
- Nurses, both general nurses with bachelor's degree and nurses with continuing specialized education in psychiatric nursing;
- Other health professionals with a university degree (e.g. clinical psychologists, social workers, etc.);
- Other health workers without a university degree.

The available data provides a limited and incomplete picture of the mental health care workforce. In 2012, the CR had 1,474 physicians (512 men and 962 women) working in psychiatry, amounting to 14 psychiatrists per 100,000 inhabitants (IHIS CR, 2013a). This number is lower than the average of 15.4 per 100,000 in OECD countries (Dvořáček, 2013). Psychiatrists represented 4% of the total 38,624 physicians in CR (IHIS CR, 2013a). In 2012, approximately 4,000 nurses worked in the mental health care system; however, only 28% of these nurses had specialized education in psychiatry (i.e. psychiatric nurses) (Česká asociace sester, 2011; Petr, 2013).

The staff of long-term psychiatric hospitals are mostly employees of the facilities and receive wages for their work. In 2012, 542 psychiatrists and 2,913 nurses worked in long-term psychiatric hospitals. This equates to about 1 physician per 17 beds and 1 qualified nurse per 3 beds (IHIS CR, 2013a). While the number of beds is high in long-term hospitals, the

---

[17] Nowadays, copayments are required for prescription drugs (those that are not fully covered by public health insurance) and as a user's fees for emergency services.

Table 4.1: Professional staff in long-term psychiatric hospitals.

Physicians	586	Health professionals with master's degree	210
Of which psychiatrists	*542*		
		Of which psychologists and clinical psychologists	*141*
		physiotherapists	*62*
Health professionals with bachelor's degree	3,140	Health professionals without university education, who have to work under the professional supervision	1,897
Of which			
nurses	*2,913*		
occupational therapists	*37*		
social workers	*115*		

Source: IHIS CR (2013a).

number of social workers, psychologists (having a master's degree in psychology and a 1-year course in psychology in health care), and clinical psychologists (those having a further 5-year specialty training in clinical psychology) are quite low according to the standards of the Czech Psychiatric Society (see Table 4.1).

In comparison, in a more acute setting, such as the 30 psychiatric departments of general hospitals, there were 188 psychiatrists[18] and 524 nurses.[19] This is the equivalence of about 1 physician per 7 beds and 1 qualified nurse per 2.7 beds (Faltus *et al.*, 2010; IHIS CR, 2013).

Outpatient psychiatrists work mostly as self-employed persons and have contracts with public health insurance companies. In addition, some outpatient psychiatrists work as employees of psychiatric hospitals, outpatient departments, and other healthcare facilities. While there has been a significant increase in the number of people seeking outpatient psychiatric care, the number of available outpatient psychiatrists has not kept pace. In 2013, 733 psychiatrists worked in outpatient settings, i.e. 7 psychiatrists per 100,000 inhabitants (see Table 4.2) (IHIS CR, 2014b). The 2008 *Revised Framework for Psychiatry* recommended 9 outpatient psychiatrists per 100,000 inhabitants in primary mental health care for adults, and

---

[18] Data from the year 2012.
[19] Data from the year 2008.

Table 4.2: Professional staff in outpatient psychiatric facilities.

Type of healthcare facility	Psychiatrists	Paramedics
Individual psychiatric outpatient units	593	225
Outpatient department of long-term psychiatric hospitals and hospitals	106	136
Other outpatient healthcare facilities	30	26
Healthcare facilities for the treatment of drug addiction	4	12

Source: IHIS CR (2013a).

10 per 100,000 in the large city areas (due to the greater concentration of psychiatric disorders in large cities) (Petr, 2013).

There are also large regional disparities in the number of outpatient psychiatrists per 100,000 inhabitants. While in Prague there are almost 9 psychiatrists per 100,000 inhabitants, in some regions the number of psychiatrists is far lower—even less than half of the recommended number (Morcinek, 2013). The main barriers to development of a network of outpatient psychiatrists include strict limits on new contracts by health insurance companies, who seek to avoid cost increases. Additionally, reimbursement rates set by the public health insurance are seen as low by practitioners and psychiatrists. They are motivated financially to see a high number of patients and in many instances not spending adequate time with each. Few psychiatrists can find the time to appropriately communicate with a patient, to arrange for social or psychiatric interventions, and to provide psychotherapy in the time allotted. The current payment system incentivizes and rewards quantity at the expense of quality (Raboch and Wenigová, 2012, p. 17).

In the CR in 2012, there were 552 outpatient clinical psychologists who had a contract with health insurance companies, i.e. 5.5 psychologists per 100,000 inhabitants. In some regions, it is only about 2.5 clinical psychologists per 100,000 inhabitants (Morcinek, 2013). According to the Czech Psychiatric Society, the recommended number should be 10 clinical psychologists per 100,000 inhabitants (Běhounek et al., 2016).

Since the EU accession in 2004, the CR has adopted 2 laws regulating health professionals' training and their continuing education in accordance with the EU legislation (Těšinová et al., 2011).[20] The first Act[21] regulates the specialty training of physicians (including specialization in psychiatry), dentists, and pharmacists. The other Law[22] determines the training of nurses' and other health professionals, including clinical psychologists, physiotherapists, occupational therapists, and social workers.

The study of general medicine takes 6 years in the CR and graduates receive an MD degree. There are 8 medical schools in the CR. In 2013, there were a total of 14,482 students and 52% of them were enrolled in a 6-year program of General Medicine (leading to an MD degree). Almost two-thirds of all students were women. There were 883 general medicine graduates in 2013 (IHIS CR, 2014e). However, the level of interest in psychiatry among these graduates is low, and issues such as stigma attached to the profession, psychiatric patients, and underfinancing of psychiatry make recruitment difficult (Praško, 2010; Höschl et al., 2010). As a result, only 4% of Czech medical students graduating in 2010 chose a career in psychiatry (Dvoracek et al., 2013).

Courses in psychiatry are part of the general medicine degree (Schefler and Potůček, 2008), however medical schools differ in how they teach psychiatry. In general, the curriculum includes combinations of lectures, clerkships, seminars, and practical training. Psychiatry is usually taught in the 4th or 5th year of study, and the courses are organized as blocks of 2 4-week periods, compared to students' exposure to general internal medicine (22 weeks), surgery (13 weeks), or gynecology (8 weeks) (Dvoracek et al., 2013). After finishing medical school, all physicians are expected to choose one of several specialty/residency trainings (see Scheme). Training is organized into 2 levels: The first level is 2

---

[20] Council Directive 93/16/EEC of 5 April 1993 to facilitate the free movement of doctors and the mutual recognition of their diplomas, certificates and other evidence of formal qualifications.

[21] Act. No. 95/2004 Coll., the Act on achieving and recognizing expert qualifications for the performance of a profession of a doctor, dentist and pharmacist pert qualifications for the performance of a profession of a "non-doctor" health care professions.

[22] Act. No. 96/2004 Coll., the Act on achieving and recognizing expert qualifications for the performance of a profession of a "non-doctor" health care professions.

Scheme: System of medical education in the CR.

years of basic training in 1 of 16 branches (internal medicine, general medicine, surgery, gynecology, psychiatry, etc.). This is just a basic training and graduates cannot practice as specialists after that. At the second level, training continues in 1 of 46 branches[23] which ranges from 1 additional year for GPs to 5 years of further training for fields such as neurosurgery or cardiac surgery. Specialty/residency training is finished by board exams/post-graduate examination (Hnilicová and Janečková, 2012).

To become a GP, it is necessary to complete 3 years of specialty training in general medicine. According to the Educational Program in General Medicine (2011), only 2 days of psychotherapeutic training are required for the candidates (Ministry of Health, 2011). According to a qualitative study of GPs (Stuchlík and Wenigová, 2007), this core group of physicians is in need of training in mental health care; they need information on individual diagnostic groups, recommended techniques of communication with persons with mental illness, types of treatment, along with a better understanding of the range of available services. The aging of GPs as a

---

[23] Incl. psychiatry, psychiatry for children and adolescents.

group further complicates workforce and training concerns; in 2013, approximately 54% of GPs were over the age of 55 (IHIS CR, 2014d).

To become a psychiatrist, 5 years of specialty training in psychiatry is necessary. The curriculum includes various practical internships at mental health care facilities, e.g. inpatient and outpatient psychiatric facilities, internal medicine departments including bed intensive care unit, neurological inpatient department, as well as departments of child and adolescent psychiatry and geropsychiatry. To become a psychiatrist, one also has to pass psychiatry board exams. The number of people passing the exams[24] is considered insufficient to meet the needs of the population and to compensate for the number of psychiatrists leaving practice. After passing the specialty board exam, psychiatrists can gain further specialization in other certified programs, including geropsychiatry, addiction psychiatry, and sexology[25] (see Scheme).

According to current legislation, nurses, occupational therapists, social workers, etc. may obtain professional qualifications in mental health after completing the 3-year bachelor's degree study. Clinical psychologists or physiotherapists must have completed a 5-year master's degree and specialized training (IHIS CR, 2014e). To become a psychiatric nurse, a general nurse must complete 12 months of field training and 18–24 months postgraduate study; only about 60 nurses a year graduate from these training programs (Blatnická *et al.*, 2011). The *Revised Framework of Psychiatry* identifies the need for 5 to 10 psychiatric nurses per 100,000 population (Koncepce oboru psychiatrie, 2008). This implies the need to train at least 500 psychiatric nurses in order to meet these guidelines (Petr, 2013).

---

[24] 38 on average per year between 2008–2011 (*Internal statistics of Czech Specialist Board of Psychiatry*, unpublished).

[25] During this training, psychiatrists gain knowledge in the field of phylogenesis and ontogenesis of sexuality, physiology and pathophysiology of the human sexual behavior and human reproduction, defects and deficiencies in physical sexual development of humans, sexual dysfunction and sexual partner discrepancies, deviations and disorders of sexual orientation and sexual identification, investigation, treatment and medical assessments of offenders and victims of sexual offenses, investigation, treatment and assessment of male fertility disorders, indications and contraindications of contraceptive methods among both men and women, counseling in family planning, counseling in connection with sexually transmitted diseases, etc.

4.7 Financing the Mental Health Care System in the Czech Republic

4.7.1 *Overview of health care financing*

Health care is primarily funded and supported by mandatory public health insurance which promotes solidarity[26] and equity. Expenditures on health in the CR represented 7.5% of GDP in 2013 (IHIS CR, 2014a). This compares to an average health expenditure as a percent of GDP in the EU region of 9.56% in 2011 (for more detailed comparison see Figure 4.5). The government covers health insurance premiums for pensioners, children up to 18, students up to 26, women on maternity leave, unemployed persons, prisoners, as well as people living below poverty levels and asylum seekers; this covers approximately 55% of the Czech population. This means that the government pays monthly premiums for these insured groups, with the amount of the premium defined by law.

Public health insurance premiums are paid as 13.5% of total income payroll tax; these costs are split between the employer who pays 9%, and the employee who pays 4.5%. Self-employed persons must contribute 6.75% of their net earnings. Czech citizens and EU citizens participate in the mandatory public health insurance. In addition, non-EU migrants may be included in the public health insurance system if they have employee status. The majority of public health expenditures (79%) are covered by mandatory public health insurance; 5.7% of the balance is paid by central and local governments and 15.3% is covered by private resources. The proportion of the private expenditures was the highest in 2008 (17%), when copayments were first introduced into the system (IHIS CR, 2014a).

Because mental health care does not have a separate or unique budget, it is very hard to estimate the amount of the overall expenditures for this portion of health spending. Mental health care is financed via the health insurance system, taxes, and regional budgets; other sources of funds include disability pensions from the pension insurance system and the sickness insurance system that protects the insured from loss of income in case of illness.

---

[26] In CR, public health insurance system is based on the recognition of the right of every citizen to equal health care and solidarity between rich and poor and healthy and unhealthy.

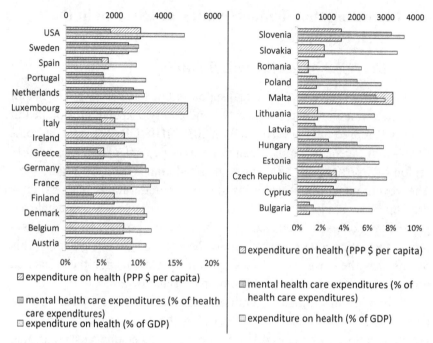

Figure 4.5: The proportion of mental health expenditures on overall health expenditures, proportion of health expenditures on GDP, and total health expenditure (PPP) per capita—comparison of EU15 countries + USA and new EU members.

Source: WHO (2011); Winkler *et al*. (2013) https://www.nudz.cz/files/common/reforma_systemu_psychiat_pece.pdf (pp. 29–30).

Psychiatric outpatient care is paid via a regulated fee-for-service mechanism; inpatient services are paid by a combination of fee-for-service and *per diem* payments, while the actual amount of reimbursed money *per diem* is dependent on the amount charged during a reference or index period (e.g. previous year); usually, the amount is higher than 100% of the reference amount. GPs are compensated through a combination of fee-per-capita and fee-for-service payments. The health insurance company reimburses prescription drugs with a copayment by the patient; in every therapeutic category, 1 drug must be fully reimbursed by public health insurance.

According to the WHO (2011), the proportion of public mental health expenditures in the CR is 2.91% of the total health expenditures. This rate is very low in comparison to other European countries (see Figure 4.5). According to Dlouhý (2011), who used a modified System of Health Accounts, the proportion of all CR mental health expenditures (public and private) in 2006 was 4.14% of overall health expenditures; 59.4% was spent on inpatient care, 12.6% on outpatient care, 25.9% on medical goods (e.g. pharmaceuticals and therapeutic appliances dispensed to outpatients), and 2.1% on other expenditures. Of the money spent on inpatient care, 88% went to psychiatric hospitals as compared to general hospitals. Dlouhý also estimated that 88% of mental health care is financed by the public sector.

As noted above, there is a comparatively low overall amount of resources dedicated to mental health care in the CR. At least in part, this reflects some reluctance by health insurance companies to establish new contracts with outpatient mental health care providers due to their cost containment efforts. An analysis by the Ministry of Health, based on data from the largest health insurer who provides coverage to 60% of the Czech population, found wide variation in the performance of psychiatric outpatient facilities. In some instances, outpatient facilities exceeded their performance targets; in others, there is significant under-performance as compared to their contracts with health insurance companies. Data collection and analysis is also confounded by the practice of psychiatric hospitals providing some level of acute care without insurance company contracts to do so.

4.8 Quality of Care, Outcomes, and Evaluation

Ongoing efforts to assure and improve the quality of care are, in many other countries, a natural and regular part of the process of providing services. This is not true in the case of CR, where efforts to evaluate quality of care have become controversial. Many facilities in the CR were examined by international organizations; however, the evaluation findings were not principally used for identification of problem areas and opportunities for the improvement of services. Rather, the media used the information for a negative critique of the system (Raboch & Wenigová 2012).

Despite a history of difficulties in assessing the quality of mental health care in the CR, the recent (2007–2010) introduction of standardized quality assessment methods and tools, such as the QUIRC (Quality

Indicator for Rehabilitative Care), will hopefully promote ongoing quality improvement efforts. These data are used mainly by mental health care facilities (e.g. Mental Health Hospitals), but unfortunately there is no institution that would systematically monitor the quality of services across all providers (Raboch & Wenigová 2012).

4.9 Advocacy, Stigma, and Self-Help

Until recently, the extent and impact of stigma related to persons with mental health issues had not been well studied in the CR. However, several papers published over the past several years have begun to shed light on the extent of the problem. A 2004 survey on public opinion about schizophrenia revealed a significant lack of knowledge about the disease; at the same time, stereotypes about the unpredictability and dangerousness of the patients were found to be common (DEMA, 2004).

Winkler *et al.* (2014) conducted a survey in the CR using the Reported and Intended Behavior Scale in an effort to determine the extent of stigma directed toward persons experiencing mental illness. The findings were compared with the results of a similar survey in the United Kingdom. In the CR, 26% of respondents reported that they would be uncomfortable in continuing a relationship with a friend who developed a mental health problem; this compared to only 4% in the UK. Czech respondents also reported a limited amount of personal experience with individuals diagnosed with a mental illness. According to the authors, there are several possible explanations for these differences: (1) the high level of "intended stigmatizing behavior" may be influenced by the lack of knowledge about mental health and illness (respondents very often chose the answer "don't know"), and (2) the institutionalized nature of the mental health care system isolates patients from the general population (Winkler *et al.*, 2014).

There have also been efforts to measure stigma toward people with mental disorders and the field of psychiatry among medical students. Stigma may play a role in the recruitment of new psychiatrists; perhaps more importantly, stigma may contribute to ineffective treatment, unsuccessful rehabilitation, and the widening of the treatment gap (due to patients who do not seek professional help). Dvořáček *et al.* (2013) investigated attitudes of medical students at just one of the Prague medical schools toward psychiatry and their intentions to choose psychiatry as their career. They found that stigma does in fact play a major role in students' career choices. They also found that psychiatry is more attractive for those who have personal or family experience with mental illness. The same pattern was also observed by Sandoval et al. (2013) who investigated attitudes toward mental illness and psychiatry at one of the regional medical schools.

Several researchers have focused on the issue of stigma toward people with mental disorders in the Czech printed media. Nawková et al. (2012) published the results of an international comparative study on the content of printed media messages related to mental health/illness in terms of stigma in 3 Central European countries (CR, Slovakia, and Croatia). In all 3 countries, negative statements reflecting stigma toward persons with mental illness were included in more than half of the articles reviewed; it is noteworthy that substance abuse was the most frequently mentioned disorder and psychotic disorders were the most stigmatized. The association of aggressive behavior with the mental illness was the lowest in the CR in comparison to the other 2 countries. Nawka et al. (2012) also investigated the association of aggression with psychiatric disorders in printed media in the CR and Slovakia in detail. They found that approximately one-third of articles dealing with psychiatric disorders, abstracted from the 6 most widely read printed newspapers and magazines in those countries, associated psychiatric conditions with either self or other-directed aggression. Psychotic disorders and schizophrenia were mostly associated with homicide, and affective disorders were associated with both homicide and completed suicide. Eating disorders were rarely associated with any kind of aggressive behavior.

A comprehensive summary of efforts to reduce stigma related to mental illness in midsize European countries was provided by Beldie et al. in 2012. In 2004, the CR joined *Open the Doors, Open your Hearts* initiative promoted by the World Psychiatric Society in an effort to reduce the stigma associated with schizophrenia. A public opinion survey was conducted by DEMA[27] to establish a pre-intervention baseline. In 2005, a destigmatization campaign called "*Změna*" (change) was conducted by the Czech Center for Mental Health Care Development, an organization

---

[27] DEMA corp. deals with public opinion research (**DE**moscopy in Greek) and **MA**rket research.

founded in 1995 in Prague by mental health care providers. Unfortunately, follow-up measurement was not conducted. Since then, the Center has become one of the leading organizations working to reduce stigma through educational courses (focused on mental health care providers, state administration, and the general public) along with the dissemination of information about mental illness on the Center's website.[28]

Another interesting and perhaps unique anti-stigma activity includes the "Mezi ploty" (Inside the Fence) festival. Every year, this event welcomes 1000s of visitors inside the psychiatric hospitals in Prague, Pilsen, and Brno and provides an opportunity for the general public to see dramatic, music, and visual performances by artists including those who are in some way disabled. Other organizations addressing the problem of stigma include the Czech Association for Mental Health, Focus Prague, Kolumbus, and Vida.

The creation of associations of psychiatric patients in the CR has been impacted by the lack of support for self-help and advocacy organizations during the communist regime. Civic organizations before 1989 are considered the "old NGOs" and were focused on organized leisure activities or advocacy of professional interests; in comparison, the "new NGOs" have attempted to advocate for human rights and provide voluntary social and health care services. This shift started after 1989, when a charter of patients' rights was adopted and various mental health NGOs were established, including the League for Mental Health, the Czech Association for Mental Health, and the Czech Society for Mental Health. According to "neziskovky.cz," an online catalogue of NGOs in the CR, there are now 57 NGOs concerned with mental health. Some are self-help organizations, while others have been established in collaboration with mental health care professionals.

4.10 Looking Forward: Challenges and Priorities in the Czech Republic's Mental Health Care System

The development of the *Strategy for Reform of Psychiatric Care* began in September 2012, and after a year of intensive work, the Strategy was

---

[28] www.stopstigma.cz.

approved and published in October 2013. Several factors that contributed to the creation of the new Strategy are as follows:

- An experience with mental illness in the family of the Ministry of Health's management;
- The head of the largest psychiatric hospital was elected president of Czech Psychiatric Society and supported the reform;
- 2 key officials at the Ministry of Health have backgrounds in psychiatric care and strategic governance;
- Support of NGOs and a large array of stakeholders related to mental health care.

The Strategy was formulated such that the resulting policy would be acceptable to key interest groups and at the same time be sustainable and capable of meeting the needs of people with mental health problems. The primary audience included the Ministry of Labor and Social Affairs, medical insurance agencies, regional governments, NGOs, and service users, along with the Czech Psychiatric Society and Czech Nurses Association.

The Ministry of Health acted as a coordinator and discussion moderator of the entire process of formulation of the new policy. A broad base of stakeholder input distinguished this from prior efforts at reform; there was meaningful input from service users themselves rather than an emphasis on plans developed by professionals without adequate input from other stakeholders. There are more than 175 million USD of pre-approved funds from the European Structural and Investments Funds (ESIF) for the transition phase of the planned reform. This money should cover equipment, education, anti-stigma, and educational programs, as well as the pilot operation of community centers and innovations in community-based services, etc. The operating costs themselves must come from national resources.

Reform of the psychiatric care system aims to systematically establish and operate Centers of Mental Health based on community, field-based multidisciplinary teams of health and social service workers. These teams are intended to provide integrated health and social interventions to people with severe mental health problems in their natural environments. The primary focus of the Centers of Mental Health are persons with SMI (Severe Mental Illness). These centers will hopefully provide a link between primary care and coordinate services including ambulatory and hospital care. If successful, the centers should prevent or shorten hospitalizations and help long-term hospitalized patients with their return to their home communities. The goal is to establish 1 Center of Mental Health for a catchment area of 100,000 inhabitants; about 100 Centers of Mental Health should be created. The hope is that by 2020, 30 such centers will be established. Additional steps needed for successful implementation of the Centers of Mental Health include the creation of standards and methods for performance evaluation; measures of quality of life, stigmatization, and cost-effectiveness of interventions should be incorporated. Evaluation of the successful implementation of primary, secondary and tertiary prevention, communication and destigmatization, establishment of acute beds in general hospitals, and education of necessary specialists will also be needed. Lastly, there is the expectation that these reforms will also help to promote research in the field of neuropsychiatry and social psychiatry.

Challenges and priorities in the mental health policy in the CR are closely related to implementation (or its absence) of a carefully planned Strategy for Reform of Psychiatric Care. Success in implementing the Strategy will require overcoming long-lasting as well as current problems in the CR that include but are not limited to:

- Demand for care is far greater than what outpatient psychiatrists can provide;
- Psychiatric hospitals are outdated, too large, and serve extended catchment areas;
- Community care resources are not sufficiently developed;
- Underfunding of the mental health care system;
- Increasing numbers of psychiatric patients and an anticipated increase in real psychiatric morbidity.

At the same time, the Strategy offers an opportunity for meaningful reform that can change the current system and benefit patients. This includes success in:

- Assisting people with their reintegration into mainstream society;
- Ensuring access to care in communities and the "natural environments" of service users;

- Reducing the risk of frequent absence from work by persons with mental illness;
- Decreasing the number of people granted permanent disability pensions;
- Fulfilling past international commitments and agreements to protect the human rights of people with mental illness;
- Increasing the possibility of introducing a stand-alone Mental Health Act;
- Introducing long-term prevention programs including the education of teachers, public institutions, general public, etc., for the timely identification of individuals with emerging mental health problems;
- Decreasing the high levels of stigma associated with persons experiencing mental illness as well as the stigma directed toward psychiatry and other mental health professions;
- Developing community-based services for other groups including people diagnosed with neurodegenerative brain disorders and addictive disorders.

While there is good reason to hope for improvements in CR policies and practices related to mental health care, critical questions remain: Will reform efforts actually be initiated? Will they succeed? The lack of clear political support for mental health is a persistent problem and has been perhaps the primary obstacle to achieving much needed system reform. Experience in other countries and jurisdictions shows that strong political support can truly make a difference and is crucial for successful implementation of any mental health care reform. The Ministry of Health has been governed by ministers from Social Democratic Party (SDP) since 2014. The SDP supports policies that include deinstitutionalization, the protection of human rights, and improving the quality of life quality for persons with mental illness.

Despite this, there are few, if any, political figures in the CR who can be identified as a champion or advocate for mental health. There are likely many reasons for this, but one may be that the mental health care reform agenda is politically unattractive. Improving mental health care requires long-ranging policy changes whose results, and potential political benefits, will require 5–10 years to be realized, while the standard election cycle is 4 years. The second obstacle to reform is the relative lack of civil associations/NGOs promoting the interests of service users and their families. This leads to insufficient lobbying with political decision makers who then feel little pressure and demand for change. For example, NGOs supporting the interests of people with diabetes, cancer, and other disease groups are much stronger in the CR than those addressing mental health. Although the Civil Association of Aid to Mentally Ill Persons CR and Sympathea are Czech organizations, they are a part of EUFAMI (European Federation of Associations of Families of People with Mental Illness). However, cooperation with this Pan-European organization is limited in large part due to language barriers.

A third obstacle may be the lack of coordination between the various entities and interests promoting the actual implementation of reform. There is also a lack of agreed upon measures and levels of performance to determine the impact and success of reforms. In 2015, National Institute of Mental Health in the CR[29] was established and fully funded by the EU. This Institute has the potential to conduct and disseminate this kind of program/policy analysis, but it needs clear direction and corresponding support from the Ministry. Obtaining this could prove to be a daunting task and requires coordination and collaboration with other stakeholders (e.g. Czech regions and other ministries).

Last but not least, there is a need for a long-term sustainable funding model to support reform implementation. While there is a general consensus that the Czech mental health care system is underfunded, a number of stakeholders must be involved to successfully address this lack of resources. Potential participants include but are not limited to the health insurance agencies, the Ministry of Labor and Social Affairs and the Association of Regions of the CR; this last group is critical because the regions are responsible for the operation of local networks of community-based social services for mentally ill people. Adequate funding of such a network of community health–social care, as defined by the Strategy, is essential for reform success.

All of these obstacles and barriers are closely interconnected, but there are many who believe that the lack of political leadership is the most critical. If reform of mental health care could gain its rightful place in the

---

[29] http://www.nudz.cz/en/.

political agenda of overall efforts to improve Czech society, this alone could substantially reduce the other barriers and help clear the path to much needed and clearly identified reforms.

References

Anderson, P., Møller, L. and Galea, G. (eds.) (2012) *Alcohol in the European Union: Consumption, harm and policy approaches.* (WHO Regional Office for Europe, Copenhagen). ISBN 978-92-890-0264-6.

Běhounek, J., Heřman, E., Hollý, M., Koblic, K., Mališ, P., Papežová, M., Papežová, S., Pěč, O., Rektor, J., Syrovátka, J., Šolle, Z. and Tuček, J. (2016) *Working materials for standards of outpatient psychiatric care and extended outpatient care for people suffering from mental disorders.* (Psychiatric Association of Czech Medical Society of Jan Evangelista Purkyně, Prague).

Beldie, A., Den Boer, J. A., Brain, C., Constant, E., Figueira, M. L., Filipcic, I., Gillain, B., Jakovljevic, M., Jarema, M., Jelenova, D., Karamustafalioglu, O., Kores Plesnicar, B., Kovascova, A., Latalova, K., Marksteiner, J., Palha, F., Pecenak, J., Prasko, J., Prelipceanu, D., Ringen, P. A., Sartorius, N., Seifritz, E., Svestka, J., Tyszkowska, M. and Wancata, J. (2012) Fighting stigma of mental illness in midsize European countries. *Social Psychiatry and Psychiatric Epidemiology* **47** (S1): 1–38. DOI: 10.1007/s00127-012-0491-z.

Blatnická, J., Petr, T. and Novotná, B. (2011) Psychiatric nurse education. Contribution on the conference "In the footsteps of psychiatric nursing XIV".

Centre for mental health care development (2005) *Mental health care policy in the Czech Republic – paths to implementation.*

Charter of Fundamental Rights and Freedoms. Constitutional Act No.2/1993 Coll. Amended by constitutional act Nr. 162/1998 Coll.

Psychiatric section of the Czech Association of Nurses (2011) Statement on the Revised Framework of Psychiatry. Available at: http://www.psychiatrickasekcecas.estranky.cz.

DEMA (2004) Attitudes towards schizophrenia: a Czech representative survey.

Dlouhý, M. (2011) Mental health services in the health accounts: The Czech Republic. *Social Psychiatry Psychiatric Epidemiology* **46**, 447–453.

Dvoracek, B., Nawka, A., Nawkova, L., Vevera, J., Lydall, G., Malik, A., Farooq, K. and Bhugra, D. (2013) Recruitment to psychiatry in the Czech

Republic: "Waiting for resuscitation"? *International Review of Psychiatry* **25** (4), 466–471.

Dzúrová, D., Smolová, E. and Dragomirecká, E. (2000) *Duševní zdraví v sociodemografických souvislostech: (výsledky výběrového šetření v České republice). Mental health in the socio-demographic context: (results of a sample survey in the Czech Republic* (Charles University and the Prague Psychiatric Centre, Prague).

European Mental Health Action Plan (2005).

European Mental Health Action Plan (2013).

European Pact for Mental Health and Wellbeing (2008).

Faltus, F., Janečková, E., Anders, M. (2010) Vývoj sítě ambulantních a lůžkových psychiatrických zařízení. *Čes a slov Psychiatr* **106** (6), 366–371.

Gustavsson, A., Svensson, M., Jacobi, F., Allgulander, C., Alonso, J., Beghi, E. and Olesen, J. (2011) Cost of disorders of the brain in Europe 2010. *European Neuropsychopharmacology* **21** (10), 718–779.

Hnilicová, H. and Dobiášová, K. (2011) Migrants' health and access to healthcare in the Czech Republic. *Central European Journal of Public Health* **19** (3), 134–138.

Hnilicová, H. and Janečková, H. (2012) Czech Republic. In: Fryed, B. J. & Gaydos, L. M. (eds.) *World Health System: Challenges and Perspectives.* (Health Administration Press, Chicago) pp. 453–473.

Höschl, C. and van Niekerk , J. (2010) Recruitment of psychiatrists: The key role of education. In: L. Gask, Coskun, B. and Baron, D. (eds.) *Teaching Psychiatry: Putting Theory into Practice* (John Wiley and Sons, Chichester), p. 5.

IHIS CR (Institute of Health Information and Statistics of the Czech Republic) (2010) *Health care about patients with diagnoses F50.0-F50.9 — eating disorders in psychiatric inpatient facilities in Czech Republic. Current information no. 3/10.* Prague: IHIS CR.

IHIS CR (2011a) *European Health Interview Survey in the Czech Republic EHIS 2008.* Prague: IHIS CR.

IHIS CR (2011b) *Health care about patients with diagnoses F50.0-F50.9 – eating disorders in psychiatric inpatient facilities in Czech Republic.* Current information no. 60/11. Prague: IHIS CR.

IHIS CR (2012) *Health care about patients with diagnoses F50.0-F50.9 (eating disorders) in psychiatric outpatient and inpatient facilities in Czech Republic between 2006–2011.* Current information no. 62/12. Prague: IHIS CR.

IHIS CR (2013a) *Psychiatric care 2012.* Prague: IHIS CR.

IHIS CR (2013b) *Terminated cases of incapacity for work for disease or injury.* Prague: IHIS CR.

IHIS CR (2013c) *Health care about patients with eating disorders in psychiatric outpatient and inpatient facilities in Czech Republic between 2007–2012. Current information no. 55/13.* Prague: IHIS CR.

IHIS CR (2013d) *Health care about patients using psychoactive substances (alcohol and other drugs) hospitalized in psychiatric inpatient facilities in the Czech Republic in the year 2012.* Current information no. 46/13. Prague: IHIS CR.

IHIS CR (2014a) *Economic information on health care 2013.* Prague: IHIS CR.

IHIS CR (2014b) *Activity of outpatient psychiatric facilities in 2013. Current information no. 28/14.* Prague: IHIS CR.

IHIS CR (2014c) *Outpatient care about patients using psychoactive substances (alcohol and other drugs) in 2013.* Current information no. 29/14. Prague: IHIS CR.

IHIS CR (2014d) *Activity of general practitioners for adults in 2013. Current information no. 16/14.* Prague: IHIS CR.

IHIS CR (2014e) *Czech Health Statistics Yearbook 2013.* Prague: IHIS CR.

Janoušková, M., Winkler, P. and Kažmér, L. (2014) Trends in Newly Admitted Disability Pensions due to Mental and Physical Disorders in the Czech Republic between 2001 and 2011." In: Psychiatrie (Psychiatry) **18** (4) 161–165.

Koncepce oboru psychiatrie (2000) Framework of Psychiatry. 2000. Psychiatric Association of Czech Medical Society of Jan Evangelista Purkyně, Prague.

Ministry of Health of the Czech Republic (2011) Educational programme in general medicine.

Ministry of Health of the Czech Republic (2013) *Strategy for Reform of Psychiatric Care.*

Ministry of Health of the Czech Republic (2014) *Zpráva o zdraví obyvatel ČR.*

Morcinek, T. (2013) *Analysis of statistical data for the specialization of psychiatry and psychology for the years 2011 and 2012.* Internal document of the Ministry of Health. Unpublished.

Nawková, L., Nawka, A., Adámková, T., Rukavina, T.V., Holcnerová, P., Kuzman, M.R., Jovanovič, N., Brborović, O., Bednárová, B., Žuchová, S., Miovský, M. and Raboch, J. (2012) The picture of mental health /illness in printed media in three Central European Countries. *Journal of Health Communication* **17** (1), 22–40. Doi:10.1080/10810730.2011.571341.

Nawka, A., Rukavina, T.V., Nawková, L., Jovanović, N., Brborović, O. and Raboch, J. (2012) Psychiatric disorders and aggression in the printed media: Is there a link? A central European Perspective. *BMC Psychiatry* **12** (19).

NMS — National Monitoring Center for Drugs and Addiction (2012) European School Survey Project on Alcohol and Other Drugs: overview of the main findings for the Czech Republic in 2011. In: *Focused on Drugs* (bulletin) 2012(1).

NMS — National Monitoring Center for Drugs and Addiction (2013) National Survey on substance use in 2012. In: *Focused on Drugs* (bulletin) 2013(2).

OECD (2014a) *How does the Czech Republic compare?* OECD Health Statistics 2014—Country Notes, available at http://www.oecd.org/els/health-systems/Briefing-Note-CZECH-REPUBLIC-2014.pdf.

OECD (2014b) Making Mental Health Count: The Social and Economic Costs of Neglecting Mental Health Care, OECD Health Policy Studies, OECD Publishing. Doi: 10.1787/9789264208445-en.

Pěč, O. (2012) Komunitní péče. (Chpt. 7) In: Raboch, J. and Wenigová, B. *Mapování stavu psychiatrické péče a jejího směřování v souladu se strategickými dokumenty* České republiky (a zahraničí). (Česká psychiatrická společnost, Praha).

Petr, T. (2013) Reforma péče o duševní zdraví v ČR (Mental health care reform in the CR). In Sestra (Nurse). 7-8/2013, 12–13.

Praško, J. P. (2010) Stigma psychiatrie. *Čes a slov Psychiatr* **106** (2), 71–72.

Raboch, J. and Wenigová, B. (2012) *Mapování stavu psychiatrické péče a jejího směřování v souladu se strategickými dokumenty* České republiky (a zahraničí) (Česká psychiatrická společnost, Praha).

Revised Framework of Psychiatry (2008) Psychiatric Association of Czech Medical Society of Jan Evangelista Purkyně, Prague.

Sandoval, A., Jelenova, D. and Prasko, J. (2013) Stigmatization of psychiatric patients by medical students. *European Psychiatry* **28** (Suppl. 1).

Scheffler, R. M. and Potůček, M. (eds.) (2008) *Mental Health Care Reform in the Czech and Slovak Republics, 1989 to the present*. (Karolinum, Prague) 258 s. ISBN 978-802-4614-663.

Stuchlík, J. and Wenigová, B. (2007) Vzdělávací potřeby praktických lékařů a ambulantních psychiatrů v oblasti péče o duševní zdraví. *Medicina Pro Praxi* **4** (12), 519–520.

Těšinová, J., Žďárek, R. and Policar, R. (2011) *Medicínské právo*. (C.H.Beck, Praha) 414 s.

UN Convention on the Rights of Persons with Disabilities (2006).

WHO (2001) *Atlas: Mental Health Resources in the World*.

WHO (2005) *Mental Health Atlas.*
WHO (2008) *Policies and Practices for Mental Health in Europe—Meeting the Challenges.* WHO Regional Office for Europe.
WHO (2011) *Mental Health Atlas.*
Winkler, P., Španiel, F., Csémy, L., Janoušková, M. and Krejníková, L. (2013) *Reforma systému psychiatrické péče: Mezinárodní politika, zkušenost a doporučení.* (Psychiatrické centrum Praha, Praha).
Winkler, P., Csémy, L., Janoušková, M. and Motlová, B. L. (2014) Stigmatizující jednání vůči duševně nemocným v Česku a Anglii: Dotazníkové šetření na reprezentativním vzorku populace *Psychiatrie* **18** (2) 54–59. ISSN 1211-7579.
World Bank. *International Comparison Program Database* cited on 15 February (2015) http://data.worldbank.org/indicator/NY.GDP.PCAP.PP.CD?Order= wbapi_data_value_2013+wbapi_data_value+wbapi_data_value-last& sort=asc.

CHAPTER 5

An Overview of Mental Health in Moldova

Cornelia Iacubovschi[*], Jana Chihai[†], and Larisa Boderscova[‡]

[*]*UNDP National Consultant, New York, US*

[†]*Department of Psychiatry, Narcology, and Medical Psychology, Nicolae Testemiţanu State University of Medicine and Pharmacy, Chisinau, Moldova*

[‡]*Health Systems Officer, WHO Country Office, Republic of Moldova*

5.1 Mental Health Status of the Moldovan Population

Mental Health is a priority in the Republic of Moldova. Moldova joined the Helsinki Declaration on Mental Health in January 2005 along with other European Union (EU) member states consistent with the country's commitment to EU accession. Moldova also ratified the United Nations (UN) Convention on the Rights of Persons with Disabilities in July 2010, and joined the European Declaration on the Health of Children and Young People with Intellectual Disabilities and their Families "Better Health, Better Lives: Children and Young People with Intellectual Disabilities and their Families" in November 2010. Together these reflect a conceptually new approach to mental health problems and intellectual disabilities (Chihai and Boderscova 2013).

In Moldova, out of a total population of 3,559,541 there are approximately 180,000 people with disabilities. Over the last 10 years, the total

Key Country Statistics

Region: Eastern Europe
Government system: parliamentary republic
Area: 33,851 square kilometers
Population: 3,510,485
Capital: Chisinau
Gender ratio: 0.95 (males to females)
Ethnic groups:
- Moldovan 75.8%
- Ukrainian 8.4%
- Russian 5.9%
- Gagauz 4.4%
- Romanian 2.2%
- Bulgarian 1.9%
- Other 1%
- Unspecified 0.4%

Literacy rate: 99.4%

Population under the age 18: 20.9%
Proportion above the age 60: 15%
Average life expectancy: 66.9 for males and 74.8 years for females
Suicide rates: 0.0176% per 100,000 populations
Economy: middle income economy
GDP annual growth rate: 8.9%
GDP per capita: 5,000 USD (PPP)
Unemployment rate (15-64 years): 5.2%
Youth unemployment rate: 9.8%
Average net salary: around 190 EUR
Total health expenditure as percentage of GDP: 10.3%
Population below poverty line: 20.8%

Source: CIA World Factbook (2016).

---

population has decreased by 2%; at the same time, the total number of Moldovans with disabilities has increased by 20%. Mental and intellectual disabilities are among the leading areas of disability. In 2010, approximately 60,000 people were under psychiatric supervision; about 3,000 are under guardianship, primarily with severe mental illness. Research indicates that individuals with mental or intellectual disabilities include people who are particularly vulnerable to exploitation, violence, and abuse along with other threats to human rights.

Institutional care remains a reality for many Moldovans with disabilities. The initial report of the Republic of Moldova to the UN focused on the implementation of the State's obligations under the UN Convention regarding the Rights of Persons with Disabilities revealed that there are more than 3,000 men and women with disabilities living in large segregated institutions located in Bender, Tiraspol, Cocieri, Badiceni, Brinzeni, and Balti. The largest group included people with intellectual disabilities; the next largest group was a combination of people with intellectual and psycho–social disabilities. Because of the extremely high rates of premature mortality in institutions, long waiting lists for admissions and lack of adequate monitoring, it is very difficult to obtain exact data; this number should be taken simply as an estimate of the total number of people in institutional care.

While mental health data (derived from both public and private health care systems) has been included in general health statistics for the last 3 years, there is not a specific mental health report. Moldova has made attempts to introduce an integrated Medical Information System, but to date this has not been successful. Thus, the existing information system collects some mental health data, but the indicators are of limited value in truly understanding the mental health of the population.[1] In Moldova, alcohol consumption and addiction come under a separate specialty, referred to as "narcology." Data regarding these conditions is separate from the data regarding mental disorders.

In 2013, the overall prevalence of mental and behavioral disorders reported in Moldova was determined to be approximately 100,000 persons. Children and youth are approximately 19% of the total population and account for 17% of the cases of mental illness (Chihai and Boderscova 2012). Women accounted for 40% of the total number of patients reported with mental disorders. From the total of all disorders, 4 major categories or groups are recognized as follows:

- Non-psychotic mental and behavior disorders—50%;
- Mental retardation—29%;
- Schizophrenia, schizotypal disorders, and deliriums—13%;
- Psychotic organic and affective mental disorders and dementia—8%.

In addition, there were 13,950 new cases of mental and behavior disorders identified in 2013. Slightly more than 30% of the new cases involved children, but further details about incidence are not available. Listed in Table 5.1 is a summary of psychiatric morbidity in Moldova over a 5-year period for which data is available.

Suicide is the 11th most common cause of mortality in the world. Monitoring the rate of suicide as a measure of population health/mental health is an increasingly important component of the evaluation and comparison of the overall health status within and across countries. Moldova, has the 22nd highest rate of suicide worldwide, and suicide accounts for 15%–20% of all causes of death (Table 5.2). The rates of suicide or

---

[1] Mental Health Atlas 2011, WHO, Moldova Country profile.

Table 5.1: Mental health and behavior morbidity in Moldova, 2009–2013.

Cases/year	2009 Total	Youth	2010 Total	Youth	2011 Total	Youth	2012 Total	Youth	2013 Total	Youth
Incidence	14,276	4,703	14,897	4,747	14,655	4,505	13,682	4,355	13,950	4,317
Prevalence	97,623	18,914	98,564	18,640	97,525	17,920	97,405	17,174	99,223	16,888

Source: Mental Health Atlas 2011, WHO, Moldova Country profile.

Table 5.2: Suicides by minors in Moldova, by years.

	2008 M	F	2009 M	F	2010 M	F	2011 M	F	2012 M	F	2013 M	F	2014 (9 month) M	F
Total	0,003	0,001	0,002	0,001	0,003	0,002	0,003	0,002	0,003	0,004	0,002	0,002	0,003	0,001
Urban	0,003	0,002	0,001	0,001	0,003	0,002	0,002	0,001	0,002	0,002	0,002	0,001	0,002	—
Rural	0,003	0,001	0,002	0,001	0,003	0,002	0,004	0,002	0,004	0,005	0,001	0,003	0,003	0,001

Note: Only 9 months of data available for 2014.
Source: National Center of Management in Health.[2]

attempted suicide by children are of particular concern. According to data from the World Health Organization, Moldova has the 15th highest total rate of youth suicides in the world based on the total number of suicides divided by the total population.

5.2 History of Mental Health Care in the Republic of Moldova

The first information on the development of psychiatry in Moldova comes from 19th century records when help was provided to those with mental illness by monasteries. The first psychiatric ward in Moldova opened in 1852 in a village hospital, and the first psychiatric hospital began construction in 1895 in the outskirts of Chisinau (*Costiujeni*), opening in 1905 with 400 beds. Although the World Wars I and II had a negative impact on psychiatric services, in the years following World War II, several new psychiatric hospitals were built. At this time, the development of

---

[2] http://www.cnms.md/ro/rapoarte.

modern psychiatry in the country began, influenced by Professor A. Molohov and the Department of Psychiatry at the Institute of Medicine starting in 1946.

As noted earlier, psychiatric services in Moldova are separated from the narcological (addiction) services. During the same time period, institutions for addictions were also created in 3 districts including: Chisinau (450 beds), Balti (75 beds), and Tiraspol (75 beds) (Boderscova and Chihai 2013).

The methods employed to treat mental health problems have significantly evolved in Moldova over the last decades of the 20th century, with the overall approach to psychiatric care shifting away from an institutional care system to a more community-oriented approach. At the end of 2000, there were only 3 dedicated psychiatric hospitals in Moldova with a total of about 3,000 beds. A factor in the evolution of mental health treatment has been outside influence. In 2003, the Stability Pact for South Eastern Europe was created in an effort to strengthen peace, democracy, human rights, and economies in the countries of South Eastern Europe. The Pact was replaced by the Regional Cooperation Council (RCC) in February 2008. While the initial Pact was driven more by outside partners, such as the European Union (EU), the RCC is more "regionally owned" than the Stability Pact. These agreements have influenced Moldova to make significant reforms in its mental health system. Perhaps most importantly, the number of psychiatric hospital beds has been reduced and community mental health centers (CMHCs) have been opened.

Moldova is currently working toward further reform of its mental health services. The overarching goal is to shift the focus toward outpatient therapy, where CMHCs have a central role in coordinating the rehabilitation and social reintegration of patients with mental health problems. While there are 27 CMHCs operating in Moldova today, they are relatively new and still in development. The centers offer a range of services including assessment, consultation, and treatment services and management and community support services. The goal of CMHCs is to ensure a timely assessment of people requiring assistance and medical attention, as well as to provide supportive services as an alternative to hospitalization. Additionally, rehab and support services to improve and ensure quality of life, active participation, and independent living in society are also provided.

As part of its reform efforts, Moldova is also working to better integrate mental health services into primary care.

Historically, prescription regulations authorize primary health care doctors to prescribe and/or to continue prescription of psychiatric medicines, but there are some restrictions. For example, the Department of Health does not authorize primary health care nurses to prescribe and/or to continue prescription of psychiatric medicines. Similarly, official policy does not permit primary health care nurses to independently diagnose and treat mental disorders within the primary care system. The majority of primary health care doctors and nurses have not received official inservice training on mental health within the last 5 years; however, officially approved manuals on the management and treatment of mental disorders are available in the majority of primary health care clinics. Established referral procedures for referring persons from primary care to secondary/tertiary care exist, as do referral procedures from tertiary/secondary to primary care, with all available specialists. The hope of reforming mental health services within primary care is to increase access to mental health services, while also reducing stigma.

5.3 Mental Health Policies and Legislation in Moldova

Mental Health services in Moldova are organized by the Ministry of Health (MoH) Order no. 591 of 20 August 2010 on the layout and operations of mental health services in the Republic of Moldova. There are additional efforts underway to better align Moldovan laws and policies with international requirements in order to provide accessible and quality services to beneficiaries (Chihai and Boderscova 2012).

Currently, there are a number of changes and initiatives to move from a relatively centralized system toward a more community-based approach to psychiatric care and community supports. The importance of mental health is highlighted in the key policy papers developed by the MoH, as well as the Ministry of Labor and Social Protection and Family, and endorsed by the Government (i.e. all existing ministries). Many of these changes have focused on de-institutionalization and include:

- *The Law on Mental Health no. 1402-XII of 16 December 1997* with subsequent changes;

- *The Health System Development Strategy of the Republic of Moldova 2008–2017*, approved by Government Decision no. 1471 of 24 December 2007;
- *The National Health Policy in the Republic of Moldova* (Chapter XII. "Enabling Conditions for Better Mental Health"), approved by the Government in May 2007 as per GD no. 886 of 6 August 2007;
- *The National Program for Mental Health 2012–2016*, approved by Government Decision no. 1025 of 28 December 2012;
- *Government Decision no. 55 of 30 January 2012* "On Approving The Minimum Standards Of Quality For Community Mental Health Centers And The Template Regulations For CMHC;"
- *Ministerial order no. 610 of 24 May 2013* "About Strategy Of Development Of Mental Health Services On Community Level And Integration Of Mental Health In Primary Health Care For 2013–2016;"
- *National Plan on Mental Health for 2012–2016*;
- *MoH Order on Community Mental Health Centers, no. 8 of 17 January 2009*;
- *MoH Order no. 591 of 20 August 2010 on Mental Health Care Layout and Operations in the Republic of Moldova*;
- *MoH Order no. 407 of 16 May 2014 on Community Mental Health Centers, Regulation and Minimum Standards*;
- *Law no. 169-XVIII of 9 July 2010*, endorsing the Strategy for Social Inclusion of Persons with Disabilities (2010–2013);
- *Law no. 60-XIX of 30 March 2012*, on the social inclusion of people with disabilities.

5.4 Organizational Structure of the Mental Health System in Moldova

The process of acquiring mental health care in the Moldovan system of mental health occurs in 3 steps: (1) family doctors/general practitioners evaluate and screen patients; those deemed in need of care are referred to psychiatrists at the district psychiatrist's offices, (2) the psychiatrists offer consultation, prescribe outpatient treatment, and make referrals to hospitals, (3) hospital-based psychiatrists provide inpatient treatment and coordinate post-discharge care with local community-based services (Boderscova and Chihai 2013).

The mental health care system itself is organized into 4 different levels of services and care: emergency psychiatric, outpatient, inpatient, and residential.

5.4.1. *Outpatient*

Outpatient care is divided into district psychiatric offices and CMCHs. Community mental health services were first developed in 2000, with the first CMHCs in Chisinau, Balti, Ungheni, and Rezina, created under different projects with international funding. The Ministry of Health Order no. 407, 16 May 2014 requires that all districts have operational CMHCs. As of the end of 2014, there are 27 CMHCs operating in Moldova, out of a total of 39 districts. Today, CMHCs offer a range of medical and social services to people with mental health problems at their place of residence, i.e. at the community level. Their focus is on evaluation, treatment and consultation, management and community support services, in an effort to ensure individuals receive help and alternative care in their community instead of hospital services.[3]

5.4.2. *Inpatient*

Psychiatric hospital services in Moldova are provided by the Clinical Hospital in Chisinau, the Psychiatric Hospital in Balti, and the Phthysiopneumology Orhei Hospital. In total, there are about 1,470 psychiatric beds, or about 58 beds per 100,000 inhabitants.

The Clinical Psychiatric Hospital is the oldest in the country. Located in the outskirts of the Moldavian capital, Chisinau, it provides 770 beds. It was founded early in the 20th century under the Russian Empire. The hospital provides treatment for chronic mental illness, alcoholism, substance abuse, mental retardation, and epilepsy. The patient population of the hospital is a fraction of what it was under the Soviet Union. Shortage

---

[3] Information Note of the Ministry of Health regarding results of evaluation of activities conducted by community mental health centers in the Republic of Moldova, 19 March 2012, Order of the Ministry of Health no. 98 of 9 February 2012.

of staff and resources allow for only a few structured activities. During the day, patients are typically either milling around the ward or lounge in enclosed yards. Patients who are allowed to leave the wards for the open grounds of the hospital are usually engaged in some form of work, such as sweeping sidewalks or cutting grass. While the availability of medications and nutritional services has improved over the past few years, the amount of money allowed for food and medication each day per patient is only 20 *lei* (approximately 1 USD). The nearby monastery supplements patients' diet with occasional donations of cooked meals. Many patients appear undernourished. Doctor's salaries are a miniscule 100–150 USD per month, while nurses and support staff earn about half this amount. Most members of the staff work 60 hours per week due to personnel shortages.

The Psychiatric Hospital in Balti was built in the 1970s and has approximately 770 patients. It appears to be in better shape than other hospitals. The Psychiatric Hospital in Balti was originally designed as a typical psychiatric hospital of the Soviet era and was distinguished by extensive vocational rehabilitation programs. While vocational rehabilitation activities have been drastically cut back, treatment with psychiatric medications has been sustained. As the hospital is unable to provide patients with more modern psychiatric drugs, patients are given older medications which are mostly phased out in Western Europe and the United States over the past 20 years. With the help of European NGOs, the hospital administration was able to establish a modern physiotherapy facility in the basement of the main building.

Finally, the Phthysiopneumology Orhei has 180 beds, and was originally used to house patients with tuberculosis. Psychiatric patients were transferred to this hospital from the grounds of the monastery at Kurki when the Eastern Orthodox Church in Moldova reclaimed the monastery. A number of patients who are stable and no longer need inpatient care continue to stay at the hospital due to a lack of alternative living arrangements, including a lack of family members willing to accommodate them. This problem is driven by the fact that there are only a few state-funded residential facilities, with the demand for supervised residential programs exceeding the availability of community-based housing (Boderscova and Chihai 2013).

5.4.3. *Residential*

The Ministry of Labor, Social Protection, and Family coordinates 6 residential social institutions for adults and children: 2 institutions for children with severe mental disabilities (including developmental disabilities/mental retardation) are located in Orhei and Hincesti, while 4 institutions for adults with mental disabilities (psycho–neurological profile) can be found in Balti, Dubasari, Soroca, and Edinet. These facilities offer residents social and medical services, accommodation (for an indefinite period), general health care, nutrition, provision of clothing and shoes, occupational therapy, cultural activities, physical therapy, etc (Boderscova and Chihai 2013).

5.5 Access to the Mental Health Care System in Moldova

Ideally, publicly funded health insurance should reduce social and health disparities through the redistribution of financial resources. However, there are problems in achieving universal access in Moldova. While overall access to primary care services and pre-hospital emergency care by vulnerable groups has improved, one-fifth of the population has no insurance coverage. The uninsured include self-employed farmers, occasional employees, and the unemployed. However, a minimum package of health services is available to the whole population, irrespective of insurance status, while the more generous package is available only for the insured.

Mental health services in Moldova are financed by the public health insurance, and there is no separate budget for mental health. Medical insurance is primarily oriented to reimbursement for health services according to detailed lists of accepted services. This is especially relevant for mental health, as the change from an institution-based to community-based system of care is dependent on a collaboration between health and social sectors in order to be successful.

Additional factors impact access to mental health care in Moldova. Workforce issues impact the availability of services, as shortages of qualified medical staff in remote areas and high numbers of elderly personnel are impediments to providing services in rural areas, and the health system remains over-centralized with unclear roles at both central and local levels of service. The high cost of medications is also a common concern. Psychiatric medications are perceived as being too expensive and their costs are only partially reimbursed. After a modification of the law in 2014, only patients with epilepsy and schizophrenia could receive medications at no expense. Caregivers for patients with other mental health conditions have been very dissatisfied with this policy.[4] Access to care in Moldova is further complicated by the expectation of informal payments. The degree of out-of-pocket payments (both formal and informal— non-legal) is relatively high and is paid mostly for medicines. Patients report that they are asked by providers for additional money and have little choice but to pay in order to get a better care for their ill relatives.

Mental health services are accessible for majority of the patients, except for those patients with multiple disabilities. Those patients that cannot be hospitalized in mental health institutions due to being severely disabled and requiring constant monitoring are under the supervision of social services.

5.6 Mental Health Workforce in Moldova

Human resources (HR) are the most valuable assets within the mental health services system; the lion's share of the recurrent annual budget is spent on staff salaries and benefits. Good care requires competent and motivated staff to promote health, prevent illness when possible, and provide services for the mentally ill. However, significant challenges in HR planning and training are an ongoing problem for the mental health care delivery system in Moldova.

The majority of districts in Moldova lack specialists in child psychiatry and some districts even lack psychiatrists for adults. Working psychiatrists face numerous challenges including: (1) high patient volume; (2) existing regulations governing patients' examination (regulated 20 minutes visits are often inadequate for addressing patients' needs); (3) the lack of telephones in psychiatric consultation rooms; (4) poor collaboration with primary medicine providers; (5) poor collaboration with district community centers that offer social services and are attended by some people experiencing mental health problems; (6) long waits for emergency psychiatric assistance; (7) poor collaboration with community social workers; and finally, (8) limited transportation to visit rural sites.

---

[4] http://auachsr.com/UserFiles/File/new%20/Domnica%20Balteanu.pdf.

Education and training of staff in mental health should ideally be aligned with overall health related human resources planning and objectives. There is a clear need for specialized mental health providers competent and capable of delivering needed services. To achieve this requires development and coordination of aligned policies across the mental health service delivery sector and the training sector. Ideally, key professional education facilities actively participate in providing mental care services in each of its facilities (e.g. community, residential, and hospital care) (World Health Organization 2011).

Additionally, developing a workforce specialized in mental health requires coordination across several professional and non-professional disciplines. Teamwork is a core competence required for all categories of mental health workers; well-functioning teams should provide motivation and support across a wide array of human and clinical challenges. As of 2012, the number of trained mental health professionals in the Republic of Moldova included the following:

- **Psychiatrists** (not including narcologists—doctors working with addiction): 232 or 0.7 to 10,000 inhabitants;
- **Nurses:** 660 in inpatient services;
- **Psychologists:** while the standard for psychiatric hospitals is 1 psychologist to 80 beds, this standard is not followed—today there are about 8 psychologists in 3 psychiatric hospitals;
- **Social workers:** there is 1 social worker in each psychiatric hospital, as well as 1 in each CMHC, as per the legislation (Governmental Decision no. 55).

Inservice training and education (ISTE) is a valuable strategy in the Republic of Moldova for helping to assure that care is provided consistent with best practice and based on the evidence of most efficient interventions. It is important that staff find their work to be rewarding and have career growth opportunities over time. Inservice education is a cornerstone of workforce development by promoting ongoing skill development and a balance between the quality of care and patient safety.

The standard curriculum for the discipline "Medical Psychology, Psychiatry, and Child Psychiatry" is for the 6th-year medical students of the general medicine track of the Medicine and Pharmacy State University

(MPSU) "Nicolae Testemitanu." The curriculum and syllabus for the 3-year residency training in psychiatry and drug addiction were first developed in 2003. Subsequently, these were updated by the Methodological Specialized Committee "Neurology, Neurosurgery, Psychiatry, Drug Addiction, Medical Psychology, Neuro-pediatrics and Traditional Medicine" in 2009. There is also a syllabus for providing training in psychiatry and addictions for Family Medicine Residents. In 2009, The MPSU Chair of Psychiatry, Addictions and Medical Psychology developed and endorsed a module on "Psychiatry and Addictions" for the Family Medicine interns and residents.

In Moldova, the inservice training of psychiatrists is carried out by the MPSU Chair of Psychiatry, Addictions and Medical Psychology. Modules are planned on a yearly basis subject to demand in Costiujeni and PH in Balti. There are about 10 modules of varying lengths covering topics such as psychosomatic disorders, and psychotherapy. Inservice training modules for psychiatrists cover the following topics: modern approaches to treatment in psychiatry, neurotic personality and conduct disorders, pediatric psychiatry, psychoactive substance abuse related mental and conduct disorders, psychosomatic disorders, forensic psychiatry, clinical features, treatment and recovery within endogenous psychoses, current issues in psychotherapy, and updates in psychotherapy.

The medical nurses have also attended the Medical Colleges. As part of their education and training, they have a general course in "Psychiatry and Neurology." However, there is no specialty training for psychiatric nurses. Inservice training programs for medical nurses are provided for nurses already working in the mental health system (Chihai and Boderscova 2013).

5.7 Financing the Mental Health Care System in Moldova

Mental health care services currently receive funding from the following sources:

- Mandatory health insurance funds, obtained after giving medical services included in the Unique Program, under contract with the National Health Insurance Company;
- State (National) Budget;

- Budget of local administrations from districts;
- Other sources of income according to current legislation.

Mental health expenditures of the government MoH are 3.24% of the total health budget. Mental hospital expenditures are 83.85% of the total mental health budget. Services provided in the CMHCs that are part of specialized medical care, as well as outpatient mental health services provided under psychiatric hospitals care, are paid from the National Health Insurance Company global budget.

For 2013, approximately 175,000 USD was spent for community mental health services. Approximately 49% (84,000 USD) and 51% (91,000 USD) came from Local Public Administration budgets. For inpatient services, about 7 million USD were expended and virtually all of this money came from mandatory health insurance funds.

5.8 Quality of Care, Outcomes, and Evaluation

In 2010, a feasibility study regarding the development of the mental health services in the Republic of Moldova provided the following findings:

- The incidence rate for mental and behavioral disorders for all age categories increased from 370 per 100,000 people in 2008 to 380 per 100,000 in 2009.
- The prevalence of mental and behavior disorders among the population is also growing, from 2,600 per 100,000 people in 2008 to 2,650 per 100,000 in 2009.
- The increase in incidence and prevalence of mental disorders can be attributed to a number of factors including but not limited to:
  o The insufficient number of specialists in the psychiatric sphere, including children psychiatry;
  o The decrease in the number of beds meant for inpatient treatment;
  o The small number of alternative mental health services as compared to traditional services provided in hospitals, etc.

There are issues related to quality of care and outcomes that are specific to inpatient services:

- Psychiatric hospital services that provide short-term help (on average of 30 days) receive 80%–85% of the funding for all mental health services;
- The extended benefit of inpatient care depends in large part on outpatient follow-up—this is often difficult to achieve, and as many as one-fourth of patients return to hospitals after discharge;
- Patients often find themselves without social support or a place to live when they leave the hospital (Patel, 2007).

Another factor impacting the quality of mental health care and outcomes in Moldova is the heavy reliance on hospital-based care. Although psychiatric hospitals provide critical services, this reliance has some drawbacks compared to community-based services, including:

- Patients are taken from their families, they are not visited by relatives, which can worsen their health resulting in the loss of their social ties;
- Psychiatric hospitals are not able to address the long-term needs of patients, these institutions only help the person to overcome the critical condition;
- The medical component of treatment is over-emphasized while rehabilitation, psychotherapy, and other recovery oriented services are only a small part of what is provided to hospital patients;
- The living conditions in many psychiatric hospitals are poor;
- Hospitals are seen not only as a place where you can undergo a treatment, but also as institutions where the family can place the patient when they want;
- There is no system for coordination of care between psychiatric hospitals and CMHCs, including between psychiatric consulting rooms and CMHCs—this negatively influences the development of the mental health service system.

Difficulties encountered by the specialists working in the CMHC can include (Chihai, Rotundu and Boderscova 2012):

- Difficult relations with doctors of the outpatient system and as a result the lack of a mechanism for coordination of care;
- The small number of beneficiaries;
- Lack of medicine for providing a supporting treatment for beneficiaries;
- Lack of nutritional services;
- Lack of national standards in this sphere;
- Lack of funding from NCMI;
- Poor remuneration for social workers and psychologists.

Patients themselves note that there are critical issues in the mental health system in the following aspects:

- In the organization and administration of psychiatric consulting rooms:
    - Doctors prescribe only reimbursed medicine and do not offer a complex treatment;
    - Confidentiality is not always respected ("when the door is open, we can hear the doctor discussing with the patient");
    - Big queues;
    - The patient is not given their medical record;
    - Patients are sometimes consulted by the medical assistant instead of the doctor;
    - There are cases when the doctor puts the person in hospital without his/her consent.
- The organization of the hospital system:
    - Lack of occupational activities;
    - Poor accommodations;
    - Lack of possibilities to walk outside the ward;
    - Staff's (nurses') discriminating attitude, etc.
- The organization of the CMHC:
    - Lack of social services;

- Lack of the information about the existence of community centers and their role in the rehabilitation and social integration of people experiencing mental health issues;
- Team of specialists is mainly women.

5.9 Advocacy, Stigma, and Self-Help

Untreated mental health problems can lead to significant distress, disability, and economic loss. This, in turn, can result in burdens on the social, education, legal, and health care systems, as well as individuals and their families. Despite the increased availability of services and treatment options, as well as recent improvements in psychiatric care, people with mental health problems and disabilities still face problems of social exclusion, stigmatization, discrimination, and violation of personal dignity and fundamental human rights. While patient groups and advocacy organizations exist in the country, their role in health policy is rather limited.

The United Nation (UN)'s Convention on the Rights of Persons with Disabilities (CRPD) was ratified by Republic of Moldova in 2010. The CRPD Convention was the result of a highly inclusive drafting process, involving not only governments but also an international groundswell of disability advocates. In its short life, it has already become one of the most ratified and adopted international human rights treaties. As of January 2017, 175 nations and regional organizations had ratified the CRPD.[5]

Article 19 of the CRDP is especially noteworthy to Moldova's mental health system development. It asserts the equal right of all persons with disabilities to live in the community, with choices equal to others. It also calls for effective and appropriate measures as needed in order to assure their full inclusion and participation in the community. Some of the specifics include:

- Persons with disabilities should have the opportunity to choose their place of residence, and where and with whom they live on an equal

---

[5] https://www.un.org/development/desa/disabilities/convention-on-the-rights-of-persons-with-disabilities.html.

basis with others and are not obliged to live in a particular living arrangement;
- Persons with disabilities should have access to a range of in-home, residential, and other community support services, including personal assistance necessary to support living and inclusion in the community, and to prevent isolation or segregation from the community. Community services and facilities for the general population should be available on an equal basis to persons with disabilities and be responsive to their needs.

These far-reaching commitments have started processes of reform worldwide, and in particular, in the countries of the former Communist bloc, such as Moldova. During the Soviet era, segregation and exclusion of persons with disabilities was intense, and large institutions were the cornerstone of highly medicalized policies. The Republic of Moldova is among the countries that have been found to be in violation of human rights by the European Court in cases concerning arbitrary detention in psychiatry, as well as forced treatment rising to the level of abuse. In 2012, the UN Special Rapporteur on Extreme Poverty and Human Rights has called for increased social inclusion of persons with disabilities in the Republic of Moldova. This is based on findings of serious human rights violations in institutional care related to neglect, harm, death, physical, sexual and other forms of abuse amounting to torture, emotional, social, and physical deprivation. During its first Universal Periodic Review by the UN (October 2011), Moldova committed to continue its efforts to combat discrimination on grounds of disability. In addition, the Moldovan Government committed to the removal of legal and social obstacles that prevent or limit the ability of persons with mental or intellectual disabilities to fully exercise fundamental human rights on equal basis with others, as recommended by the UN Committee on the Economic, Social, and Cultural Rights.

However, along with these problems, the Republic of Moldova has also seen some recent progress in the promotion and protection of rights of persons with disability. In September 2011, the Government launched a national program of inclusive education for all children in an effort to eliminate discrimination on grounds of disability. In November 2011,

3 ministries (Health; Justice; Labor, Social Protection and Family) initiated a Working Group to amend the Civil Code and provide supported decision-making according to CRPD Article 12 requirements. In 2012, the Government adopted a comprehensive *Law on Ensuring Equality*, and, for the first time, established a domestic legal requirement for reasonable accommodation for persons with disabilities. Also in 2012, the *Law on the Social Inclusion of Persons with Disabilities*, which incorporated many pieces of the CRPD, became part of Moldovan policy. In 2013, an anti-stigma body was established, and has been extensively supported by multiple UN agencies during its first year of existence.

Along with the legislative and policy initiatives described above, the Moldovan Government has agreed to transform psychiatric care by increasing community-based services and support (Article 19). This commitment is included in the *National Mental Health Program*. In November 2013, the College of the Ministry of Health—the overall body for all health policy matters in the Republic of Moldova—decided that the Government would move from a system focused on large institutions to a model of community-based care over the next few years. Similar efforts are underway to address concerns about residential institutions, which are operated under the direction of the Ministry of Labor, Social Protection and Family. In early 2014, several individuals in long-term institutional care were reintegrated into communities as part of pilot supported by the UN country team in Moldova (Chihai and Boderscova 2012).

There is still much work to be done if a major transformation in the treatment of persons with disabilities is to be realized. Challenges include a need to further develop the resources and infrastructure needed for community-based care and services along with developing community support for reintegration. There is a need to assure that such services are accessible and to also improve the access to community-based vocational training. The need for continuing development of grass-roots organizations to support service users and survivors of mental illness has also been identified. There is some evidence of a true commitment by the government to these changes, as reflected in the adoption of legislation and policy documents consistent with international standards. Government representatives have repeatedly stressed their commitment to carry through CRPD-based reforms along with the redesign of systems needed to ensure the long-term sustainability of these reforms. While discrimination and mistreatment of persons with disabilities is of genuine concern in the Republic of Moldova—no other group faces such serious threats of complete exclusion from the effective exercise of rights, or is as directly affected by complete removal from human society via placement in institutions—the proposed actions are promising. They are person-centered, comprehensive, context-specific, and prevention-oriented. They involve measures that seek to reduce the likelihood of conflicts, help overcome the obstacles to development, and promote human rights for all, with specific attention to the particular segments of the community which are most marginalized, stigmatized, and at risk of threats to personal security.

5.10 Looking Forward: Challenges and Priorities in the Moldovan Mental Health Care System

There are many challenges and opportunities that are faced by the mental health services delivery system in the Republic of Moldova. All future actions should build upon, and take advantage of, recent achievements in advancing respect for the fundamental human rights and the ratification of the Convention on the Rights of Persons with Disabilities (CRPD). Success in these efforts will require a continued strong political will to bring domestic law, policies, and practices in line with international standards in the field of human rights for persons with disabilities. Moldova's desire for European integration should help promote a constructive dialogue between national authorities that is needed to adequately address issues related to the rights of persons with disabilities, although this dialouge must include broader engagement in civil society as well as greater participation by stakeholders and representatives from organizations representing persons with disabilities.

Advancing the rights of individuals with mental illness and disabilities include future initiatives to support the transition toward community-based care, which fall within the commitments under the National Action Plan (2014–2016) for the implementation of the EU-Moldova Association Agreement. Hopefully, the agreement will strengthen coordination and implementation of deinstitutionalization, along with steps towards the protection of human rights consistent with the United Nations CRDP, along with the laws on Social Inclusion of Persons with Disabilities and the Law on Ensuring Equality. These actions sit at the heart of the far-reaching transformations needed to shift the treatment of persons with disabilities from medical models to social models of support. Success in these endeavors will require the inclusion of community-based systems of independent and supported living that can deliver better outcomes, such as an improved quality of life, better health and the ability to contribute to society. By supporting deinstitutionalization and improving the accessibility of mainstream services, more people will have the opportunity for social inclusion and the ability to contribute to the communities' social and economic growth.

Moldova has the potential to be a model for the transformation into a disability-rights-based system among the countries of the former Soviet Union and beyond. As countries work to implement the CRPD Convention's commitment to ensure the right for all persons to live in the community with dignity, Moldova can become a recognized leader in achieving and sustaining this much need change.

Thus, going forward, priorities in the Moldovan mental health care system include:

- Psychiatric beds in general hospitals;
- Mental health services in primary care system;
- Reduced number of beds in psychiatric hospitals;
- Deinstitutionalization.

Challenges in the Moldovan system, moving forward, will include:

- Lack of historical data;
- Data for 2014;
- Data from Transnistria.[6]

---

[6]Unrecognized by any United Nations member state, Transnistria is designated by the Republic of Moldova as the Transnistria autonomous territorial unit with special legal status.

References

Boderscova, L. and Chihai, J. (2013) Assessment of Psychiatric Hospital Care Services in the Republic of Moldova Subordinate to the MoH. In: *Gulbenkian Mental Health Platform*.

Boderscova, L. and Chihai, J. (2013) Report on the Performance of Residential Facilities for People with Mental Disabilities in the Republic of Moldova. In: *Gulbenkian Mental Health Platform*—http://www.gulbenkianmhplatform. com/conteudos/00/66/00/00/MH-hospital-care_-ENG_7622.pdf, p. 15.

Chihai, J. and Boderscova, L. (2012) Assessing Primary Healthcare Services in the Republic of Moldova as to the integration of mental health services into PHC In: *Gulbenkian Mental Health Platform* -http://www.gulbenkianmhplatform.com/conteudos/00/66/00/00/PHC-and-MH_-ENG_5243.pdf, p. 22.

Chihai, J. and Boderscova, L. (2012) Evaluation of Community Mental Health Services in Republic of Moldova. In: *Gulbenkian Mental Health Platform* - http://www.gulbenkianmhplatform.com/conteudos/00/66/00/00/community-based-mental-health-services-in-Moldova_ENG_3242.pdf, p. 22.

Chihai, J. and Boderscova, L. (2013) Review of Mental and Behavior Disorders Morbidity in the Republic of Moldova, 2007–2011. In: *Gulbenkian Mental Health Platform*—http://www.gulbenkianmhplatform.com/conteudos/00/66/00/00/epidemiological-data-revision_ENG_9620.pdf, p. 6.

Chihai, J. and Boderscova, L. (2013) Review of the Mental Health Graduate and Residential Syllabus in the Republic of Moldova. In: *Gulbenkian Mental Health Platform* – http://www.gulbenkianmhplatform.com/conteudos/00/66/00/00/review-of-MH-Graduate-and-Postgraduate-syllabus_3285.pdf, p. 33.

Chihai, J., Rotundu, D. and Boderscova, L. (2012) Defining the Package of Mental Health Services Appropriate for Being Integrated into Primary Health Care. In: *Gulbenkian Mental Health Platform* – http://www.gulbenkianmhplatform.com/conteudos/00/66/00/00/MH-packages-of-services-for-PHC--professionals_based-on-FGDs_ENG_8616.pdf, p. 10. European OBSERVATORY on Health System and Policies/Health System in transition, p. 14.

Ministry of Health of RM. National Strategy of Health System for 2008–2017, Chisinau, 2008, pp. 81–87.

Ministry of Health of RM. National Policy of Health of RM for 2007–2021, Chisinau 2007, p. 65.

National Center I Health Management. Public Health in Moldova. Chisnau 2012, p. 312.

Programul Național privind Sănătatea Mintală aprobat prin hotărârea de Guvern nr.353 din 30.12.2012 Publicat la 11.05.2013 în Monitorul Oficial Nr.064, art. Nr. 493.

Patel, V. (2007) Mental Health in Low-and-Middle-Income Families Republic of Moldova Mental Health System Review. In: *Gulbenkian Mental Health Platform*, 2013.

World Health Organization (2011) *Atlas: Mental Health Resources in the World* (World Health Organization, Geneva), p. 239. Available at: http://www.who.int/topics/mental_health/eng/.

CHAPTER 6

An Overview of Mental Health in Romania

Raluca Sfetcu* and Marius Ungureanu[†]

*Faculty of Psychology, Spiru Haret University, Bucharest, Romania

[†]Health Policy and Management Department, Cluj School of Public Health, Babeş-Bolyai University, Cluj-Napoca, Romania

6.1 Mental Health Status of the Romanian Population

Sound epidemiological data regarding psychiatric disorders in Romania are still sparse or non-existent. The best available data sources include international indicator databases, the World Mental Health Survey Initiative and service use data.

The WHO indicators database for the year 2015[1] reports an incidence rate of all mental disorders of 1,178 cases per 100,000 population and a prevalence rate of 2.2%.

Epidemiological data collected in the framework of the World Mental Health Survey Initiative (WMSHI)[2] indicate a lifetime prevalence of any disorder of 13.4%, with 4.5% of respondents having 2 or more lifetime disorders and 1.4% having 3 or more (see Figure 6.1) (Florescu *et al.*, 2009). The same study also identified anxiety disorders as the most

---

[1] WHO Mental Health Indicators, Health for All Database. Available at: http://data.euro.who.int/hfadb/profile/profile.php?w=1600&h=900.

[2] See http://www.hcp.med.harvard.edu/wmh/.

Key Country Statistics

Region: Southeast Central Europe
Government system: semi-presidential republic
Area: 238,391 square miles
Population: 20,599,736
Capital: Bucharest
Gender ratio: 0.95 male to female
Ethnic groups:
- Romanian 83.4%
- Hungarian 6.1%
- Roma 3.1%
- Ukrainian 0.3%
- German 0.2%
- Other 0.7%
- Unspecified 6.1%

Literacy rate: 98.8%

Population under the age 15: 15.6%
Population above the age of 65: 15.73%
Average life expectancy: 71.7 for men and 78.8 for women
Suicide rates: 12.5 per 100,000 residents
Economy: upper middle-income economy
GDP annual growth rate: 3.8%
GDP per capita: 20,900 USD (PPP)
Unemployment rate (15-64 years): 6.8%
Youth unemployment rate: 24%
Average net salary: 497.5 (USD) or 398 (EUR)
Total health expenditure as percentage of GDP: 5.6%
Population below poverty line: 22.4%

Source: CIA World Factbook (2016).

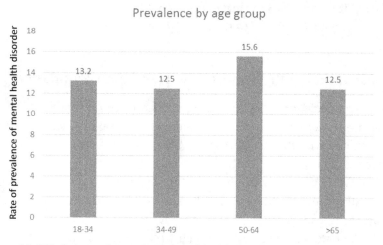

Figure 6.1: Lifetime prevalence of any mental health disorder by age group.
Source: Authors' analysis from data from Florescu *et al.* (2009).

prevalent class of disorders (6.9%), followed by mood disorders (4.3%), substance use disorders (3.4%), and impulse-control disorders (2.1% overall and 2.9% for those 44 years old or less). Lastly, the data highlight a substantial treatment gap for mental illness; the median time between onset of symptoms and first contact with the medical system for most such conditions is oftentimes decades rather than years.[3]

An international study comparing 10 WMHI countries, shows that Romania has the lowest prevalence of any lifetime internalizing disorder[4] for both women (10.8%) and men (5.9%), as well as for any lifetime mood or anxiety disorder (Boyd *et al.*, 2015). A similar study comparing the prevalence of psychotic experiences (PE) in the general population of the 18 WMHSI countries, reports a lifetime prevalence of 1% for any type of psychotic experience (0.9% hallucinatory experience and 0.1% delusional experience) and a 12 month prevalence of any psychotic experience of 0.3%. Romania ranked last among the included countries, with the study average of any PE being 5.8% for lifetime prevalence and 2.0% for a 12-month period (McGrath *et al.*, 2015).

National level service use data from an ongoing study[5] of psychiatric morbidity among hospitalized patients across the country found that the overall percentage of patients discharged with a main ICD 10-F diagnosis was of 7% (247,196 out of 3,564,272). According to these data, mood disorders represent more than a third of hospitalized psychiatric cases, while psychotic disorders come second, accounting for 21.34% (for details, see Table 6.1).

Outpatient service use data[6] for the year 2013 indicate that a total of 527,700 individual patients with mental health problems were treated by a psychiatrist either in private practice or in community centers, and that 43,477 of these represented new cases. The same source also reports that a total number of 234,888 new cases of mental and behavioral disorders

---

[3] Economist Intelligence Unit. Mental Health and Integration. Provision for supporting people with mental illness: A comparison of 30 European countries. Country report: Romania. Available at: http://www.mentalhealthintegration.com.

[4] Mental disorders were broadly grouped into internalizing disorders (including mood disorders: major depressive episode, dysthymia with hierarchy; and anxiety disorders: panic disorder, specific phobia, social phobia, agoraphobia with or without panic disorder, generalized anxiety with hierarchy, post-traumatic stress disorder) or externalizing disorders (including attention-deficit, conduct, alcohol-use, and drug-use disorder).

[5] Unpublished report; data collected in the framework of the CephosLink EU study.

[6] Centrul Național de Statistică și Informatică în Sănătate Publică (CNSISP).

Table 6.1: International statistical classification of diseases and related health problems.

ICD-10 Codes	Total (% column)	Male (% row)	Female (% row)
F0—Dementia in Alzheimer's disease	21.30	63	37
F1—Vascular dementia	5.98	88	12
F2—Dementia in other diseases classified elsewhere	21.34	50	50
F3—Unspecified dementia	36.44	33	67
F4—Organic amnesic syndrome, not induced by alcohol and other psychoactive substances	6.43	35	65
F5—Delirium, not induced by alcohol and other psychoactive substances	1.25	39	61
F6—Other mental disorders due to brain damage and dysfunction and to physical disease	3.62	75	25
F7—Personality and behavioral disorders due to brain disease, damage and dysfunction	3.37	59	41
F9—Unspecified organic or symptomatic mental disorder	0.05	33	47

Table 6.2: Mental health service use data in inpatient, outpatient, and primary care settings for 2013.

Service type	Total no of cases treated in 2013 (N/rate per 1000 population)	New cases in 2013 (N/rate per 1000 population)
Inpatient	247,196 (12.55%)	NA
Psychiatrist in OP	527,700 (26.79%)	43,477 (2.21%)
GP	NA	234,888 (11.93%)

were identified by general practitioners (GPs) in the year 2013 (see Table 6.2).

There has been a reduction in the average suicide rate. In 2011, the rate for males was 21.52 per 100,000 inhabitants and for females was 3.77, while the average suicide rate for the year 2013 was 13.52 overall, with males accounting for 82% of the cases. For 2014, the total standardized death rates due to intentional self-harm (per 100,000 inhabitants) was 11.4, with rates of 20.6 for males and 3.2 for females.[7]

---

[7] Report mina minovici, 2013.

6.2 History of Mental Health Care in Romania

6.2.1 *General context*

At present, Romanian citizens benefit from universal health insurance coverage, provided via a Bismarckian model.[8] The Social Health Insurance (SHI) program provides for all persons legally residing in Romania access to a basic package of health care services. This system was gradually implemented in the post-1989 period as an alternative to the previously existing Semashko system[9] (1949–1989), whose aim was to generalize access to care. The transition from a centralized service provision model to a SHI model occurred over a long period of time and was achieved through several legislative initiatives following the breakup of the Soviet Union. The process started in 1995 with the organization of the College of Physicians[10] followed by the implementation of the Social Health Insurance in 1997[11] and the reorganization of the public health system in 1998.[12] This initial legislative package was completed by a law regarding the organization of hospitals.[13]

Since 2000, the basic laws regulating the health system have been modified and adjusted several times to reflect the political vision of the ruling parties in relation to issues of finance. While these changes have addressed relatively small and isolated problems within the health care system, the need for a more comprehensive approach required a new health reform law[14] which was passed in 2006. This law represents the core of the country's health-related legislation and it addresses the organization of various components of the Romanian health care system; including social health insurance, private health insurance, hospitals, community

---

[8] The Bismarckian system is based on a compulsory health insurance system controlled by the State with additional coverage provided by profit or non-profit private health insurance companies. The health services are a mix of private market and public sector.

[9] A resource intensive model where the state is directly providing health care services to all members of society in a highly regulated, standardized, and centralized system.

[10] Law 74/1995 concerning the organization of the College of Physicians.

[11] Law 145/1997 on Social Health Insurance.

[12] Law 100/1998 on Public Health.

[13] Law 146/1999 on Hospital Organization.

[14] Law 95/2006 on the Reform of the Health System.

care, primary health care, pharmaceuticals, emergency services, public health, national and European health cards, national health programs, professional liability, as well as the establishment of a national school of public health and management. At a systems level, these changes have meant that primary health care services are mostly provided by family doctors, who operate as independent practitioners contracted by the public health insurance fund; secondary care is provided by hospital outpatient departments (e.g. centers for diagnosis and treatment) and by specialists in private offices (i.e. ambulatory care). Inpatient and tertiary care is provided in hospitals, which, for the most part, remain publicly owned and administered by the state.

Reform efforts were furthered in the period between 2009 and 2011 with the transfer of responsibility for health care provision from central to local governments. This change was intended to, as much as possible, align decision-making and accountability mechanisms with the provision of health services. As might be expected, these measures have also resulted in the reduction of overall health care spending by the central budget and increases from local budgets.

Impacted by global economic decline, Romania's economy contracted in 2009 and stagnated in 2010; from 2008 to 2012, per capita public spending declined. As a result of unemployment and falling wages, health insurance revenue declined. In response, the budget of the Ministry of Health (MoH) was cut and government budget transfers to the health insurance scheme were made. For the hospital sector, this required measures to reduce hospital spending and included abandoning or scaling down planned investment, decreasing the number of beds (with 2% beds cut in 2013 and another 2% beds cut by 2015) or borrowing to increase investment.[15] For primary care, these economic challenges resulted in an initial decline in funding (2009–2011) and a subsequent increase (by 15% in 2012); this was achieved by reducing the per capita component of GP revenue in favor of fee for service (FFS).

In 2015, the public fraction of health care spending in Romania was 4% of GDP, 1.1% higher than it had been 15 years ago (2.9% in 1999).

---

[15] Economic crisis, health systems and health in Europe: impact and implications for policy, Policy summary 12, 2014.

However, this rate of spending remains about half of the EU average (6.8% in 2011). This level of chronic under-financing represents important challenges to be addressed in the future and indicates that unresolved imbalances in the structure of the service delivery system remain. For example, there are still too many hospitals with too many beds and very few facilities for specialized outpatient services and secondary ambulatory care.

6.2.2 Historical development of mental health services

The first "modern" mental health establishment in Romania was the "Marcutza Asylum," created near Bucharest in 1839. Over time all the patients from the "Malamuci" monastery[16] were transferred there (Buda et al., 2013). From 1839 to 1950, several other psychiatric hospitals were established (e.g. Socola in 1905, Obregia in 1923). By 1930, legislation established a standard of care that required "the treatment and care of psychiatric disorders [...] in specialized hospitals or health houses." However, it was during the period spanning from 1955 to 1975 that most of the current existing psychiatric hospitals and psychiatry departments in general hospitals were established.

Community mental health services were first introduced in Romania in the 1970s under the name "Laboratoare de Sanatate Mintala" (LSM).[17] LSM sites were organized in accordance with WHO recommendations, and were created "in the county hospitals and clinical hospitals, separately for adults and children, in order to provide comprehensive outpatient team care[18] for the mentally ill." Treatment included medical consultation and treatment, psychotherapy, psychological testing, speech therapy treatments, etc.[19]

---

[16] Medieval mental health care was monastic, consisting of isolation and detention.

[17] Ministry of Health Order no. 86/1974 regarding the approval of the plan of actions for 1974–1975 and 1975–1980 with respect to the protection and promotion of the mental health of the population.

[18] The multidisciplinary team included psychiatrists, psychologists, speech therapists, and other professionals.

[19] cf. Article 117, MHO 86/1974.

Besides treatment, the services provided by the LSMs included[20] efforts at the identification of risk factors impacting psychiatric disorders. This effort included early detection of psychiatric disorders, providing medical assistance through multidisciplinary teams (psychiatrists, psychologists, etc.), as well as orientation for insertion and socio-professional reinsertion. Psychiatry and child neuropsychiatry offices were integrated into LSM's structure, while other program and services, called "stationare de zi" and functioning similar to day hospitals, were also established. This was done to provide "specialized mental health care to the mentally ill by combining inpatient treatment at the clinic in the general hospital or psychiatric hospitals with specialized treatment, such as psychological assessment, physiotherapy, occupational therapy, etc."[21] Most of the existing LSMs and day hospitals in Romania were established between 1975 and 1985. However, less than 25 community service sites were functional before 1989. This was due in part to staffing problems (psychology and social work were banned from Romanian universities from 1977 until 1990). In addition, during this time many professionals had only limited access to international literature and knowledge of advancements in their fields.[22] The decline in the activity of the LSMs led to their loss of autonomy and, consequently, to their integration into the structure of the hospitals.[23]

6.3 Mental Health Policies and Legislation in Romania

Although efforts for reform of mental health laws by the Romanian parliament can be traced back to 1996, it was not until 2002 that a mental health law was introduced.[24] However, lack of regulations and policies delayed its implementation for another 4 years. Eventually a Mental Health National

---

[20] cf.art.146 MHO 86/1974.

[21] cf. Article 90, MHO 86/1974.

[22] From hospital to community: The stony way of Romania (2009); presentation by Mugur Ciumageanu and Heinz Katschnig retrieved on 21 September 2015 from: http://ec.europa.eu/health/archive/ph_determinants/life_style/mental/docs/ev_20090528_coll_en.pdf.

[23] Ministerial Order 276/1996.

[24] Law 487/2002.

Strategy was created[25] and adopted by the MoH[26] in 2005. In 2006, an EU-funded project[27] supported the creation and promulgation of a package of regulations in response to several international reports.[28] The package consisted of:

- The approval of the *Action Plan for the implementation of the Mental Health Policy of the Romanian Ministry of Health*;[29]
- The establishment, organization, and functioning of Mental Health Centers (MHCs);[30,31]
- The establishment and functioning of the National Mental Health Center[32] as a department of the National Public Health School (SNSPMPDS);
- The implementation of regulations and procedures for the mental health law.

The legislative initiative also provided a 5-fold increase in the budget allocated to the National Program for Mental Health in the year 2006 (from 21 to 100 billion RON), allocated to the development of 8 pilot MHCs. More recently, specialty mental health services for children and adolescents were also impacted by legislation which addressed the

---

[25] Through the project "Enhancing Social Cohesion through the Development of Community Mental Health Structures in South East Europe," within the cooperation framework of the Stability Pact.

[26] Minister Order no. 639/14.06.2005.

[27] Twinning light PHARE project (RO03/IB/OT 09 TL) "Action Plan for the implementation of the Mental Health Policy of the Romanian Ministry of Health."

[28] Amnesty International report (2004), Comprehensive Monitoring Report on the state of preparedness for EU membership of Romania issued by the European Commission in May 2006.

[29] Ministerial Order no. 426/19.04.2006.

[30] MHCs are defined as public health units, without legal personality, organized within hospitals in order to provide care in the community for people with mental disorders through a team of multidisciplinary specialists.

[31] MO 375/10 April 2006.

[32] MO 373/10 April 2006.

A Policymaker's Perspective

What experiences have you had that you consider representative of the way the mental health system works?

I was involved in developing a number of occupational profiles, such as community nurses and clinical psychologists, that are necessary in implementing the reform of the mental health system. Through this, I made contact with people in the system and I noticed a significant degree of resistance to change. I also worked on the reform strategy for the mental health service, especially for children, to create a Stepped Care Mental Health System. At the present moment, the system is barely starting to work. I would say it exists largely on paper.

How has the mental health care system evolved over the last 25 years?

It is changing, but as any other system, it changes slowly. The change is slower with regard to service provision for children and teenagers. In the case of adults we have seen some progress. The system is still too focused on hospitals and on inpatient treatment, and is uninterested in the intermediate level, the community centers, or in empowering family physicians to do their part of the job; interaction between these levels of care is very weak. Most people go to their family physicians, who don't have screening instruments, can't write prescriptions and keep their patients on all sorts of vitamins and medication substitutes instead of treating them adequately. Thus, it's still an extremely inefficient system, but it's changing.

What is your opinion of the reforms addressing the Romanian mental health system?

The law on mental health that passed after the 1990s is good; unfortunately, implementation is unsatisfactory and budgeting for implementation is even more unsatisfactory.

What are the obstacles to fully implementing this reform or making further reforms?

One obstacle is inertia, and the reliance on old practices typical of the system. Psychiatrists tend to only work with inpatients. So even if they understand the changes on a conceptual level, it is hard for them to apply them all at once. Second, payment is very often dependent on the percentage

(*Continued*)

(Continued)
of occupied hospital beds, so psychiatrists have a tendency to admit people who shouldn't be otherwise admitted in order to meet a percentage of occupied hospital beds. Third, there is still some resistance to doing other types of therapy in clinics, especially in those where they treat more severe conditions. Forth is money—not enough funds are directed toward implementing the reforms. And fifth would be the lack of will to apply what is already written down. I'm referring to managerial will starting from the government level (i.e. political will), all the way down to managerial will at the level of hospital managers and of county public health agency managers, who should implement the law.

What is the influence of politics on the mental health care system and reforms in Romania?
Unlike how things were back in the '90s, politics no longer interferes with psychiatric practice. In the past, people were admitted to the psychiatric clinics because of their problematic political profile, and psychiatrists were sometimes used (not all of them, of course) to protect the system and its ideology from those who were ideologically deviant. This is no longer the case—the system is independent. It was the political system that adopted the mental health reform at the European Union's recommendations, but the political system is not efficient in implementing and financing it—the main drawback of the political system.

So reforms aren't necessarily sustainable?
They don't have sufficient backup from the political system. The mental health reform was initiated because of the insistence of the European Union, it wasn't a process where people would say "look, this is the reform, this is how we want to do it."

integrated management of autism and associated mental health problems[33] as well as the initial development of a national strategy for the mental health of children and adolescents.[34]

---

[33] Law 151/2010 on integrative health, education, and social services for people with Autism and associated mental disorders, revised in 2013.

[34] A draft version was proposed to the Ministry of Health in order to be adopted.

In 2009, the National Mental Health Center (established in 2006) was transformed into an independent institution and changed its name to the National Mental Health and Antidrug Centre/Centrul National de Sanatate Mintala si Lupta Antidrog (CNSMLA) to reflect the additional focus on the treatment of substance use disorders.[35] Today, the CNSMLA coordinates the yearly National Mental Health Program (NMHP). In 2014, the NMPH identified 3 priorities and established policy objectives for the treatment of depression and suicide prevention, the promotion of mental health in the workplace, and improving access to specific mental health programs for children and adolescents.

In order to implement these objectives, CNSMLA was allocated 51,363 EUR in 2013 and 58,409 in 2014[36] and further increases in funding are expected in the near future (Figure 6.2). However, there is concern that these amounts of money are still not sufficient to meet the identified needs.

The national health strategy for the period 2014–2020[37] includes a separate sub-chapter for mental health. 3 main strategic priorities are:

- Increasing the level of evidence informed decision-making for a better selection of interventions for particular groups (children, elderly) and assessing their impact at population level;
- Increasing access to and quality of mental services designed for the prevention, detection, treatment, and follow-up of mental health problems;
- Further development and diversification of available mental health services.

---

[35] Hotararii de Guvern nr. 1424 din 18 noiembrie 2009.
[36] Official letter from 20 February 2015 issues in response to Active Watch inquiry 427/05.02.2015; retrieved from: http://www.decidpentrumine.ro/uploads/raspuns%20adresa%20ACTIVE%20WATCH.pdf.
[37] Ministerul Sanatatii (2014). Strategia Națională de Sănătate 2014–2020. Retrieved from www.ms.ro.

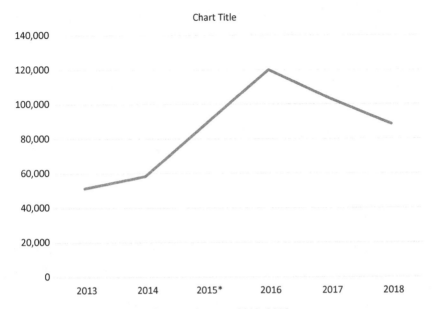

Figure 6.2: CNSMLA budget in Euros by year, 2013–2018.

Note: For year 2015 the budget represents an approximation as the real data was not available; for the rest of the year the data is extracted from the yearly reports of CNSMLA.

An action plan to support the implementation of the strategy has also been developed,[38] with 4 specific budget allocations for mental health care and a total estimated budget of 7,180,682 EUR.

It should also be noted that Romania has made real efforts to align its mental health policies and practice with relevant international agreements and standards initiated by the World Health Organization,[39] the European Union,[40] and the European Council.[41] Additionally, Romania is a collaborating partner in the Joint Action "Mental Health and Wellbeing,"

---

[38] Ministerul Sanatatii (2014). ANEXA 2 Plan de acțiuni pe perioada 2014–2020 pentru implementarea Strategiei naționale.

[39] The Mental Health Declaration and the Action Plan prepared within the European Conference for Mental Health in Helsinki in 2005.

[40] The European Pact for Mental Health and Well-being (2008).

[41] Recommendations on the human rights and the dignity of people with mental disorders, (2004 and 2009).

cofunded by the Health Program of the European Union and National Health Ministries from 28 EU Member States.[42]

6.4 Organizational Structure of the Mental Health System in Romania

The structure of the mental health system in Romania can be divided into 4 categories: primary care, outpatient care, inpatient care, and specialized services.

6.4.1 *Primary care*

In Romania, most general practitioners (GPs) work in small solo private practices. Their services are funded by the National Insurance House on a contractual basis (a capitation and fee for service mixed model is in place). GPs play a gatekeeping role for the health care system, both for physical and mental health problems. They often provide initial assessment and treatment for common health conditions and refer those needing more specialized care (i.e. secondary, tertiary services).

According to a recent study, GPs report being the first point of care for 66% of adults with anxiety problems and 84% of older patients with memory problems; they are also involved in the treatment and follow-up of depression in 74% of cases.[43] Currently, GPs have the right to initiate anti-depressant and anxiolytic treatment using a limited list of medications and can follow-up on all types of treatment for most psychiatric disorders if a psychiatrist develops a treatment plan for the GP to implement. Since 2009, a treatment guideline for depression in primary care has been available. More recently, mental health training sessions for GPs and nurses were conducted, and a pilot screening program for the diagnosis and treatment of depression in primary care was financed through the National Mental Health Program as well (2013–2015).

---

[42] http://www.mentalhealthandwellbeing.eu/.
[43] Butu, A. C., Tomoaia-Cotisel, A., & Olsavski, V. (2014). Are Romanian family doctors ready for Health 2020?. *Management in Health*, 18(2).

Access to secondary and tertiary care services requires a formal physician referral in order to be covered by insurance. However, no additional mechanisms to insure the continuity of care are in place. Collaboration with mental health professionals other than psychiatrists is also limited. GPs can employ additional staff, and roughly 75% engage a practice nurse.[44] However, these assistants rarely assume a significant role in patient management and are primarily responsible for administrative tasks (Chanturidze, 2012).

6.4.2 *Outpatient care*

Outpatient care is largely provided by psychiatrists in private practice and, for a small number, by multidisciplinary teams in community mental health centers—facilities that provide services to a designated catchment area (100,000–150,000 inhabitants for adults and 200,000–400,000 inhabitants for children). A third option, the so-called "integrated ambulatory" care, represents an outpatient service offered by an inpatient unit in order to increase the continuity of care. However, this option is rarely available in actual practice.

Outpatient psychiatrists are the main provider of aftercare services for all types of psychiatric patients. Currently, there are approximately 2,000 psychiatrists working in private offices across Romania. They are self-organized as Cabinete Medicale Individuale—CMI (individual medical offices), and are in direct contract with the National Health Insurance House. They are not unlike GP practices and, similarly, can employ additional staff (such as psychiatric nurses) or can buy additional services (psychological assessment or treatment). The possibility of forming group practices (by joining 2 or more CMI) is also an option. Nevertheless, due to bureaucratic requirements, psychiatrists rarely choose to subcontract in this way to expand psychiatric services.

MHCs aim to provide more intensive care for patients with more complex needs but these are still an underdeveloped segment of care in Romania. In 2012, there were only 52 centers available in all of Romania, with 16 designated for children. The staff working in MHCs are multidisciplinary (psychiatrists, nurses, psychologists, social workers), directly employed by the

---

[44]Groenewegen, P., Heinemann, S., Greß, S., & Schäfer, W. (2015). Primary care practice composition in 34 countries. *Health Policy*, 119(12), 1576-1583.

MHC and paid from tax revenues. MHCs provide a wide range of services, including home visits and interventions aimed at prevention. However, due to insufficient financing, their operations are typically constrained.

6.4.3 *Inpatient care*

Psychiatric departments in general hospitals are the primary source of inpatient psychiatric care in Romania, and free-standing psychiatric hospitals for chronic care and psychiatric departments in university hospitals are common. Some free-standing psychiatric hospitals for acute care can also be found. In general, the psychiatric departments of general hospitals and university hospitals typically see less severely ill patients; in free-standing psychiatric hospitals, there may be a broader range of patients receiving treatment.[45]

According to Eurostat,[46] in 2013 there were 16,540 psychiatric beds in Romania; this is almost 20% lower than in 1993 (20,418). Previously published data report similar declines in inpatient capacity; for the period 1989–2009, a 22% decrease was observed (Mundt *et al.*, 2012). However, while the overall number of beds has declined over the past 25 years, there has also been a decline in the total population (due to population ageing and migration). Accordingly, the number of beds per 100,000 inhabitants has actually increased over time (Figure 6.3). The majority of these beds are located in free-standing psychiatric hospitals rather than in psychiatric departments of general hospitals (12,027 beds as compared to 4,373 beds); the capacity of the 36 existing psychiatric hospitals ranges from 50 to 1,250 beds (Figure 6.4).

Approximately 50% of these beds are located in large institutions, while 35% are located in average-sized institutions. Only 15% of the beds are located in small psychiatric hospitals. By comparison, the size of the psychiatric departments of general hospitals is much smaller (ranging from a minimum of 21 to a maximum of 300). Around two-thirds of the

---

[45] Report on the result of the REFINEMENT project (see http://cordis.europa.eu/result/rcn/149791_en.html).

[46] *Source of data*: Eurostat; Last update: 30 July 2015; Date of extraction: 21 September 2015 13:44:02 CEST; Hyperlink to the graph: http://ec.europa.eu/eurostat/tgm/graph.do?pcode=tps00047&language=en.

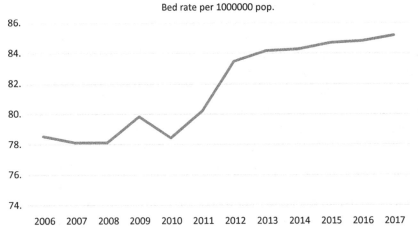

Figure 6.3: Psychiatric bed rates per 100,000 inhabitants, 2006–2017.

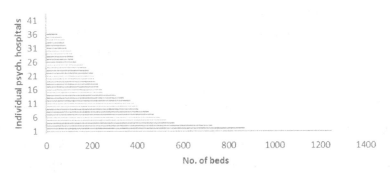

Figure 6.4: Number of beds in psychiatric hospitals.
Note: minimum = 50, maximum = 1,250.
Source: Authors' analysis of data from Eurostat.

beds located in psychiatric departments are acute and a third are reserved for providing long-term care.

In many of the psychiatric hospitals, housing conditions are relatively low, with little concern for the privacy and the environment of the patient (Junjan et al., 2009). The primary focus of inpatient care is psychopharmacotherapy, supplemented to varying degrees with individual and group counseling.

6.4.4 *Specialized services*

The availability of child and adolescent mental health care and treatment services is unevenly distributed in the country. With few exceptions, each of the 42 counties of Romania has an outpatient service located mostly in the district capital. In 16 counties, the outpatient services are located in Mental Health Centers. The others are found in pediatric hospitals or in general county hospitals. Some health care units offer a wide range of services for children and youth that include outpatient clinics, pharmacological treatment, inpatient beds on a children's psychiatric ward, and social services for children (e.g. child protection). At the same time, in some areas there are significant gaps in available services and there is a pressing need for expansion and improvement. There are 27 acute inpatient facilities for children throughout the country and 1 hospital for long-term children's inpatient treatment. In total, there are 464 beds for child and adolescent psychiatry in Romania. This translates into 8.4 beds per 100,000 for persons of 0–18 years of age.

Specialized services for the elderly are scarce in Romania (only 245 beds for the whole country) and are unequally distributed; most of the existing bed capacity is concentrated in Bucharest at the Ana Aslan Institute (Ames *et al.*, 2005). A few other psychiatric hospitals have small units of 5–10 beds dedicated to the care of the elderly. In Romania psycho-geriatrics is a shared competency,[47] and several geriatric units have specialized beds for the mental health problems of the elderly as well. In Bucharest, there is also a memory center for patients diagnosed with dementia.

There are 144 inpatients beds in all of Romania available for the inpatient treatment of alcohol and substance use disorders. These are distributed in small units of 5–10 beds located in the psychiatric departments of either general or specialized hospitals. Specialized state-funded outpatient services for substance use problems are almost non-existent. Currently, a

---

[47] Shared competnency i.e. both psychiatrists and MDs specialized in gerontology and geriatrics that can more specifically treat the mental health problems of the elderly. There are only 281 individuals specializing in pyschogeriatrics in Romania.

wider array of services (such as outpatient care, harm reduction programs, prevention, residential care, etc.) is provided by an NGO (ALIAT) and are funded by European Funds through competitive programs. However, these are available only in a few areas and have limited capacity.

6.5 Access to the Mental Health Care System in Romania

Despite universal coverage of services, many people still have difficulties gaining access to both general health care and mental health services. This is largely due to geographic and financial barriers, as well as issues of accessibility, service availability, and the acceptability of services. A recent report by The Economist Intelligence Unit[48] places Romania in the last place among 30 countries assessed in terms of access to mental health care on the basis of quantity of services; Romania scored 11 out of 100. This score was calculated on the basis of a set of 5 distinct indicators, including: (a) availability of assertive community outreach, (b) mental health workforce (rates of psychiatrists, psychologists, nurses, and social workers per 100,000), (c) public funding for patient advocacy schemes for mental health service users, (d) access to therapy and medication, and (e) support in prisons.

Geographical accessibility is particularly low in mountainous areas and territories surrounded by water (Danube Delta), a problem for both for primary (Chanturidze, 2012) and secondary care. Additionally, access to tertiary care is also difficult, as psychiatric hospitals are often located in remote rural areas (Predescu, 2008). This also creates transportation barriers for access to health care outside of the psychiatric hospital (Huber *et al.*, 2008). A report entitled "Quality in and Equality of Access to Healthcare Services" highlights difficulties patients with mental illness encounter when trying to access general health services, including delays in scheduling appointments, longer wait time to see a doctor, poor physical access to the doctor's office, and affordability.

---

[48] Romania Country Report Mired in an unhealthy past, The Economist Intelligence Unit 2014; Available at: http://mentalhealthintegration.com/#!/countryreport/RO.

Those with mental illness encounter difficulty in accessing counseling and routine check-ups, as well as specialized services including dental care, eye care, etc.

Cost sharing also impacts access to health care, be it formal copayments or informal "under the table" payments (Huber *et al.*, 2008). This is reflected in the amount of out-of-pocket (OOP) medical spending as a share of final household consumption.

Availability of day services and community mental health services, often needed for care of persons with severe and persistent mental illness, is limited or non-existent (WHO Regional Office Europe, 2008). This could potentially lead to higher readmission rates as well as individual suffering and family burden. Some special populations are more impacted by mental disorders than others. A recent study shows that Roma children, when compared to non-Roma children, are up to 6 times more likely to experience mental health problems. Stigma and discrimination, poor living conditions, and segregation seem to contribute to this situation and create additional barriers to access for this vulnerable group (Lee *et al.*, 2014).

6.6 Mental Health Workforce in Romania

Currently, the Romanian health workforce faces major challenges reflected in systemic staff shortages, widening availability gaps between urban and rural areas[49] and increased out-migration of physicians and nurses.[50] However, despite being a clearly identified need for many years (Mladovsky and Leone, 2010), a comprehensive human resources policy is still not in place. The need for urgent action is addressed in the National Health Strategy 2020 which calls for the implementation of a sustainable human resources policy in health care. There are 2 prongs to this priority area of policy and funding: (1) optimization of existing human resources

---

[49] In rural areas, the number of practicing physicians is 5 times lower than in the urban areas.

[50] Even if the data on medical doctor's migration are scarce, some estimations show that over 9,000 doctors (from a total of 48,000) have requested verification certificate since 2007.

by conducting human resources (HR) audits and developing specific HR strategies along with other interventions; and (2) insuring that adequate numbers of specialists are trained, especially in specialties where shortages have been identified.

Both adult and child psychiatry are included as priorities in the list of medical specialties with workforce shortages. Currently, there are 10.22 psychiatrists per 100,000 population working in Romania.[51] While this rate is slightly higher than the WHO average for 41 countries of 9 psychiatrists per 100,000 population,[52] the data in all likelihood does not adequately reflect the impact of emigration by physicians and does not take into account high regional disparities. For example, almost 25% of Romania's 2,157 psychiatrists are located in Bucharest. The rate of psychiatric trainees is also low, as per a study conducted in 35 European countries estimating a rate of 4.7 trainees per 100,000 inhabitants in Romania, compared to an average of 5.5 for the EU (Nawka et al., 2015). For psychiatrists and trainees, this difference can be explained in part by high emigration rates of the existing workforce, and partly by negative perceptions about psychiatry/psychiatrists, resulting in reduced numbers of psychiatric trainees.

Migration represents a system wide problem in Romania. A recent study shows that after family medicine and intensive care, psychiatry has the highest outflow migration rates among all medical specialties (Galan et al., 2011). Frequently mentioned determinants of the decision to emigrate are poor infrastructure—this includes working conditions, the availability or quality of facilities, and the lack of equipment in the medical system, low salaries and the under-financing of the health care sector in Romania (Boncea, 2014). On the other hand, the declining interest in psychiatry is not particularly unique to Romania. Several authors have identified factors that impact the recruitment and retention of psychiatrists. The factors such as poor working conditions, low recruitment of psychiatric trainees, insufficient training opportunities, and inadequate

---

[51] http://www.cmr.ro/registru/.
[52] http://www.euro.who.int/en/health-topics/noncommunicable-diseases/mental-health/data-and-statistics.

psychotherapy training are demotivating factors for psychiatric residents (Katschnig, 2010; Nawaka et al., 2010).

Psychiatric residency programs in Romania require 5 years of training (Rojnic et al., 2012). Topics include inpatient psychiatry (short, medium, and long stay), outpatient psychiatry (community psychiatry, day-hospital), liaison and consultation psychiatry, and emergency psychiatry in general adult psychiatry, old age psychiatry, psychiatric aspects of substance misuse, developmental psychiatry, and forensic psychiatry. The MoH has complete responsibility for organizing and granting certification of specialists, while the Ministry of Education has partial responsibility through the medical schools for the curricula and training. However, all too often, opportunities for career development are limited and the criteria for promotion are subjective and unclear (Mladovsky and Leone, 2010)—this also contributes to the problems of recruitment and retention. An official specialization program is not generally available for nurses working in mental health care; however, approximately 300 nurses have been trained in the last 20 years by a pilot psychiatric nursing school in Bucharest.

6.7 Financing the Mental Health Care System in Romania

All persons legally residing in Romania are covered by the national health insurance fund, as long as they have made the necessary contributions for at least 6 of the 12 previous calendar months. A package of basic medical services is covered by the health insurance, which is updated periodically by the MoH. Services not included in the package (e.g. dental and ophthalmological services) can be purchased individually.

The total public health expenditure in Romania accounted for 4.3% of GDP in 2014, and 4% for the year 2015. Approximately 80% of health care costs in Romania are paid for with public funds (mandatory health insurance contributions and transfers from the national budget) and only 20% of the total expenditure on health comes from other sources, such as copayments, informal patient payments, and payments from private insurance companies. The main financing source for health care in the public sector is the National Unique Social Health

Insurance Fund (Romanian FNUASS, often referred to simply as "the Fund"), which administers 85% of the total financing. Additionally, the MoH and local administrations contribute to the total Government spending.

The main sources of income for the FNUASS (as stated in its Budget Execution statements) are the contributions to the mandatory insurance fund (66.94% of the total FNUASS income), the claw-back tax (4.61%), non-tax revenues, EU funds, and public budget subsidies. Employees contribute 5.5% of their monthly wage to the mandatory social health insurance and employers add an extra 5.2% for each employee. Children under the age of 18, students, the unemployed, and low-income persons are exempted from health insurance contributions. Adults are considered uninsured if they do not contribute to the health care fund, meaning they can only benefit free of charge from a basic health package which covers emergency care, pregnancy care, communicable disease diagnosis, prevention, and treatment.

6.7.1 *Primary care*

As private for-profit providers, GPs are paid by the National Health Insurance House through a mixed risk adjusted capitation and fee-for-service payment mechanism. While the social insurance program largely covers the cost of services, small user charges are paid by patients when using primary care services.

6.7.2 *Psychiatric ambulatory care*

Solo self-employed psychiatrists are paid from the National Health Insurance House (CNAS) on a fee-for-service basis; this also applies to psychiatrists in group practices. However, Community Mental Health Centers, outpatient services of hospitals, and stand-alone outpatient services are publicly owned and receive a global budget for the salary of their staff from the MoH. In addition, patients are required to pay user charges.

6.7.3 *Inpatient care*

All subtypes of inpatient care are publicly owned and the payer is the Health Insurance House (CNAS). Stand-alone psychiatric hospitals for acute care are paid a flat rate for each hospital admission, regardless of the length of stay or specific services provided. This payment mechanism also applies to stand-alone psychiatric hospitals providing long-term care. Psychiatric departments in general hospitals and university hospitals are paid based on the diagnosis of the patient. Patients have to pay user charges for all subtypes.[53] The DRG hospital payment in Romania is a mixture of prospective and retrospective reimbursement systems. At the beginning of the year, hospitals contract with the Health Insurance House for an annual budget based on the previous year's activity and reflected in the number of cases and case mix index (CMI). Then, every month, hospitals receive sums from the Health Insurance House according to the number of actually discharged patients and the contracted (predicted) CMI. Every quarter, there is a reconciliation of the sums, based on the number of actually discharged patients and the CMI of these cases. However, given the budgetary constraints in the system, hospitals entitled to larger payments based on actual treatment rates will only receive that additional money if savings are made in other hospitals with fewer cases than predicted. If a hospital has fewer cases and is therefore entitled to less money than in its contracted budget, it will receive funding only for the discharged cases. The actual payments consist of a tariff per individual treated; the average weighted national tariff for 2012 was 1,444 RON.

6.8 Quality of Care, Outcomes, and Evaluation

Mental health care in Romania does not have quality indictors separate from those used in evaluating general health care services. For all types

---

[53] Report on the result of the REFINEMENT project. Available at: http://cordis.europa.eu/result/rcn/149791_en.html.

of inpatient care (including psychiatric), an accreditation program is in place which involves the expertise of independent external evaluators. The National Commission for Hospital Accreditation is charged with the operation of this program.[54] Accreditation standards are grouped into several categories, such as organizational strategic management, information management, human resources management, quality management, patient data management, risk prevention and management, transplant and transfusion safety, and nosocomial infection management. The Commission had planned for all public and private hospitals in Romania to have an accreditation survey completed by the end of 2014, but this was not accomplished. Moreover, no aggregated data is available to offer an overview of the status of accreditation up to the present.[55]

A paper evaluating the technical efficiency and performance of 20 health systems by using an output-oriented Data Envelopment Analysis (DEA) has found that Romania has a high level of technical efficiency but poor health outcomes.[56] These findings further support the evidence that the Romanian health care system is severely underresourced; even efficient utilization of existing resources falls short of achieving optimal health outcomes. That said, an ever-greater degree of efficiency is possible by improving the mix of health care resources (doctors, hospital beds, and pharmaceuticals) in order to offer greater access to medical services. More specifically, this would require management of the cost of drugs and a reduced reliance on hospital care while further developing the human resources, both numerically and qualitatively, to provide quality care.[57]

---

[54] http://anmcs.gov.ro/web/ro/.

[55] See National Commission for Hospital Accreditation website, www.conas.gov.ro.

[56] Anton, S. G. (2013). Financing health care in Romania and implications on the access to health services. *The USV Annals of Economics and Public Administration*, 12(1 (15)), 195–200.

[57] Antón, S. G., & Onofrei, M. (2012). Health care performance and health financing systems in countries from Central and Eastern Europe. *Transylvanian Review of Administrative Sciences*, 8(35), 22–32.

A Patient's Perspective

S.D., user of mental health services for 34 years and president of a mental health service organization

Could you describe a particular moment that illustrates your interaction with the medical personnel?
When I was subjected to electric shock treatment. I knew where they were taking me, I knew what they were going to do, I disagreed, yet they forced me on a bed, tied my hands. I only remember them putting a wooden tongue inside my mouth, so I wouldn't swallow my own tongue, and I only remember them turning on the electric shock. I felt my body shaking completely and remember nothing afterward.

And it was so significant because it had a physical effect or...?
Because I was completely ignored as an individual, from a human rights perspective, as a patient, you name it. Being ignored happens quite often.

Has there been improvements in psychiatry over time?
Yes, things have improved. Not radically, but there have been improvements. During my last 2 stays in the hospital, there were no beatings. In the 1990s, they were pretty common.

Could you describe the accommodation conditions in the psychiatry hospital?
In the 1990s, we were 3 people sleeping in the same bed. This even happened in the 2000s. Today, on average, there are 5–6 beds in 1 room. At the new clinic, there are 4–5 beds. Before, there was a big room with 15 to 18 or 20 beds. Usually, if you were admitted unwillingly, you would end up locked in one of the 15 beds rooms.

At "rehabilitation centers" subordinate to the Ministry of Work, I have seen conditions comparable to Auschwitz. The toilet was dirty, the isolation room was a dirty mattress thrown on the floor, everything smelled of urine, there was a door... there was no door, actually, there were some bars that could be locked and unlocked, and everyone was staring at the man behind them as if he was a lion or a monkey locked behind bars at the zoo.

(Continued)

> *(Continued)*
> **What's your experience with stigmatization?**
> The main stigma perpetuators are the media. Because of the media's focus on scandals, they cover stories like a schizophrenic person killing for some sweets and so on. On the contrary, most times, people suffering from mental health problems are the victims of violence, not perpetuators, meaning the media only publishes isolated cases, but this selective published leads leaders to wonder how come there are so many crazy people walking free.
>
> **Do you have any other observations or things you want to add?**
> I had an unofficial discussion with the state secretary and I asked how come it's so difficult to finance these services. And he told me frankly, "Have we ever had a psychiatrist as a minister? Until the health minister will be a psychiatrist, there will be no financing for you." So what if there will never be one?

Although these studies address the whole health care system, taking into account the commonality of challenges both the general health and the mental health system face, the above presented findings can be extrapolated to provide at least an approximate assessment of performance within the mental health care sector.

6.9 Advocacy, Stigma, and Self-Help

6.9.1 *Stigma of the general population*

In Romania, the negative image of mental illness is more frequently associated with schizophrenia, while depression and anxiety are tolerated by society and commonly ascribed to stress and daily worries. A nationally representative study (Stănculescu *et al.*, 2008) evaluated the public recognition of mental illnesses by using the vignette method. The results indicate that only 50% of participants identified major depression as mental illness and 75% did so for schizophrenia. The same paper reports that about 80% of participants identified stressful circumstances as the most likely cause of mental illnesses. A similarly low mental health literacy rate was documented by a study on stigma levels in an adolescent population

(Zlati *et al.*, 2011). This greater level of acceptance of mild and moderate mental health problems by the general population has the potential to reduce stigma and improve the self-image of persons with mental health problems; an international study comparing 6 European countries shows that Romanians suffer less from internalized stigma (Krajewski *et al.*, 2013).

On the other hand, there is a strongly perceived association between schizophrenia and mental illness that leads to higher social distance (Stănculescu *et al.*, 2008), as well as generalized stereotypes of dangerousness, need for exclusion, incurability, and the possibility of some kind of mysterious contagion (Beldie *et al.*, 2012). There is an urgent need for research and interventions to reduce the negative impact of stigma; fear of stigma and labeling has been identified as a significant factor that discourages people from seeing a mental health professional during a first episode of psychosis (Ienciu *et al.*, 2010).

To address these issues, several anti-stigma projects were developed with EU support after Romania joined the European Union. In addition, a few regional and temporary stigma reduction initiatives have been financed by the National Mental Health Program. Beldie *et al.* (2012) provide a detailed description of these efforts. There has also been the development of resources to support anti-stigma programs in schools[58] consistent with the EU-funded Twining program.[59] Nevertheless, civil society remains an essential catalyst for action in reducing stigma. ActiveWatch NGO,[60] which monitors portrayals of mental health problems in the media, is a good example of such efforts as is the National Committee Against Discrimination.[61] The increased awareness of the role that media plays in shaping public perceptions of mental illness has also encouraged young journalists to try and depict a more accurate reflection of mental health issues in Romania. There have been 3 Romanians who

---

[58] See http://cnsm.org.ro/documente/manual3.pdf.

[59] "Sprijin pentru dezvoltarea serviciilor comunitare de sănătate mintală şi de instituţionalizarea persoanelor cu tulburări mintale", RO2006/018-147.03.12-RO/06/IB/OT/02.

[60] See http://www.activewatch.ro/.

[61] See http://www.activewatch.ro/ro/antidiscriminare/reactie-rapida/sesizare-cncd-schizofrenicii-isi-macelaresc-familiile/.

have been awarded Rosalynn Carter Fellowships for mental health journalism and are a good example of this approach.[62] ActiveWatch, often in partnership with The Romanian Association of Community Psychiatry,[63] has also been involved in developing and implementing a large number of anti-stigma, anti-discrimination and advocacy projects. "I make my own decisions! Equal rights through self-representation for beneficiaries of mental health care services"[64] or "Trust their mind"[65] are both good examples of what is possible.

6.9.2 *Stigma of the health care providers*

Despite these recent initiatives, the stigma of health care providers in Romania is still high and the attitudes of non-psychiatric physicians are more negative than the attitudes of the general population (Huber *et al.*, 2008), with a significant proportion of non-psychiatry doctors feeling more uncomfortable with mentally ill patients than their counterparts in United States or Spain (Voinescu *et al.*, 2010). In the opinion of Romanian mental health professionals, this often leads to reduced access to both general and mental health care, especially in the case of patients with a history of psychiatric hospital admission (Stănculescu *et al.*, 2008).

6.9.3 *Initiatives by service users*

Currently, there are only 2 user-led NGOs in Romania: Aripi in Bucharest and Orizonturi[66] in Campulung Moldovenesc. These NGOs were the initiators of Local and National Policy Forums;[67] these events brought together (ex)users and other stakeholders, including local

---

[62] See http://www.cartercenter.org/health/mental_health/fellowships/index.html.
[63] See http://www.psihiatriecomunitara.ro/prctRO2.htm.
[64] See http://www.fondong.fdsc.ro/financed-project-107.
[65] See http://www.mintealor.ro/.
[66] See http://www.orizonturi.org/.
[67] See http://www.forumulsanatatiimintale.ro/.

government, as well as business and the media, to initiate changes in mental health policies at local and national levels. The aim is to develop campaigns to influence locally identified health issues, as well as develop literature and good practice guidelines that have the potential to influence the national policy debate through greater user involvement.[68] Other types of user involvement initiatives are rare or non-existent in Romania.

6.9.4 *Social inclusion*

Between 2007 and 2013, the European Social Fund[69] supported efforts to promote the development of social and economic resources to better support the integration of different vulnerable groups into the community—including initiatives for persons with mental health problems. Many NGOs working in the field of mental health have seized the opportunity and accessed these funds for service development. ESTUAR[70] and ALIAT[71] are 2 examples of NGOs that have been very successful in attracting EU funds for a diverse array of new mental health services that include: respite care, job-clubs, supported employment, vocational and occupational counseling. However, the sustainability of these programs and services is highly dependent on the availability of future funding.

6.10 Looking Forward: Challenges and Priorities in the Romanian Mental Health System

Mired in an unhealthy past (the Economist Intelligence Unit, 2014), many of the challenges the Romanian mental health care system faces are not much different from those in other countries. This includes, but is by no means limited to, a lack of data, low level of financing, and the continued emphasis on inpatient care as compared to adequate funding of

---

[68] See http://chafea-mental-health-event.eu/files/MHiAP_Background.pdf.
[69] See http://ec.europa.eu/regional_policy/en/funding/social-fund/.
[70] See http://www.estuar.org/servicii-oferite-de-catre-fundatia-estuar.
[71] See http://aliat-ong.ro/english-version/.

community level services (the Economist Intelligence Unit, 2014). However, it is the failure to reform the large psychiatric facilities that sets Romania apart from other countries and further widens the gap between population needs and the type and quality of services provided. This lack of adequate reform creates additional challenges in improving the capacity of the mental health workforce, more rational resource allocation and better access to care.

In conclusion, there are 3 priority policy issues that will need to be addressed moving forward:

- Many of the psychiatric hospitals are remotely located in old buildings; they are costly to maintain and even costlier to upgrade. These attributes alone make them unattractive for recruitment and retention of skilled staff and difficult to access by patients. This is a serious challenge for Romania's efforts to reform mental health services as these institutions represent 75% of the total number of psychiatric beds in the country. The development and implementation of concrete plans for disinvestment in this area and for the redistribution of existing financial resources to staff and treatment in more appropriate settings should be a major priority.
- While staff shortages in mental health care are seen in many other countries (Bruckner *et al.*, 2011), the massive outgoing migration of young psychiatrists and nurses (often in the early training years) in Romania has a double negative impact on the mental health workforce—it decreases the number of available providers and increases the average age of mental health professionals. Therefore, a second priority should be to initiate adequate policy measures and funding in order to actively and timely manage the workforce crisis.
- While state-funded mental health care has been very slow in adjusting to post-1989 realities, the not-for-profit sector has built expertise and resources that could be used to expand and strengthen community services. Creating better links to primary components of care should also constitute a priority (Junjan *et al.*, 2009).

With attention to these issues, there is great potential for improvement and growth in the mental health services system in Romania.

References

Ames, D., Burns, A. and O'Brien, J. (2005) *Dementia* 3rd Ed. (CRC Press).

Beldie, A., Boer, J., Brain, C., Constant, E., Figueira, M., Filipcic, I., Gillian, B., Jakovljevic, M., Jarema, M., Jelenova, D., Karamustafalioglu, O., Kores, P. B., Kovacsova, A., Latalova, K., Marksteiner, J., Palha, F., Pecenak, J., Prasko, J., Prelipceanu, D., Ringen, P. A., Sartorius, N., Seifritz, E., Svestka, J., Tyszkowska, M., Wancata, J. and Ringen, P. (2012) Fighting stigma of mental illness in midsize European countries. *Social Psychiatry and Psychiatric Epidemiology* **47**, 1–38. Available at: http://doi.org/10.1007/s00127-012-0491-z.

Boncea, I. (2014) Brain drain in Romania : Factors influencing physicians' emigration, *Journal of Community Positive Practices* **14** (1), 64–74.

Boyd, A., Van de Velde, S., Vilagut, G., de Graaf, R., O'Neill, S., Florescu, S., Alonso, J. and Kovess-Masfety, V. (2015) Gender differences in mental disorders and suicidality in Europe: Results from a large cross-sectional population-based study. *Journal of Affective Disorders* **173**, 245–254. Available at: http://doi.org/10.1016/j.jad.2014.11.002.

Bruckner, T. A., Scheffler, R. M., Shen, G., Yoon, J., Chisholm, D., Morris, J., Fulton, B. D., Dal Poz, M. R. and Saxena, S. (2011) The mental health workforce gap in low- and middle-income countries: A needs-based approach. *Bulletin of the World Health Organization* **89** (3), 184–194. Available at: http://doi.org/10.2471/BLT.10.082784.

Buda, O., Hostiuc, S., Drima, E. and Ghebaur, L. (2013) The institutionalization of asylum and forensic psychiatry in Bucharest, 19th Century. A historic outline. *Romanian Journal of Legal Medicine* **21** (1), 79–84. Available at: http://doi.org/10.4323/rjlm.2013.79.

Chanturidze, T. (2012) *Technical Assistance for Project Management Unit APL 2, within the Ministry of Health of Romania, in order to develop a Strategy for Primary Health Care in Underserved Areas and the Related Action Plan*. Final report No. http://www.opml.co.uk/sites/default/files/Technical%20Assistance%20for%20Project%20Management%20Unit%20APL%202%2C%20within%20the%20Ministry%20of%20Health%20of%20Romania%20-%20Final%20Report.pdf. Oxford Policy Management.

Florescu, S., Ciutan, M., Popovici, G., Gălăon, M., Ladea, M., Pethukova, M. and Hoffnagle, A. (2009) The Romanian mental health study. *Management in Health* **13** (3). Available at: http://doi.org/10.5233/mih.v13i3.30.

Galan, A., Olsavszky, V. and Vladescu, I. A. (2011) Emergent Challenge of Health Professional Emigration: Romania's Accession to the EU. In Wimsar, M.

(ed.) *Health Professional Mobility and Health Systems: Evidence from 17 European Countries* (World Health Organization).

Huber, M., Stanciole, A., Wahlbeck, K., Tamsma, N., Torres, Jelfs, E. and Bremner, J. (2008) *Quality in and equality of access to healthcare services* (p. 160). Retrieved from http://www.euro.centre.org/data/1237457784_41597.pdf.

Ienciu, M., Romosan, F., Bredicean, C. & Romosan, R. (2010) First episode psychosis and treatment delay–causes and consequences. *Psychiatr Danub*, 22:540–3.

Junjan, V., Miclutia, I., Popescu, C., Ciumageanu, M., Sfetcu, R. and Ghenea, D. (2009) The provision of psychiatric care in Romania—Need for change or change of needs? *Transylvanian Review of Administrative Sciences* (26E), 81–93.

Katschnig, H. (2010) Are psychiatrists an endangered species? Observations on internal and external challenges to the profession. *World Psychiatry* **9** (1), 21–28.

Krajewski, C., Burazeri, G. and Brand, H. (2013) Self-stigma, perceived discrimination and empowerment among people with mental illness in six countries: Pan European stigma study. *Psychiatry Research* 210:1136–1146.

Lee, E. J., Keyes, K., Bitfoi, A., Mihova, Z., Pez, O., Yoon, E. and Masfety, V. K. (2014) Mental health disparities between Roma and non-Roma children in Romania and Bulgaria. *BMC Psychiatry* **14** (1), 297. Available at: http://doi.org/10.1186/s12888-014-0297-5.

McGrath, J. J., Saha, S., Al-Hamzawi, A., Alonso, J., Bromet, E. J., Bruffaerts, R., Caldas-de-Almeida, J. M., Chiu, W. T., de Jonge, P., Fayyad, J., Florescu, S., Gureje, O., Haro, J. M., Hu, C., Kovess-Masfety, V., Lepine, J. P., Lim, C. C., Mora, M. E., Navarro-Mateu, F., Ochoa, S., Sampson, N., Scott, K. and Vian, K. R. (2015) Psychotic experiences in the general population: A cross-national analysis based on 31,261 respondents from 18 countries. *JAMA Psychiatry* **72** (7), 697–705. Available at: http://doi.org/10.1001/jamapsychiatry.2015.0575.

Mladovsky, P. and Leone, T. (2010). Specialist human resources in Europe. *Euro Observer* **12** (2), 1–12.

Mundt, A. P., Frančišković, T., Gurovich, I., Heinz, A., Ignatyev, Y., Ismayilov, F., Kalapos, M. P., Krasnov, V., Mihai, A., Mir, J., Padruchny, D., Potocan, M., Raboch, J., Taube, M., Welbel, M. and Priebe, S. (2012) Changes in the provision of institutionalized mental health care in post-communist countries. *PloS One* **7** (6), e38490. Available at: http://doi.org/10.1371/journal.pone.0038490.

Nawka, A., Kuzman, M. R., Giacco, D. and Malik, A. (2010) Mental health reforms in Europe: Challenges of postgraduate psychiatric training in Europe: A trainee perspective. *Psychiatric Services (Washington, D.C.)* **61** (9), 862–864. Available at: http://doi.org/10.1176/appi.ps.61.9.862.

Nawka, A., Kuzman, M. R., Giacco, D., Pantovic, M. and Volpe, U. (2015) Numbers of early career psychiatrists vary markedly among European countries. *Psychiatria Danubina* **27** (2), 185–189.

Predescu, M. (2008) *Quality in and Equality of Access to Healthcare Services— Country Report for Romania*. The Institute of Public Health, Bucharest, Romania.

Rojnic, K. M., Norstrom, K. B., Colin, S., Oakley, C., Stoklosa, J. and Kuzman, M. R. (2012) Training in Psychiatry Today: European and US Perspectives. In: Fiorillo, A., Calliess, I. and Sass, H. (eds.) *How to Succeed in Psychiatry: A Guide to Training and Practice* (John Wiley & Sons), pp. 1–17.

Stănculescu, M. S., Nițulescu, D., Preotesi, M., Ciumăgeanu, M. and Sfetcu, R. (2008) Persons with mental health problems in Romania: stereotypes, causes and perceived care, attitudes and social distance, (13), 284–316.

The Economist Intelligence Unit. (2014) Romania Country Report: Mired in an Unhealthy Past. Mental Health and Integration.

Voinescu, B. I., Szentagotai, A. and Coogan, A. (2010) Attitudes towards psychiatry: A survey of Romanian medical residents. *Academic Psychiatry: The Journal of the American Association of Directors of Psychiatric Residency Training and the Association for Academic Psychiatry* **34** (1), 75–78. Available at: http://doi.org/10.1176/appi.ap.34.1.75.

WHO Regional Office Europe (2008) *Policies and practices for mental health in Europe: Meeting the challenges*. WHO Regional Office Europe.

Zlati, A., Oh, J. and Baban, A. (2011) Mental illness stigma among Romanian adolescents. *Journal of Child and Adolescent Psychology* **3**, 67–76.

CHAPTER 7

An Overview of Mental Health in Serbia

Aleksandra Milićević Kalašić[*], Olga Kalašić Vidović[†],
and Ivana Anđelković[‡]

[*]Institute of Gerontology Belgrade, Serbia; Department of Social Work, Faculty of Media and Communications, Singidunum University, Serbia

[†]NIRAS International Consulting, Serbia

[‡]Group for Children and Youth "Indigo", Serbia

7.1 Mental Health Status of the Serbian Population

Mental health in Serbia has been a growing public health issue since the 1990s; while mental and behavioral disorders have been the second most common health problem (after the cardiovascular diseases) of the Serbian population for many years. In 2013, approximately 10% (or 540,000) of people examined in the primary health setting were diagnosed with some kind of mental or behavioral disorder (ICD-10, WHO; Institute of Public Health of Serbia "Dr. Milan Jovanovic Batut,"[1] 2014).[2]

---

[1] This is the same institution that was established in 1861 and changed several names throughout history.

[2] Since 1997, this Institute has published the Health Statistical Yearbook of the Republic of Serbia, which provides a picture of the mental health status of the Serbian population.

Key Country Statistics

Region: Southeast Europe
Government system: parliamentary republic
Area: around 77,474 square kilometers
Population: 7,143,921
Capital: Belgrade
Gender ratio: 0.95 (men to women)
Ethnic groups:
- 83.3% Serbs
- 3.5% Hungarians
- 2.1% Roma
- 2% Bosniaks
- 5.7% other
- 3.4% undeclared or unknown

Literacy rate: 98.1%
Population under the age 18: 19.7%
Proportion above the age 60: 24.5%

Average life expectancy: 72.6 for men and 78.5 years for women
Suicide rates: 12.6% for men and 4.1% for women per 100,000 population
Economy: emerging upper-middle income economy
GDP annual growth rate: 0.7%
GDP per capita: 13,700 USD (PPP)
Unemployment rate (15–64 years): 19.3%
Youth unemployment rate: 49.4%
Average net salary: around 370 EUR
Total health expenditure as percentage of GDP: 10.4%
Population below poverty line: 9.2%

Source: CIA World Factbook (2016).

The most commonly diagnosed mental disorders included stress-related, adjustment, and somatization disorders; mood (affective) disorders were the second most common (Table 7.1).

Table 7.2 provides a summary of hospital utilization for a 5-year period, from 2009 through 2013.

On average, 0.5% of the general population were treated in hospitals for mental and behavioral disorders. More men than women received inpatient care, with a male to female ratio of 1.25:1 (Table 7.2).

A recent survey, conducted by the Institute of Public Health of Serbia using the Patient Health Questionnaire (PHQ-8), revealed that, on average, 4.1% of the population reported at least some symptoms of depression. The study also showed that symptoms of depression were significantly more prevalent in women (5.3%) than in men (2.9%), and that depression is more common among the elderly and the poor (Table 7.3). Over half the survey respondents reported exposure to stress; this is significantly higher than what was found in 2006 (43%), with women, again, being more exposed to stress than men (Institute of Public Health of Serbia "Dr Milan Jovanovic Batut," 2014). It is perhaps noteworthy that from the mortality rates in 2013 alone, 1,219 or 1.22% of deaths were caused by mental and behavioral disorders, at a rate of 17 per 100,000 residents (Institute of Public Health of Serbia "Dr Milan Jovanovic Batut," 2014).

Table 7.1: Number of diagnosed mental and behavioral disorders (ICD-10; F00-F99).

ICD-10 classification	Total number	Rate per 1,000 population
Mental and behavioral disorders (F00-F99)	539,013	93.77
Dementia (F00-F03)	12,016	2.09
Mental and behavioral disorders due to use of alcohol (F10)	10,361	1.80
Mental and behavioral disorders due to psychoactive substance use (F11-F19)	8,016	1.39
Schizophrenia, schizotypal and delusional disorders (F20-F29)	42,235	7.35
Mood (affective) disorders (F30-F39)	149,885	26.07
Stress-related and somatoform disorders (F40-F48)	252,593	43.94
Mental retardation (F70-F79)	3,708	0.65
Other mental and behavioral disorders (F04-F09, F50-F69, F80-F99)	60,199	10.47

Source: Authors' analysis of data from Institute of Public Health of Serbia "Dr. Milan Jovanovic Batut" (2014).

Table 7.2: Patients treated in hospitals for mental and behavioral disorders by gender in the period 2009-2013.

	2009	2010	2011	2012	2013
Total	35,058	39,050	36,967	34,642	34,566
Male	19,850	22,006	20,364	18,834	19,560
Female	15,208	17,044	16,603	15,808	15,006

Source: Authors' analysis of data from Institute of Public Health of Serbia "Dr. Milan Jovanovic Batut" (2014).

Table 7.3: Population signs of depression (PHQ-8), Serbia 2013.

Category of depression	% of the population
Not suffering from depression (score 0-9)	95.9
Suffering from depression (score 10-24)	4.1
Moderate depression	2.4
Moderately severe depression	1.1
Severe depression	0.6

Source: Authors' analysis of data from Institute of Public Health of Serbia "Dr. Milan Jovanovic Batut" (2014).

Table 7.4: Suicide rate per 100,000 residents.

	1998	2000	2005	2007	2009	2012
Total	19.3	20.6	19.4	15.1	18.8	16.15
Men	27.5	29.3	27.9	23.4	18.1	15.66
Women	11.5	12.3	11.3	7.8	10.0	16.62

Sources: Institute of Public Health (2009); Penev and Stankovi (2007); WHO (2012).

Suicide is an increasing public health problem globally. According to data from the World Health Organization, Serbia is ranked 43rd internationally in the rate of suicides (WHO, 2012). The burden of suicide is higher in men. On average, suicide rates in Serbia were 3 times higher for men than women (Institute of Public Health of Serbia "Dr. Milan Jovanovic Batut," 2009). Suicide rates derived from various sources are summarized in Table 7.4.

7.2 History of Mental Health Care in Serbia

The public health system in Serbia was conceived with the foundation of the Serbian Medical Society in 1872. Following World War I, the School of Medicine was founded as part of the Belgrade University in 1920. The expansion of a network of health centers, clinics, and major medical centers followed later in the mid-20th century. A social protection system developed along with the public health system, and by the end of the 1960s, centers for social work had been established in almost all of Serbia's municipalities (SeConS Development Initiative Group, 2009). However, the last decade of the 20th century was marked by social and economic crisis, which resulted in neglect and deterioration of the health system, as well as a decline in the overall health of the population. Today, Serbia is undergoing a process of reform to create a more efficient and sustainable health system.

The first mental health care in Serbia was provided in the 12th century by religious organizations (Backović, 2010). In 1861, mental health extended beyond the church with the establishment of the Doctor's Tower in Belgrade. 20 years later, this became a hospital for the mentally disabled (Munjiza, 2011). Laza Lazarević, a 19th century physician, is recognized for his efforts to promote mental hygiene, and one of the largest psychiatric hospitals in Serbia is named after this pioneer. After World War I, a Neuropsychiatric clinic was established in Belgrade in 1923. This was followed by the opening of clinics in Popovača, Kovin, Gornja Toponica, and Vršac in 1934, 1924, 1927, and 1952, respectively. Eventually, these centers evolved into being psychiatric hospitals (Munjiza, 2011). At the time, there were virtually no outpatient psychiatric services, nor a sufficient number of qualified mental health professionals.

After World War II, mental health in Serbia substantially deteriorated and the overcrowded hospitals became asylums (Munjiza, 2011). However, in 1963, the Institute of Mental Health was established and became the country's first psychiatric institution to provide community-based psycho–social care, including the first day-hospital as well as mental health dispensaries. The institute also introduced new methods of treating patients and provided psychiatric education. Subsequently, mental health dispensaries in primary care settings, day-hospitals within psychiatric hospitals and psychiatric wards, and clinics in general hospitals were established (Bukelić, 2004). Thus, the period between 1960 and 1990 saw the rapid development of psychiatry in Serbia, as well as in other parts of Yugoslavia. There was an investment in infrastructure, as well as improvement in hospital conditions and gains in the quality of mental health care—it was a "golden era" of the so-called sectorial psychiatry. A fruitful connection with centers for social work, as well as with residential institutions for social protection of people with disabilities was established (Munjiza, 2011).

In the period spanning from 1990 to 2000, Serbia was significantly affected by a number of regional developments including the civil war in the region and the breakup of the Socialist Federal Republic of Yugoslavia, as well as the NATO bombardment in 1999. This decade was also marked by international and United Nations (UN) economic sanctions. The mental health care system in Serbia was particularly impacted by these events—the quality of the service was reduced, mainly as a result of inadequate funding, and the prevalence of mental health and behavioral disorders increased by 13.5% (Lečić et al., 2007).

Since the 2001 WHO report *Mental Health: New Understanding, New Hope*, Serbia has been actively engaged in reforming its mental health system. The National Strategy for Development of Mental Health Care was approved by the Government in January 2007, and this initiated a process of mental health reforms that focus on improved cooperation and collaboration between primary, secondary, and tertiary healthcare levels, definition of catchment areas and responsibilities, continuing education of general practitioners in mental health issues, as well as better cooperation between psychiatric and social welfare institutions (National Commission for Mental Health of Ministry of Health of Republic of Serbia, 2007). To date, there has been some progress in the implementation of the Strategy; the opening of the Mental Health Centre (MHC) in Nis, the third largest city in Serbia, is especially noteworthy. In addition, anti-stigma campaigns have been launched and in 2013, the Law on Protection of Persons with Mental Disabilities was adopted, while continuing education in mental health is being provided for general practitioners, and considerable funds have been invested in psychiatric hospitals. Projects for deinstitutionalization of residential institutions are also underway (Pejaković and Zajić, 2014).

While these improvements are significant, there is still room for improvement, as a number of goals defined in the National Strategy were not achieved in the planned time frame.

7.3 Mental Health Policies and Legislation in Serbia

It has been said that mental health policies and legislation are the foundation upon which action and services are built (WHO, 2008). Thus, the development and implementation of national mental health policies and the related legal framework is essential for improving mental health services in Serbia. Most of the European policies and strategies were based on documents; the Declaration and the Mental Health Action Plan for Europe from 2005 is but one example (WHO, 2008). In Serbia, essential mental health legislation is included in the *Law on Protection of Persons with Mental Disabilities*, and the *Strategy on Development of Mental Health*. Other laws, such as the *Law on Public Health*, the *Law on Health Care*, and the *Law on Social Welfare* also provide a framework for the mental health system.

The Law on Public Health was adopted in 2009, creating the conditions for the preservation and improvement of public health through a range of initiatives and activities. These efforts include a focus on maintaining the physical and mental health of the population, prevention and early intervention, improvements in the organization, and implementation of public health campaigns.[3] With regard to mental health, there are 2 especially important parts of the legislation:

- *Article 2 of the Law* establishes the definitions and scope of mental health and mental disorders, and emphasizes the importance of individuals' mental health;
- *Article 8 of the Law* establishes mental health as a fundamental part of public health, equivalent to physical and social health.

The Law on Health Care was first adopted in 2005 and has been amended several times since then, including recent changes made in October 2014. The broad scope of the law includes the regulation of the health care system along with organization of health services, social care for the health of the population, general interest in health care, rights and responsibilities of patients, as well as health protection.[4] In relation to mental health, this Law:

- Recognizes that health care at the primary level[5] is responsible for the protection of mental health (*Article 88 of the Law*);
- Obligates primary care providers to provide health services in the field of mental health, with these providers defined as a medical doctor or a specialist in general medicine, or specialist in occupational medicine; specialist in pediatrics; specialist in gynecology; and or dentist (*Article 99 of the Law*).

---

[3] Official Gazette of the Republic of Serbia No. 72/2009 (2009). Law on Public Health.
[4] Official Gazette of the Republic of Serbia No. 107/2005, 72/2009, 88/2010, 99/2010, 57/2011, 119/2012, 45/2013 and 93/2014 (2014). Law on Health Care.
[5] Primary level of health care in the Republic of Serbia is provided in 157 state-owned primary health centers, which cover the territory of 1 or more municipalities or towns, with a developed network of outpatient facilities and offices.

The Law on Social Welfare was adopted in 2011. This law regulates social protection, financing, and provision of services, along with quality improvement efforts.[6]

The Law on Protection of Persons with Mental Disabilities was passed in May 2013; it is the single piece of legislation dedicated solely to mental health in Serbia. This law closely regulates basic principles, organization and implementation of mental health care, organization and conditions of treatment methods and procedures for providing services, including instances when persons with mental disabilities are unable to provide consent.[7]

- The principles defined by this law include: protection of mental health, prohibition of discrimination, protection of dignity, and prohibition of abuse (*Articles 3, 4, 5, and 6*);
- The rights of persons with mental disabilities under this law include: the right to improvement of mental health, the right to equal treatment conditions, the right to privacy, and the right to the exercise civil and other rights (*Articles 7, 8, 9, and 10*).

However, *the Law on Protection of Persons with Mental Disabilities* also addresses the restriction of rights if and when the health and safety of a mentally disabled person are threatened. It provides guidance to mental health institutions regarding the voluntary and involuntary placement of individuals with mental disabilities and addresses the rights and obligations for these individuals in psychiatric institutions. In Serbia, involuntary admission can occur when a doctor or psychiatrist believes that, due to a mental disability, the person might endanger his own life and/or the safety and well-being of others.

Primary care has the responsibility of preventing mental disorders, as well as providing treatment and rehabilitation; psychiatric institutions provide specialty care when it is indicated.[8] The law also allows for special

---

[6] Official Gazette of the Republic of Serbia No. 24/2011 (2011). Law on Social Welfare.
[7] Official Gazette of the Republic of Serbia No. 45/2013 (2013). Law on Protection of Persons with Mental Disabilities.
[8] *Ibid.*

A Policymaker's Perspective

Interview with Dragana Dinić, PhD in sociology

In your opinion, is the mental health system influenced by the political system? In what way?

From a global point of view, we are just collateral damage of the political system, due to the disintegration of the political system, like many other Eastern European countries, including Czechoslovakia and the Balkan countries. I believe that there has not been much progress in the mental health system in any of these countries, and we are lagging 20 years behind the world as a result. Specifically, when it comes to the influence of the political system in Serbia, of course the mental health care system is influenced. Although each political party promises to not to have their interests interfere with professional interests before coming to power, ultimately, the party in power yields immense influence on the system. This influence is negative, because it leads to the demotion of experts in favor of the promotion of party people, who generally lack expertise in the field of mental and the relevant knowledge for the positions they are placed in.

Would you say things have changed in the mental health system in the past 25 years?

25 years ago, Serbia was part of SFR Yugoslavia, and we had a developed economy, an adequate budget, low unemployment rates, and taxes were paid based on real income. Thus, the budget was relatively satisfactory and as a result, we had a very high quality health care, and most importantly—it was free, for all segments of society. After 25 years, with the disintegration of Yugoslavia and the total collapse of the system, we have had to start all over again. The economy collapsed, the budget was emptied, and people worked in the shadow market, so taxes were not paid fully. With empty coffers, we cannot expect a good mental health system. We are far below the level of the mental health system that existed 25 years ago.

Are there any upcoming reforms in the mental health system, and what are the main setbacks in implementation of reforms?

Many reforms have been passed in recent years, ever since we decided to join the European Union. These reforms were made in order to meet

(Continued)

> (*Continued*)
> the requirements of the European Union and, in the formal sense, we have implemented them—but the fact that we cannot put them into practice is another story.
>
> **Is the current mental health care system financially sustainable? If not, what is the "way forward?"**
> It is not. And the "way forward?" Volunteer work cannot be an alternative for professional work, as much as we would like the work to be transferred to other organizations, such as the civil sector organizations, voluntary associations, etc., to close the gaps in the system. All this is terribly superficial, *ad hoc*, and short-term. We do not have a systemic solution and we have no alternative system. The eyes of experts and those who expect a change are pointed at that the European Union, counting on favorable loans. However, looking at the situation in Greece and some other countries, there is little chance that there will be any changes based on EU support. Thus, I'm quite pessimistic at this point.

treatments of persons with mental disabilities (i.e. electroconvulsive treatment, medical research); however, psychosurgery and sterilization of mentally disabled persons is strictly forbidden. Provisions for assuring the privacy and confidentiality of health care data of individuals with mental disabilities are also included.

The Strategy on Development of Mental Health (2007), referenced above, is the predecessor of the dedicated mental health law[9,10] and was accompanied by a 10-year *Action Plan*. The Strategy was based on relevant documents of the World Health Organization (WHO, 2001, 2003), as well as scientific studies and surveys regarding mental health in Serbia (Lečić and Draganić-Gajić, 2005; Milićević-Kalašić, 2003). The strategy recognizes that mental health must be promoted through

---

[9] One of the main goals of the strategy was the formulation of the Law on Protection of Persons with Mental Disabilities.

[10] Official Gazette of the Republic of Serbia No. 8/2007 (2007). Strategy on Development of Mental Health.

joint efforts of the whole community and all relevant stakeholders, including patients (users), their associations, and family groups. The 3 main goals of the strategy include: improvement of health, enhanced response to the demands of vulnerable persons, and provision of better financial support.

In addition to its domestic laws and policies, Serbia ratified the *Declaration and Action Plan on Mental Health* from the Convention on the Rights of Persons with Disabilities (CRPD) in 2009. This was a result of Serbia's participation in the WHO European Ministerial Conference on Mental Health held in Helsinki in 2005.

7.4 Organizational Structure of the Mental Health System in Serbia

Serbia, like other parts of the former Yugoslavia, inherited a health system which was designed to provide easy access to comprehensive health services for the entire population. However, the political problems that negatively impacted the country's economy during the 1990s resulted in a substantial reduction of health system resources. In response, Serbia was forced to initiate reforms to create a more efficient health system (Stošić and Karanović, 2014).

Health care in Serbia is provided through a wide network of public health care institutions operated by the Ministry of Health and owned by the state. The backbone of the Serbian health system is the Public Healthcare Provider Network. This network includes 355 health institutions and some 112,000 employees, and is principally financed by the National Health Insurance Fund (NHIF) (Institute of Public Health of Serbia "Dr Milan Jovanovic Batut," 2011). The private health care sector is still not included in the public funding scheme; however, there has been some consideration of including this as a supplementary component of the public system (Gajić-Stevanović, 2014). There is no data about mental health care in the private sector (Radivojević, 2011).

Health care for the population is directly provided through a network of health care institutions and depends on the level of organizational and operational development. In general, there are 3 levels of health care: primary, secondary, and tertiary.

Health care at the primary level is provided by state-owned primary health centers, which cover 1 or more municipalities or towns. If the primary health center is unable to provide adequate health care, the general practitioner will refer the patient to a specialist and the secondary level of health care (hospitals). Each patient can get treatment—either outpatient or inpatient—in one of Serbia's 77 general or specialty hospitals. The tertiary level of health care has the most specialized personnel and technological equipment, and provides quality diagnostic and treatment. Thus, this level cooperates closely with the secondary level by providing technical assistance and support, engaging in research and activities of medical education (such as the Clinic Research Institute, Clinical Hospital Center, and Clinical Center).

7.4.1 Primary health care

Primary health care in the Republic of Serbia is provided by 157 Primary Health Centers or Municipal Health Centers, called Dom Zdravlja (DZ) (Institute of Public Health of Serbia "Dr Milan Jovanovic Batut," 2011), with a developed network of outpatient facilities and offices throughout the country. In this way, primary health care for the population in Serbia is relatively decentralized. Primary health care in the centers is provided by a selected general practitioner or a specialist in general medicine, gynecologists, pediatricians, psychiatrists, and dentists, as well as specialists in occupational medicine.[11] There are 73 outpatient facilities staffed by a total of 170 psychiatrists/neuropsychiatrists.

7.4.2 Secondary and tertiary health care services

These services include general hospitals (GH), specialized hospitals (SH), including 5 psychiatric hospitals, clinics (CL), clinic–hospital centers (CLHC), and clinical centers (CLC), as well as institutes and academic hospitals. There are 46 psychiatric facilities in Serbia, which include specialized hospitals, psychiatric institutes, psychiatric clinics, clinics for

---

[11] Article 98, Official Gazette of the Republic of Serbia No. 107/2005, 72/2009, 88/2010, 99/2010, 57/2011, 119/2012, 45/2013 and 93/2014 (2014). Law on Health Care.

child and adolescent psychiatry, and psychiatric departments in GH (National Commission for Mental Health of Ministry of Health of Republic of Serbia, 2007).

7.4.3 Inpatient

In 2007, the entire mental health sector (MH) had a total of 6,247 beds at its disposal, 50% of which were in psychiatric hospitals (PH). By 2013, this had fallen to 5,237 beds, representing 13% of all hospital beds intended for mental health care (see Table 7.5) (Institute of Public Health of Serbia "Dr Milan Jovanovic Batut" (2014)). This reduction of inpatient psychiatric beds has not been accompanied by a steady and incremental development of community-based outpatient facilities.

7.4.4 Outpatient

Day hospitals are one of the most common types of outpatient facilities in the Serbian mental health system.

Some of the longstanding mental health community services, like the Mental Health Department in the Institute of Gerontology and Palliative care are not clearly identified in health system, nor in the NHIF (meaning they are not recognized by law and thus not paid), so they face insecurity and imparity instead of promoting the good example of almost 30 years of practice, regarded as reputable by many experts (Milićević-Kalašić, 1993, 2008). In current psychiatric institutions, diagnosis based on established diagnostic criteria (ICD-10), as well as DSM-5 for research purpose, using contemporary guidelines (Lečić et al., 2012b).

Table 7.5: Distribution of beds in mental health care.

Psychiatry departments in inpatient facilities	Number of beds
Psychiatry department in general hospitals	1,081
Psychiatric hospitals	3,435
Institutes	120
Clinics	45
Clinical-hospital centers	91
Clinical centers	465

Source: Institute of Public Health of Serbia "Dr. Milan Jovanovic Batut" (2014).

Pharmacotherapy is provided in accordance with professional guidelines and is subject to both internal (within the institution) and external (Ministry of Health) supervision and evaluation. All healthcare settings collect and maintain data on all patients, including: date of birth, place of residence, address, employment data, marital status, and parents' names. Information about each patient's health is also recorded in the following categories: subjective complaints/problems, objective findings, diagnoses, and therapy. Computerized information systems are used, but the data is also entered manually into paper records, which are kept in a special file registry. Integrated electronic health care records have been introduced, but are still in progress. Routine collection and analysis of clinical data, as well as service use data are performed by the Public Health Institute.

Primary prevention activities are in the domain of non-hospital psychiatric institutions comprising marital and pre-marital counseling and services for adolescent and juvenile population. At schools, these activities are carried out by full-time psychologists and pedagogues. There are also some NGOs working with addiction-related issues and promotion of healthy life styles.

There are often problems with secondary prevention activities, such as early diagnosis, and due to prevalent negative attitudes toward mental disorder. Because of family members' shame, inability to recognize mental disorders, and fear of stigmatization, persons with mental disorders usually come late to mental health care. Tertiary prevention, i.e. rehabilitation, takes place in hospitals and non-hospital institutions and comprises protected workshops, as well as numerous psycho–socio–rehabilitative activities. Work on tertiary prevention is fragmented and insufficiently organized which contributes to hospitalization and stigmatization.

Current mental health institutions do not have organized activities related to mental health promotion, i.e. these institutions are not subject to the clearly defined obligation in terms of mental health promotion.

Routine collection and analysis of service management data are performed by Health Insurance Fund Services. The existing information system does not provide easy access to data, especially data that is not collected by the Public Health Institute and Health Insurance Fund. The reason for this is insufficient integration of the informational system, i.e. lack of information exchange among medical institutions, even among those dealing with the same health problems and treating the same patients. There is a need for an integrated system of communication and information flow within the health care system, especially within the mental health system, to guide increases in service quality. This need was specified within the Mental Health Policy (WHO Europe—Mental Health Network, 2008).

7.4.5 Residential

In the 17 residential institutions for persons with mental disability, the mentally ill and people with physical disabilities, 5,574 beneficiaries were accommodated under coordination of the Ministry of Labor and Social Policy (Pejaković and Zajić, 2014).

7.4.6 Inter-sectorial linkage

At present, there is practically no formal institutional linkage between mental health services and related organizations in the community. Cooperation does occur between mental health services and other organizations in the community (social work centers, gerontology centers, orphanages, correctional institutions, schools, the Church, etc.), however, cooperation is occasional and is orientated toward particular cases.

For example, Figure 7.1 considers the case of a patient who develops a first episode of psychotic illness. The patient lives with parents and younger siblings and has been unemployed for the past 18 months. The patient's family is quite poor and have had no previous experience with the mental health service. If the patient is willing to accept medical assistance, a primary health care physician in the Health Center will refer him/her to a Mental Health Care Clinic psychiatrist. Depending on the seriousness of the clinical picture and cooperation on the part of the patient and family, the patient can receive outpatient treatment, treatment in the day hospital, or he or she could be sent to the Psychiatry Clinic for inpatient treatment. In all cases, both pharmacotherapeutic and psychosocial rehabilitation interventions could be delivered. However, if the patient refuses medical assistance, the only option is involuntary hospitalization

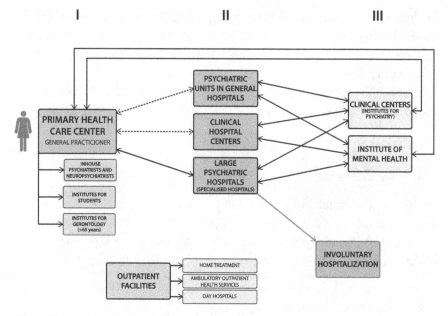

Figure 7.1: Pathway of the patient through the mental health system.
Source: Authors' interpretation of patient experiences.

according to the Mental Health Law.[12] After discharge from the hospital, if the patient still refuses to cooperate, possibilities for further assistance practically do not exist. Existing services are also incapable of addressing the problem of low income in the family or the patient's unemployment problem, which can affect therapy, rehabilitation, and the overall outcome.

7.5 Access to the Mental Health Care System in Serbia

The term "access to mental health and substance abuse (MH/SA) services" refers to the ability to obtain treatment with appropriate professionals for MH/SA disorders (Varmus, 1998). Accessibility includes 5 elements: affordability, availability, accessibility, acceptability, and equity of care

---

[12]Official Gazette of the Republic of Serbia No. 45/2013 (2013). Law on Protection of Persons with Mental Disabilities.

(WHO, 2006). However, it is difficult to find data about access to Mental Health services Serbia; accordingly, the analysis of accessibility below is based upon data from the health system as a whole.

Affordability of health care refers to the financial impact on individuals and families seeking and receiving treatment (Balkans Primary Health Care Policy Project, 2008). As noted above, 10% of Serbian people live in absolute poverty, while the percentage of the population at risk of poverty is 17.7% (Vidanović, 2012). According to official statistics, more than 95% of the population is covered by health insurance. Coverage differs by population subgroup as shown in Figure 7.2 (Republic Institute for Social protection, 2012).

The majority of mental health services are formally covered by health insurance, although only around 4.75% of the health budget is allocated for mental health services. A majority of those with health insurance are required to pay small "participation fee" for services. This participation fee is paid at every visit to health services; there is a price list determined by NHIF and users pay for services according to that list. About 5% of the population report that these fees are a barrier to accessing mental health services.

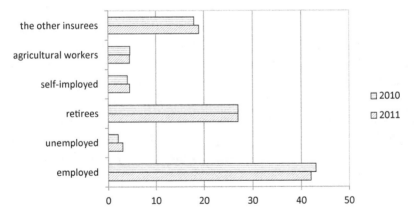

Figure 7.2: Profile of the insured population in Serbia.

Note: The "other insurees" group includes: children up to 18 years old; pregnant women and those who are on maternal leave; persons older than 65 years of age; persons with disabilities; persons who receive social security benefits; Roma people without a permanent residence; single parents with children up to 7 years old; other vulnerable groups defined in Article 22 of the Law on Health Care.
Source: Author's interpretation of data from Republic Institute for Social protection (2012).

7.5.1 Availability

The adequacy of resources (e.g. qualified staff, medications, technology, etc.) to actually provide care is referred to as availability (Balkans Primary Health Care Policy Project, 2008). The health system in Serbia faces serious shortages in terms of facilities, staffing, and the range of services available. Pharmacotherapy is the most commonly available service, however, there are frequently changing restrictions and gaps. For example, the so-called positive list of medicaments represents a list of medications whose costs are reimbursed fully or partially by the NHIF. However, the list is changed several times a year, and in the most recent alteration of the list, several frequently prescribed psychiatric medications were removed, meaning that users must now pay the full price. Psychotherapy is available in some institutions, but rarely implemented, due to the lack of resources (Danas, 2015).

7.5.2 Accessibility

Accessibility is defined as delivering health care that is timely, geographically reasonable, and provided in a setting where skills and resources are appropriate to medical needs (WHO, 2006). Data shows that every 7th household (13.7% of all households) is situated 4 kilometers or more from the nearest institution of primary health care and that 6% of households are located more than an hour away (Balkans Primary Health Care Policy Project, 2008). Around 41% of villages have an ambulance, while 41% of village populations state that health care they need is not available for them. Despite the Law on Health Protection, the majority of health institutions are not accessible for persons with physical disabilities and a majority of disabled persons report being dissatisfied with health care access (Tatić, 2007).

7.5.3 Acceptability

Acceptable health care is responsive to the preferences and priorities of individual service users and the cultures of their communities

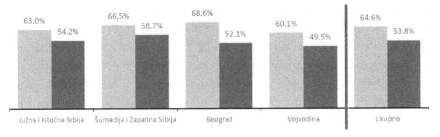

Figure 7.3: Satisfaction with state-owned and private health service according to the regions.

Note: The regions of Serbia are as follows: South and Eastern Serbia; Central and West Serbia; Belgrade and Vojvodina (Northern Serbia). The differences between private and public health services are statistically significant, as well as those among the regions. Satisfaction with public health services is the highest among those living in Central and Western Serbia and the lowest among those who live in Vojvodina (Northern Serbia).
Source: Ministry of Health of Republic of Serbia (2014).

(WHO, 2006). The European Health Consumer Index (EHCI Index)[13] is a measure of service user satisfaction; according to research from the EHCI Index of 2006, 78.6% of persons were satisfied with service in state-owned primary care settings (Balkans Primary Health Care Policy Project, 2008). There are also differences in satisfaction observed in comparing state-owned and private health services (see Figure 7.3). Estimates for users' satisfaction specifically with mental health services are not available.

7.5.4 *Equity of care*

This refers to assuring that the quality of care does not vary due to personal characteristics, such as gender, race, ethnicity, geographic location, or socioeconomic status (WHO, 2006). In Serbia, the most vulnerable

---

[13] It is comprised of 5 indicators: patients' rights and information, accessibility, outcomes, prevention, and pharmaceuticals.

population groups Roma people, homeless people, people in rural areas, and people below the poverty line. Homeless persons are faced with the harshest life conditions and numerous health problems. A recent study of the homeless in Belgrade revealed that 35.6% of those surveyed had a lifetime diagnosis of a psychiatric disorder; depression was the most common problem along with suicide attempts, affecting 27% of study participants (Sarajlija *et al.*, 2014).

7.6 Mental Health Workforce in Serbia

Human resources (HR) are the most valuable assets within the mental health services system. Developing a workforce specialized in mental health requires coordination across several professional and non-professional disciplines. Teamwork is a core competence required for all categories of mental health workers, encompassing psychiatrists/neuropsychiatrists, psychologists, social workers, nurses, and occupational therapists. Accurate data about the mental health workforce in Serbia is difficult to obtain, but Table 7.6 provides a summary of the workforce and shows a decline in availability across all disciplines. Table 7.7 includes data about the numbers of medical specialists in mental health.

Education of mental health professionals occurs in different settings. Some training in Psychiatry is provided to 6th year medical students and more extensive training in General Psychiatry, as well as Child and Adolescent Psychiatry, is available. There is concern that stigma plays a role in engaging doctors in psychiatric practice and thus, efforts at

Table 7.6: Human resources–health professionals working in the MHS in Serbia, rate per 100,000.

Type of MH professionals	2007	2011
Psychiatrist	12.6	9.61
Nurses	21.6	15.98
Psychologist	2.3	1.70
Social worker	1.6	1.17
Occupational therapist	n/a	n/a

Source: Author's analysis of data from Lečić and Draganić-Gajić (2005); WHO (2011).

Table 7.7: Medical doctors by specialization in MHS in Serbia and their gender distribution.

MDs by specialization in MHS	Total numbers	% of MDs	Male	Female
Neuropsychiatrist	359	1.70	129	230
Psychiatrist	434	2.06	119	315
Child psychiatrist	13	0.06	1	12
Specialist in MHS	806	3.82	249	557
MD in the public health care sector	21,098	100	7,459	13,639

Source: Author's analysis of data from Institute of Public Health of Serbia "Dr. Milan Jovanovic Batut" (2014).

destigmatization are underway (Lečić et al., 2012b). Continuing education is mandatory for all licensed medical doctors and nurses, and includes some mental health focus.

In 1928, the Psychology Group was established within the Faculty of Philosophy in Belgrade, while Departments of Psychology evolved later in Novi Sad and Nis. Today, graduate, master, and doctoral programs are offered and include specializations such as General and Experimental Sociology, Social Psychology, Clinical Psychology, Psychology of Development and Education, Psychology of Work, and Methodology in Psychology Research. In addition, education for social workers is provided at several universities, and undergraduate and masters level training is available.

Mental health reform in Serbia will inevitably require further workforce development and continuing education of professionals, especially of general practitioners. Packages for continuing education in mental health care for general practitioners have been developed. However, primary care physicians are overburdened with daily patient demands in general and are challenged in their ability to provide more specialized psychiatric care (Lečić et al., 2007). Moreover, chronic stress due to poor working conditions and low salaries is an ongoing problem for the Serbian health care workforce. As a consequence, many professionals have left Serbia to work in more economically developed countries, while others have established non-governmental organizations (NGOs) or opened private practices (Lečić et al., 2007).

> **A Provider's Perspective**
>
> *Interview with Dušica Marković Žigić, MD PhD, psychiatrist at CHC "Dragiša Mišović"*
>
> **What are, in your opinion, the particularities of the patients of the mental health care system?**
> We have quite an assortment in every aspect, from employed to unemployed, although, until a few years ago, there was a large percentage of patients who came motivated by external incentives such as compensation. In recent years, this is much less of the case. Many receive social assistance. In most cases our patients are compliant, although some have poor compliance. We do not pass on all patients who are poorly compliant to the closed-type institutions, because the reasons for their non-compliance are not always the result of their severe mental illness, but rather their character, misconceptions, family relationships, etc. When we notice this, we provide psychotherapeutic work to improve compliance.
>
> **Would you say that things have changed in the last 25 years? If yes, in what way?**
> Regarding the beliefs, they have changed for the better, at least a little. Prejudices have decreased and so has the stigma. There is higher influx of patients seeking help, who otherwise would not have come due to their prejudices and fear of stigmatization. As far as the system is concerned, I think that it has worsened, mostly for financial reasons. The political situations led to financial problems, which impacts staffing; there are not enough personnel, so the staff is far from being paid enough for the workload, and in the end, the patients are the ones that suffer.
>
> **Would you say that there is a need for any other type of services in the mental health system?**
> Yes. Social psychiatry (also referred to as psychiatry in the community) is extremely undeveloped. It has never been realized.

7.7 Financing the Mental Health Care System in Serbia

Financing is a critical factor in the realization of a viable mental health system. Without adequate financing, mental health policies and plans remain in the realm of rhetoric and good intentions (WHO, 2003).

However, accurate data on mental health care financing in Serbia remains scarce.

As noted above, the overall health care system in Serbia is based on universal health coverage from the NHIF. In 2014, almost 7 million Serbians had health insurance (Institute of Public Health of Serbia "Dr Milan Jovanovic Batut," 2014),[14] providing coverage to over 95% of the population.[15] According to the Law on Health Care, compulsory health insurance includes insurance covering diseases and injuries not related to work, and/or insurance covering work-related injuries or diseases.[16] However, the law also defines the services that are excluded from insurance (i.e. extended care in specialized hospitals), so there are additional costs for some types of health services. This can present a cost barrier for certain social categories of the population in Serbia.

The NHIF is funded through contributions from employees and employers and supplemented from various budgetary sources, such as the Pension Fund and Ministry of Finance Fund for the Unemployed.[17] Together, these funds are the basis for the National Health Account (NHA) of Serbia, the financial framework of the health system. Funding of staff salaries, medical supplies, and medicines is under the jurisdiction of the NHIF and/or the Ministry of Health (MoH), regional and local governments. A small portion of the funds for health care are provided by the Ministry of Defense, Military Health Insurance Fund, and the Ministry of Justice.[18] Figure 7.4 depicts the flow of the multiple funds that make up the overall health budget.

In contrast, private health insurance is still not fully developed in Serbia, so private funding is mostly based on "out-of-pocket" payments or provided by a small number of private companies. The military has a

---

[14] Institute of Public Health of Serbia 'Dr Milan Jovanovic Batut'. (2014). *Health Statistical Yearbook of Republic of Serbia 2013*. Belgrade: Institute of Public Health of Serbia 'Dr Milan Jovanovic Batut'.

[15] The NHIF collects revenues from obligatory insurance, which represent the largest source of its incomes (about 70%) and distributes them to health providers. However, additional funds are transfered from the general budget, and some services have to be paid by out-of-pocket money (for mental health these include services such as sobering, placement at geriatric psychiatric institutions longer than a week, etc.).

[16] Official Gazette of the Republic of Serbia No. 107/2005, 72/2009, 88/2010, 99/2010, 57/2011, 119/2012, 45/2013 and 93/2014 (2014). Law on Health Care.

[17] *Ibid.*

[18] *Ibid.*

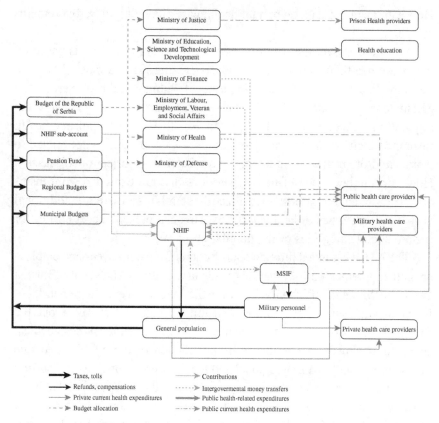

Figure 7.4: Flow of funds in the Serbian health system.
Source: Author's interpretation of data from Gajić-Stevanović *et al.* (2009).

separate health insurance fund, called the Military Social Insurance Fund (MSIF), which functions similar to the NHIF.

As of 2015, there is no published NHA accounting, so accurate, systematized, and internationally comparable data on health care financing in Serbia is not readily available. Serbia currently uses a line-item budgeting system; however, budget lines are synthesized in such a way that monitoring and analyzing of flows of resources and assessing the implementation of specific strategic objectives are not allowed. For instance, the Budget of the Republic of Serbia indicates that 5,692,373 EUR and 112,484,022 EUR[19]

---

[19] The total amount in RSD were 668,000,000 and 13,200,000,000, respectively. The average exchange rate in 2014 was 117.35.

were allocated to the NHIF and the Ministry of Health, respectively, in 2014, but there are no further explanations as to how the resources are assigned.

The total health expenditure (THE) of Serbia as percentage of its GDP was 10.59% in 2013; this number has not varied significantly over time.[20] The general government expenditure for health as a percentage of THE was 60.5% in 2013. This has decreased considerably since the year 2000, when it was 78.5%. Private sector expenditures on health (PvtHE) as a percentage of THE have increased from 20.9% in 2000 to 39.5% in 2013; out-of-pocket expenditures as a percentage of THE were 37.9% in 2013, a significant rise from 27.4% in 2000 (Institute of Public Health of Serbia "Dr Milan Jovanovic Batut," 2010). A recent study by the Institute of Public Health of Serbia, by Dr Milan Jovanović Batut (2012), on health care service expenditures according to the international disease classification provides more substantial data on health care and mental health care expenditures. Between 2003 and 2011, overall health expenditures have increased significantly (see Figure 7.5).

There has also been an upward trend in mental health expenditures during the same observed period, with an exception of the year 2008,

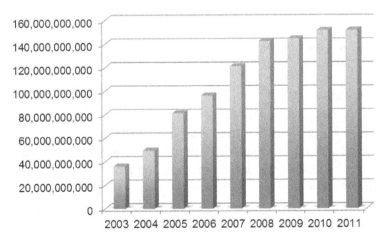

Figure 7.5: Total healthcare expenditures (in RSD) in the period 2003–2011.
Note: RSD is the local currency, the Serbian dinar.
Source: Author's analysis of data from Institute of Public Health of Serbia "Dr Milan Jovanovic Batut" (2012a).

---

[20] In 2000, the total health expenditure as percentage of GDP was 10.29%.

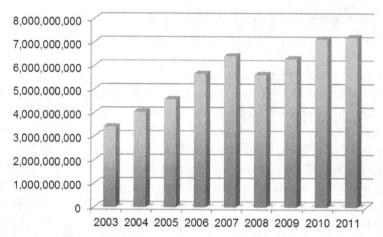

Figure 7.6: Healthcare expenditures (in RSD) for mental disabilities (F00-F99) in the period 2003–2011.

Source: Author's analysis of data from Institute of Public Health of Serbia "Dr Milan Jovanovic Batut" (2012a).

Table 7.8: Mental health care expenditures as percentage of total health care expenditures in the period 2003–2011.

2003	2004	2005	2006	2007	2008	2009	2010	2011
9.44	8.18	5.64	5.89	5.30	3.95	4.36	4.72	4.75

Source: Institute of Public Health of Serbia "Dr Milan Jovanovic Batut" (2012a).

when mental health expenditures slightly declined (see Figure 7.6). However, if mental health care expenditures are converted to a percentage of total health care expenditures, one can observe, in Table 7.8, that the expenditures for mental health have decreased throughout the years, with only 4.75% of total health expenditures allocated to mental health in 2013. The year 2008 was especially critical, as only 3.95% was distributed to mental health. This allocation is substantially less than that in other more developed countries.[21]

---

[21] For instance, Australia spends around 8% on mental disorders, which is almost double than that of Serbia.

Table 7.9: Breakdown of expenditures in mental health care as percentage of the overall mental health care expenditures in the period 2003–2011.

	Hospital healthcare services	Ambulatory healthcare services	Home healthcare services	Other healthcare services	Medications and other goods	Total (in RSD)
2003	82.86	0.84	0.01	16.29	n/a	3,412,266,460
2004	82.91	0.79	0.01	16.29	n/a	4,054,615,887
2005	84.23	0.82	0.01	14.94	n/a	4,671,131,238
2006	58.68	1.52	0.01	18.35	21.43	5,663,075,593
2007	49.34	1.38	0.01	19.43	29.84	6,409,806,945
2008	70.80	1.67	n/a	27.54	n/a	5,626,752,727
2009	57.95	1.56	n/a	40.49	n/a	6,296,441,774
2010	62.03	2.26	n/a	35.71	n/a	7,139,887,203
2011	62.07	2.55	n/a	35.39	n/a	7,204,353,642

Source: Institute of Public Health of Serbia "Dr Milan Jovanovic Batut" (2012a).

A breakdown of the expenditures in mental health care can provide a clearer picture of how the total budget is allocated (see Table 7.9).

7.8 Quality of Care, Outcomes, and Evaluation

The quality of mental health care can be measured on the basis of whether or not services increase the likelihood of desired mental health outcomes (in other words, do service recipients experience improvements in the quality of life, social inclusion, reduction of symptoms, etc.) (WHO, 2003). Outcomes can further be divided into administrative measures, clinical measures, and economic measures.

7.8.1 *Administrative measures*

Administrative measures are based on data gathered in health centers which record their everyday activities. They encompass 3 domains: the structure of mental health services, evaluation of system capacities, and the process of health care service delivery. Process measures frequently examine the interactions between consumers and structural elements of the health care system (for example, are consumers actually receiving

Table 7.10: Indicators of quality in specialist consultations services (Bjornberg, 2014).

Specialist service	Number of health institutions which sent data	Percentage of health institutions which do not schedule appointments	Average number of days spent waiting for the first visit for services	Percentage of scheduled visits compared to total number of visits	Percentage of patients who were seen by the doctor within 30 minutes of the scheduled time
Surgery	82	26.8	12.3	33.2	67
Internal medicine	97	19.6	13.3	47.8	77.2
Pediatrics	45	57.8	8.6	30.4	83.7
Gynecology and obstetrics	40	72.5	4.2	21.1	74.9
Psychiatry	46	50	6.2	43.2	80.7

Source: Official Gazette of Republic of Serbia No. 49/10 (2010) Rules on Health Care Quality Indicators.

high quality services in a way that conforms to the evidence base) (Kilbourne et al., 2010). In the Serbian health system, these measures are defined by the Rules on Health Care Quality Indicators.[22] Every health institution is required to collect and report data to the Institute of Public Health of Serbia, who publishes a comprehensive annual report.

Table 7.10 provides a summary of available indicators and comparisons between specialty services. The data shows that the majority of specialty services are consistent with Ministry of Health guidelines.[23] However, compared to other European countries, indicators related to waiting time for treatment have remained low (Bjornberg, 2014). A Serbian study conducted in 2013 showed that 16.6% of Serbians had not accessed health protection services due to prolonged waiting times (Ministry of Health of Republic of Serbia, 2014). However, this showed improvement during 2017, due to the implementation of electronic system for direct specialist booking (mojdoktor.gov.rs) which significantly shortened waiting times (Bjornberg, 2014).

As Figure 7.7 illustrates, the timely delivery of health services differs between regions in Serbia. The residents of Belgrade and Vojvodina face

---

[22] Official Gazette of Republic of Serbia No. 49/10 (2010) *Rules on Health Care Quality Indicators* retrieved on 27 January 2015, from: http://www.iohbb.edu.rs/files/dokumenti/Pravilnik%20o%20pokazateljima%20kvaliteta%20zdravstvene%20zastite.pdf.

[23] *Ibid.*

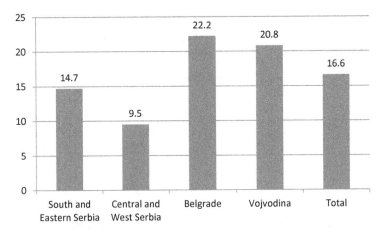

Figure 7.7: Percentage of population which didn't satisfy their health needs due to prolonged wait times for care (Bjornberg, 2014).
Source: http://www.zdravlje.gov.rs/downloads/2014/jul2014/Jul2014IzvestajPreliminarni.pdf.

great difficulty in satisfying their health needs due to prolonged waiting times, while the situation is different in other regions. This difference can be explained by the fact that Belgrade and Vojvodina have a higher population density, and thus higher number of health service users, leading to congested services.

7.8.2 *Clinical measures*

These are comprised of data collected from medical records to evaluate whether care is positively impacting individuals and society (Kilbourne et al., 2010). Indicators include:

- *Diagnosis*: Assessment of the physical, emotional, cognitive and behavioral signs, and symptoms related to a disorder;
- *Disabilities*: Functional ability to fulfill social roles, work, self-care, etc.;
- *Life satisfaction and fulfillment*: Quality of life and well-being assessed by the users themselves; Welfare and safety including suicide, substance abuse, homelessness, victimization, etc.;
- *Treatment effects*: *Changes that users of the system experience, e.g. quality of life, social inclusion, reduction of symptoms, etc.*

Clinical measures in mental health are difficult to assess as a substantial amount of mental health services are delivered outside the health care sector (e.g. criminal justice, education, social services, etc.). As a result, there is insufficient evidence for some mental health treatments (Kilbourne et al., 2010).

A part of clinical measures is the consideration of *quality of life*, which can be defined as patients' perception of how a disorder and its treatment may influence his/her physical and psychological well-being, work ability, social communication, and physical health (Schipper, 1990). Functional ability to fulfill social roles and to work plays a major role in determining the well-being of persons with mental health disorders, but it is very difficult to quantify that impact. Qualitative data gathered through interviews with psychiatric patients show that they faced stigma, rejection, and difficulty in finding work (BKV Fond, 2014). Individuals requiring guardianship or those who are institutionalized face additional challenges in their quality of life and sense of well-being, often related to their loss of basic human rights and ability to make decisions for themselves. When a person is placed under guardianship, as per Serbian family law, a guardian is appointed to take care of that person and to ensure that they are capable of living an independent life as much as possible. The role of the guardians is to represent the individual in legal matters, acquire funds for their living expenses, and manage their property. Guardians are usually the parents of the person put under guardianship, but they can be also other family members or even directors or employees of residential institutions (Mental Disability Rights Initiative, 2014). More than half of the persons placed in institutions are deprived of their ability to make legal decisions for themselves, such as decisions regarding marriage or representation in legal matters (Mental Disability Rights Initiative, 2014).

A review of studies in Serbia on the quality of life for psychiatric patients shows that in the period between 2000 and 2009 patients diagnosed with schizophrenia suffered more from bad moods, fear, and hallucinations, but were significantly happier with their living conditions and incomes in comparison to healthy subjects (Opalić and Nikolić, 2008). Another study involving patients with recurrent depression shows that in comparison to individuals diagnosed with somatic illnesses and healthy controls, patients with depression report a lower quality of life than individuals from both other groups (Stanković, 2006). Another procedure for assessing impact of illness on quality of life is by the calculation of DALYs (Disability Adjusted Life Years) to quantify the burden of disease and to compare disease burden across a range of diseases, injuries, and risk factors. Research conducted in Serbia in 2000 showed that depression is the leading cause of non-fatal disease burden in Serbia and the fourth leading cause of years lived with disability (Janković *et al.*, 2006).

7.8.3 *Economic measures*

Economic measures of quality in health care delivery systems are usually concerned with issues of efficiency and effectiveness based on some form of economic analysis, such as cost-benefit, cost-effectiveness or cost-utility. Unfortunately, health economics, health management, and measurements of sector efficiency are almost non-existent at the micro and macro levels of health care organization in Serbia; accordingly, only some partial estimates can be made.

Actual total revenue of National Health Fund in 2012 amounted to 1.9 billion EUR, which is 261 EUR per capita for the Republic of Serbia. Efficiency of the system would be higher if all potential revenues were actually collected. For example, if all of the contributions of health insurance payers and budget transfers were collected, Serbian health insurance revenues per capita would have amounted to 363 EUR, almost 40% higher than actual collections (National Health Insurance Fund Republic of Serbia, 2013). The most common reason for failure in collection of revenues is that some employers do not or did not pay health insurance taxes (for example, former state-owned companies that went bankrupt). The amount of money per capita for mental health services is unknown; however, the median value for upper-middle countries, where Serbia belongs, is approximately 3.8 USD per year (WHO, 2011). To resolve these discrepancies, the Serbian Health Insurance Development Strategy proposes a whole new system of health service financing that will contribute to a more efficient health system by 2020 (National Health Insurance Fund Republic of Serbia, 2013).

7.9 Advocacy, Stigma, and Self-Help

Stigma associated with people diagnosed with mental illnesses can be defined as social labeling and discrimination, along with being viewed as socially undesirable, harmful, and dangerous (Thornicroft et al., 2008). The process of stigmatization can be observed from 2 perspectives: (1) the personal feeling of being stigmatized (i.e. self-stigma and feelings of anger, depression, fear, anxiety, guilt, and embarrassment), and (2) labeling another person (i.e. "public stigma" including stereotypes, prejudices, and discrimination) (Totić et al., 2011).

According to the research conducted in 2012 on a representative sample of Serbian citizens, persons with mental disabilities are perceived as the most stigmatized group in the population (CeSid, 2012). An overview of earlier studies shows that social distance toward this group has always been high and dependent on age, education, and socio-economic status; those with higher levels of education and better socio-economic status show less prejudice. Conversely, older individuals in Serbia tend to discriminate more (Svilanović, 2013). This data is consistent with research findings from other countries which demonstrate that mentally disabled people still encounter a great deal of public rejection and stigma to this day.

Since stigma and discrimination have negative effects on the users of mental health services, participation of family members and mental health professionals in public anti-stigma activities are critical components of change. In Serbia, the majority of these activities are state-sponsored or conducted by NGOs in cooperation with state institutions. These campaigns consist of public lectures, forums, roundtables, TV advertisements, and various actions in public places. This has included celebrations of the Day of Mental Health and organizing "living libraries," events where visitors can approach people from different backgrounds and "borrow" them for one-on-one conversation during which they can challenge their preconceptions and learn about the experiences of others; a very useful tool in fighting prejudice and stigma. All actions are aimed at promoting positive attitudes and eradicating prejudices toward mentally ill individuals.

The efforts of NGOs dedicated to protecting human rights of mentally disabled persons are also important in bringing about changes in attitudes

A Patient's Perspective

What is the first thing that comes to your mind when we mention "mental illness?"
Torment. During the bouts of illness, the person is tormented and living in hell, torturing himself, while people are avoiding him and he's avoiding them, thus further alienating himself. What hurts is that even his family becomes tired of all that. Mental illness is like living in hell without a hell, where psychiatric hospitals serve as the entrance. Some people from the association ("Duša," the association of psychiatric users) who had that experience said that the hospitals are even worse than prison.

What did the whole experience of being a patient in a psychiatric facility mean to you?
Collapsing of my life and of my advancement in life, constant slowdowns, going backwards. Nothing positive. When I think about times I stayed in the ward, I see it as a catastrophe and I wish I had never been there.

Do you think that psychiatry is effective in dealing with mental illness?
I don't know what to think. From my own experience I can say that I was in very upset state, with frayed nerves, when I was in the psychiatric ward and they helped me become functional again. So, psychiatry was useful to me. But on the other hand, I am bothered that they don't offer more psychotherapy instead of just medicines. And the checkup lasts only 5 to 10 minutes—what can you say in that time?

Could you briefly describe one significant medical examination that you were subjected to?
The first time I was hospitalized the nurse gave me medicines after briefly talking to me, and I saw the doctor for the first time only after couple of days. I didn't have any important medical examinations. The psychiatrist barely talks to you, he just gives you medicines. I could not open myself and talk honestly about my problems, because if I did, he would only give me higher dosage of medicines. Significant examination to me would be conversation with empathy, care, and consolation. But I didn't have that.

(Continued)

> *(Continued)*
>
> **Did you experience any discrimination due to your condition?**
> I felt discrimination, first and foremost in the hospital. Every psychiatric patient is discriminated against there, because we have no rights. There was also a period when I was taking medicines and it was obvious, my appearance gave it away (I was sleepy, with slow movements and unfocused, wandering look). I heard unpleasant comments in the street. But, generally, I think I was discriminated against less than some other users, people have far worse stories. I am sure, for example, had I been looking for a job, I would also be discredited and rejected.
>
> **Would you like to make any additional comments?**
> I hope I will live to see the shutting down of large psychiatric hospitals and opening of mental health centers. I wish the whole system was humanized in a way that if someone has mental problems, it doesn't mean that he should spend his whole life in psychiatric hospital. We are capable to work, maybe not full-time, but part-time for sure, and working brings us back to the community. We are part of the society and we should be included in it, as much as is possible, instead of being locked away.

and behavior. Two of the most active organizations in Serbia include Caritas Republic of Serbia and the International Aid Network (IAN). Caritas Republic of Serbia is a member of a wider organization, Caritas Internationalist, which serves as a charity organization of the Catholic Church. Their work is aimed at helping those who live at the margins of society, especially those who are poor and oppressed. In addition to organizing 2 anti-stigma campaigns in 2014, Caritas Serbia initiated a project called Pro.Me.Ne (Promotion of Mental Health Network). This effort focused on promoting democratic dialogue between Serbian institutions and organizations representing users of mental health services, with a goal of empowering service users and developing mutually supported mental health policies (Caritas Republic of Serbia, 2015). The International Aid Network (IAN) is a local NGO whose mission is to support survivors of human rights violations, along with other marginalized and vulnerable groups, in order to help these individuals better achieve peace and satisfaction in their lives (IAN, 2015). IAN has convened a Mental Health Group, which includes psychiatrists, psychologists, and lawyers working to develop programs for protection and rehabilitation of individuals with mental disorders (IAN, 2015). The most important activities of this group include: (1) the organization of psychosocial rehabilitation services for various vulnerable groups (e.g. torture survivors, refugees, Roma, mentally ill), (2) implementation of projects connected to mental health system reform in Serbia, (3) monitoring the state of mental health institutions, and (4) empowering organizations of users of mental health services (IAN, 2015).

Associations of users of mental health services also represent an important contribution to mental health advocacy and the fight for human rights. Currently in Serbia, there are 9 associations of mental health services users, the majority of which are located in Belgrade. The most active groups include: "Duša" ("Soul")—The Association of Psychiatry Consumers, "Herc"—The Association for People with Neurosis, "ULOP"—The Association for Persons with Psychosis, and "Zvono" ("Bell")—The Association of Citizens, Friends and Family Members of Persons with Psychosis. Some of these organizations restrict membership to persons with experience in psychiatric treatment, while others allow family members and friends to take part in activities (Dimitrijević and Božović, 2011). Associations are primarily funded through national or international grants, along with membership fees. A majority of these associations convene in weekly meetings for members, while some like "Duša" and "ULOP" provide daily activities. These meetings and activities include self-help groups, educational programs, informal conversations, psychological, literature, and art workshops, picnics and walks, visits to the theatre or cinema, etc. (Dimitrijević and Božović, 2011). The objectives of these associations are 2-fold: first, to promote recovery and self-empowerment of mental health consumers through peer support, thus addressing self-stigma; and second, to promote advocacy, education on mental health topics, and destigmatization, thus addressing public stigma.

Overall, both NGOs and users' associations are making efforts to influence mental health policies and reform the system in Serbia.

A Patient's Perspective

What is the first thing that comes to your mind when we mention "mental illness?"
Stigma. If you say you have a mental illness, you are automatically labeled and stigmatized as someone who is not normal. Everybody looks differently at you. Everything changes. That's why nobody knows about my mental illness, except for my doctor, my mother, my girlfriend, and people in the association ("Duša"—The Association of Users of Psychiatric Services).

Do you think that psychiatry is effective in treating mental illness?
Psychiatry is becoming more flexible. When I first became ill, it wasn't like that. Now psychiatrists are listening to you and even accept your suggestions; they don't use insulting words. People are feeling better because the doctors have become more accessible. When we organized a "Hearing Voices" conference, doctors came and were listening to our experiences, they were very open and eager to find out what we, as psychiatric users, have to say. So yes, I would say that psychiatry is more effective now because it finally acknowledges our attitudes and opinions.

Did your own knowledge and understanding about psychiatry change over time?
Yes, it did. I have learned many things. As a member of "Duša," I took part in seminars about mental health where I listened to psychiatrists, but I also had a chance to share my thoughts on the topic. In the beginning of my treatment I had very negative attitudes, I believed that psychiatry has no value and that doctors only stuff you with medicines, but with time I changed my opinion. Now, I can see that the medicines have positive effects. Psychiatry has also changed, as I mentioned; now the doctors acknowledge me as a human being, not only as a patient. Nowadays, when I go to my doctor, we don't only discuss my illness, she is also interested in finding out about "Duša's" activities, too. Fourteen years ago, she didn't even discuss with me the therapy that she was prescribing me; for example, she didn't notify me when she changed the medications.

Do you experience any discrimination due to your illness?
Mostly no, because only a select group knows about it. However, ever since I became active in "Duša," I am much more visible in public, because I take

(Continued)

(Continued)
part in public events, I give interviews for the radio, TV, newspapers, and I even acted in a theater performance. In the beginning, I felt constrained and timid, but gradually I have become more relaxed when I talk about my illness. Still, I wouldn't admit my illness to my own cousins.

Could you describe the accommodation at the psychiatric hospital?
"Dragiša Mišović" is a hotel. Patients stay in double bed rooms, where everything is perfectly organized and clean, without bars on the windows or locked doors. It is possible to walk freely. In Palmotićeva, I was in the closed ward and there they have bars on the windows, which I didn't like because they created prison-like atmosphere.

Was group therapy available and did you participate in any sessions during your last episode of care?
In "Mišović," group therapy is available every day from 9 to 10 AM. Besides the psychiatrist, both the psychologist and the social worker are present. Usually, there is a topic which is discussed, mostly connected to the problems of the users or the doctor explains something regarding the mental health. I took part and really enjoyed those sessions. In contrast to that during my stay in Palmotićeva there were no such activities organized, people were playing chess or just sitting and talking.

However, neither NGOs nor users' associations have representatives in the government committees and groups responsible for organizing and providing mental health services, and therefore, no voice in the decision-making process (WHO, 2008). Despite this lack of representation, non-governmental groups dealing with mental health issues and associations of mental health consumers are very active in addressing these topics. When the Law on Protection of Persons with Mental Disabilities was passed in May 2013, Caritas and IAN issued comments regarding their concerns and identified the law's shortcomings. The NGOs' concerns centered around what they perceived as the law's failure to promote deinstitutionalization and closure of the major psychiatric hospitals, as well as the limited role of NGOs and associations of mental health users in tertiary health care services (Pro.Me.Ne, 2014). One outcome of these efforts included the establishment of a national platform to connect all mental health users' associations in October 2013, in order to support the ongoing advocacy for Serbian mental health system reform.

7.10 Looking Forward: Challenges and Priorities in the Serbian Mental Health Care System

There are many challenges and opportunities that face the mental health services delivery system in the Republic of Serbia. The vision, values, principles, and goals of mental health in Serbia are expressed in the strategy, as well as the strategic challenges and priority areas of work. The 3 main goals of the strategy include:

- Improvement of health;
- Enhanced response to the demands of vulnerable persons;
- Provision of better financial support for services.

However, insufficient cooperation between sectors and mental health associations, insufficient financial support, inadequate work conditions, and the need for more professional staff development remain some of the greatest challenges in reform efforts.

The values and principles from the strategy are somewhat embedded in the aforementioned Law on Mental Health and they include:

- Protection of mental health;
- Prevention of mental and behavioral disorders and promotion of mental health;
- Quality of service;
- Availability and equality;
- Protection of human rights;
- Health care in the community;
- Care for vulnerable groups;
- Community participation;

- Integration of physical and mental health;
- Inclusion of relevant institutions and resources;
- Destigmatization.

Establishing these values and principles in mental health legislation and protection of human rights represents significant progress toward reform. The next step is to transfer this vision into everyday practice—legislation and policy should not become mere documents of reference; rather, they need to become roadmaps for change.

To this end, there is a need for the reorganization of mental health services to be in better alignment with the needs of the population, as well as with international standards. Inevitably, this will require more resources allocated to mental health, as well as a new and different manner of distribution. For example, the process of deinstitutionalization should be a joint effort of the health and social sectors with a coordinated allocation of funds. By supporting deinstitutionalization and improving accessibility of mainstream services, more people will have the chance to be included in society and contribute to its social and economic growth. This will require thoughtful reallocation of existing resources with a balance between greater efficiency and the preservation of key services.

Development of programs aimed at prevention of mental disorders and promotion of mental health have been identified as another priority area, especially for the vulnerable groups, such as children, the elderly, substance abusers, members of minority groups, refugees, and displaced persons. Moreover, development of human resources, education, and research was highlighted as a need in order to meet the increased demand for mental health services. These developments should include consideration of the undue burdens placed on service providers and the potential toll on their well-being due to working in chronically under-resourced systems.

Finally, an overall improvement of quality will require access to improved information and communications technology, better inter-sectorial cooperation, as well as enhanced public representation and advocacy. Technology should be harnessed to help—rather than constrain—health professionals. The implementation of the strategy is a long-term process, which involves the whole community, relevant ministries, local self-governments, professional associations, NGOs, and the media; this is where the development and improvement of inter-sectorial linkages and communication becomes essential. In conclusion, an improved mental health care system for Serbia will require the alignment of all stakeholders to shared goals and a genuine commitment to change for all involved.

References

Backović, D. (2010) Mental health and mental hygiene between two milleniums. *Medicinski pregled*, **63** (11–12), 833–838.
Balkans Primary Health Care Policy Project. (2008) *Accessibility of primary health coverage in Serbia*. Presented at Second round of dialogues for health policy.
Bjornberg, A. (2014) *Euro health consumer index 2012 report*. Health Consumer Powerhouse.
BKV Fond. (2014) *Human rights and democracy alert*, BKV Fond, Belgrade.
Bukelić J. (2004) Social psychiatry. Zavod za udžbenike, Belgrade.
Caritas Republic of Serbia. (2015) *On Caritas*. Retrieved on 20 January 2015, from http://caritas.rs/caritas/?page_id=7.
Central Intelligence Agency. (2014) *The World Factbook: Serbia*. Retrieved on 14 November 2014, from https://www.cia.gov/library/publications/the-world-factbook/geos/ri.html.
CeSid (2012) *Survey of public opinion—Citizens' attitudes toward discrimination in Serbia,* CeSid, Belgrade.
Danas (2015) *More than 120 medications will not be available for discounted price.* Retrieved 13 January 2015, from http://www.danas.rs/danasrs/drustvo/vise_od_120_lekova_nece_moci_na_recept.55.html?news_id=295093.
Dimitrijević, A. and Božović, M. (2011) Actual status of psychiatry consumer associations in Serbia. *Engrami* **33** (1), 79–91.
Gajić-Stevanović, M. (2014) Health care system of the Republic of Serbia in the period 2004–2012. *Serbian Dental Journal* **61** (1), 36–44.
Gajić-Stevanović, M., Dimitrijević, S., Vuksa, A. and Jovanović, D. (2009) *Health care system and spending in Serbia from 2004 to 2008.* (Institute for Public Health of Serbia "Dr Milan Jovanović Batut," Belgrade).
International Aid Network (IAN). (2015) *Mental Health Group*, retrieved on 20 January 2015, from http://www.ian.org.rs/mentalhealth/index.htm.

Institute of Public Health of Serbia "Dr Milan Jovanović Batut." (2009) *Health of Population of Serbia: Analytical Study 1997–2007*. Institute for Public Health "Dr Milan Jovanović Batut," Belgrade.

Institute of Public Health of Serbia "Dr Milan Jovanović Batut." (2010) *Serbian Experience with National Health Accounts*. Institute for Public Health "Dr Milan Jovanović Batut," Belgrade.

Institute of Public Health of Serbia "Dr Milan Jovanović Batut." (2011) *Statistical Yearbook of Republic of Serbia*. Institute of Public Health of Serbia "Dr Milan Jovanović Batut," Belgrade.

Institute of Public Health of Serbia "Dr Milan Jovanović Batut." (2012a) *The expenditures of health protection in Serbia according to the international classification of illnesses for the period 2003–2011*. Institute of Public Health of Serbia "Dr Milan Jovanović Batut," Belgrade.

Institute of Public Health of Serbia "Dr Milan Jovanović Batut." (2012b) *Methodology on research of users' satisfaction with health insurance in republic of Serbia*. Institute of Public Health "Dr Milan Jovanović Batut," Belgrade.

Institute for Public Health of Serbia "Dr. Milan Jovanović Batut." (2013) *Report on improvement on quality of work in health institutions of Republic of Serbia in year 2012*, Belgrade.

Institute of Public Health of Serbia "Dr Milan Jovanović Batut." (2014) *Health Statistical Yearbook of Republic of Serbia 2013*. Institute of Public Health of Serbia, "Dr Milan Jovanović Batut," Belgrade.

Janković, S., Vlajinac, H., Bjegović, H., Marinković, J., Šipetić-Grujićić, S., Marković-Denić, Lj., Kocev, N., Šantrić-Milićević, M., Terzić-Šupić, Z., Maksimović, N. and Laaser, U. (2006) The burden of disease and injury in Serbia. *European Journal of Public Health* **17** (1), 80–85.

Jašović-Gašić, M., Lacković, M., Dunjić-Kostić, B., Pantović, M., Cvetić, T., Damjanović, A., Vuković, O., Ceković, J. and Jovanović, A. (2010) Critical review of studies on quality of life in psychiatric patients published in Serbian medical journals from 2000 to 2009. *Psychiatria Danubina* **22** (4), 488–494.

Jovanović M. (2014) *Legal status of persons with disability*. Retrieved on 29 January 2015, from: http://pescanik.net/pravni-polozaj-osoba-sa-invaliditetom-2/.

Kilbourne, A., Keyser, D. and Pincus, H. A. (2010) Challenges and opportunities in measuring the quality of mental health care. *Canadian Journal of Psychiatry* **55** (9), 549–557.

Kohn, R., Saxena, S., Levav, I. and Saraceno, B. (2004) The treatment gap in mental health care. *Bulletin of the World Health Organization* **82** (11), 858–866.

Lečić, T. D., Đukić D. S., Pejović M. M., Crnobarić, C., Špirić, T. and Mihajlović, G. (2012a) Treatment of Depression: Serbian National Guidelines of Good Clinical Practice. *Psychiatry Today* **44** (2), 171–191.

Lečić, T. D., Draganić, D. and Milovančević, M. (2012b) State of psychiatry in Serbia: problems, advances and perspectives. *International Review of Psychiatry* **24** (4), 341–246.

Lečić, T. D., Pejović, M. M. and Popović D. S. (2007) Reform of the mental health care in Serbia: Ten steps plus one. *World Psychiatry* **6** (2), 115–117.

Lečić, T. D. and Draganić-Gajić, S. (2005) The Serbian Experience. In: Lopez-Ibor, J. J., Christodoulou, G., Maj, M. and Sar, N. (eds.), *Disasters and Mental Health*. (John Wiley & Sons, Chester, UK).

Mental Disability Rights Initiative. (2014) *Serbian country report on legal capacity reform*. Retrieved on 29 January 2015, from: http://www.eu-person.com/publication/serbian-eu-person-country-report/wppa_open/.

Milićević-Kalašić, A. (2003) *Neuropsychiatric Disorders in Elderly at Home Treatment and Care*. Belgrade.

Milićević-Kalašić, A. (1993) Home care and promotion of mental health for the elderly in Belgrade. *International Psychogeriatric Association Newsletter* **10** (1), 21–22.

Milićević-Kalašić, A. (2008) Mental Health Services of Older people. *Gerontologija*, (1), 218–228.

Ministry of Health of Republic of Serbia. (2014) *Research on health of citizens of republic of Serbia* Retrieved 12 December 2014, from: http://www.zdravlje.gov.rs/downloads/2014/jul2014/Jul2014IzvestajPreliminarni.pdf.

Munjiza, M. (2011) *Historical Development of Psychiatry: History of approaches and concepts to a mentally disturbed person throughout history and at present*. Official Gazette, Belgrade.

National Bank of Serbia. (2014) Sector of Insurance in Serbia: Report for the Third Quartal of 2014. National Bank of Serbia, Belgrade.

National Health Insurance Fund Republic of Serbia. (2014) About Us. Retrieved on 23 February 2014 from National Health Insurance Fund: http://www.eng.rfzo.rs/index.php/about-us.

National Health Insurance Fund Republic of Serbia. (2013) *Serbian health insurance development strategy by 2020*. Retrieved on 06 February 2015, from: http://eng.rfzo.rs/images/baneri/Strategija_english_final.pdf.

Ogbuja, G. (2012) *Correlation between Poverty and Mental Health: Towards a Psychiatric Evaluation* Available at SSRN: http://ssrn.com/abstract=2152161.

Opalić, P. and Nikolić, S. (2008) Assessment on quality of life of schizophrenic patients. *Vojnosanitetski Pregled* **65** (5), 383–391.

Paunović-Milosavljević, G., Nenadović, M. and Klidonas, N. (2012) Frequency of involuntary hospitalization in the urgent psychiatric treatment. *Engrami* **34** (3), 69–76.

Pejaković, Lj. and Zajić, G. (2014). *Deinstitutionalization of residential institutions of social protection*. (Republic Institute for Social Protection, Belgrade).

Penev, G and Stankovi, B. (2007) Suicides in Serbia at the beginning of the 21st century and trends in the past fifty years. *Stanovništvo* **45** (2), 25–62 (Serbian).

Pro.Me.Ne (Promotion of Mental Health Network) (2014) *Comments on existing legislation of mental health protection on European and national level*, Caritas Republic of Serbia, Belgrade.

Priebe, S., Janković-Gavrilović, J., Matanov, A., Francisković, T., Knežević, G., Ljubotina, D., Bravo-Mehmedbasic, A. and Schutzwohl, M. (2010) Treatment Outcomes and costs at Specialized centres for the treatment of PTSD after the war in former Yugoslavia. *Psychiatric Services* **61** (6), 598–604.

Radivojević, B. (2011) Half Serbians treated by private owners. UPKLS Retrieved on 20 March 2015, from: http://uplks.com/pola-srbijelece-privatni-doktori.

Republic Institute for Social protection (2012) *Structure of the insured users*. Retrieved on 11 December 2014, from: http://www.zso.gov.rs/doc/statistika/zdravstveno/Struktura%20osiguranika%202011.pdf.

Sarajlija, M., Jugović, A., Živaljević, D., Merdović, B. and Sarajlija, A. (2014) Assessment of health status and quality of life of homeless persons in Belgrade, Serbia. *Military Health Journal* **71** (2), 167–174.

Schipper, H., Clinch, J. and Powell, J. (1990) Definitions and conceptual issues. In: Spilker, B. (ed.), *Quality of life assessments in clinical trials*. (Raven Press, New York), pp. 11–25.

SeConS Development Initiative Group (2009) Social Inclusion. Retrieved on 8 January 2015. Available at: http://www.inkluzijakurs.info/onlinekurs.php.

Sedmak, T. (2010) Social positioning of psychiatry and psychiatrists. In Branko Ćorić (ed.), *Value system and psychiatry* (Faculty for Special Education and Rehabilitation (FASPER), Belgrade), pp. 169–240.

Stanković, Z., Nikolić-Balkoski, G., Leposavić, Lj. and Popović Lj. (2006) Perception on quality of life and social adaptation of patients with recurring depression. *Srpski Arhiv za Celokupno Lekarstvo* **134** (9–10), 369–374.

Statistical Office of the Republic of Serbia (2014) *Statistical Yearbook of the Republic of Serbia—Population*. Statistical Office of the Republic of Serbia, Belgrade.

Statistical Office of the Republic of Serbia (2014) *Statistical Yearbook of the Republic of Serbia—Labour Market.* Statistical Office of the Republic of Serbia Belgrade.

Statistical Office of the Republic of Serbia (2014) Data from: http://webrzs.stat.gov.rs/WebSite/Public/PageView.aspx?pKey=2.

Statistical Office of the Republic of Serbia (2008) Living *Standards Measurement Survey 2007.*

Stošić, S. and Karanović, N. (2014) Health care economics in Serbia: Current problems and changes. *Vojnosanitetski Pregled* **71** (11), 1055–1061.

Svilanović, T. (2013) *Stigma and discrimination toward persons with psychosis: Survey on attitudes of citizens of Belgrade,* Doctoral dissertation, Belgrade.

Tatić, D. (2007) *Report on the position of persons with disabilities in Serbia.* Center for Independent life of disabled persons, Belgrade.

Thornicroft, G., Brohan, E., Kassam, A. and Lewis-Holmes, E. (2008) Reducing stigma and discrimination: Candidate interventions. *International Journal of Mental Health Systems* **2** (1), 3.

Totić, S., Stojiljković, D., Pavlović, Z., Zaric, N., Zarkovic, B., Malic, L., Mihaljevic, M., Jasovic-Gasic, M. and Maric, N. P. (2011) Stigmatization of 'psychiatric label' by medical and non-medical students. *International Journal of Social Psychiatry* **58** (5), 455–462.

UNDP. (2014) *About Serbia.* From UNDP in Serbia: http://www.rs.undp.org/content/serbia/en/home/countryinfo/.

Varmus, H. (1998) *Parity in Financing Mental Health Services: Managed Care Effects on Cost, Access and Quality.* (National Institute of Mental health).

Vidanović, V. (2012) Problems of poverty and social exclusion. *Magazine of the Institute for crime and sociological research* **31** (2), 179–198.

WHO (2001) *Mental Health: New Understanding, New Hope.* WHO, Geneva.

WHO (2002) *Prevention and Promotion in Mental Health.* WHO, Geneva.

WHO (2003) *Mental Health Financing, Mental Health Policy and Service Guidance Package.* WHO, Geneva.

WHO (2003) *Mental Health Policy and Service Guidance Package: Mental Health Legislation & Human Rights.* WHO, Geneva.

WHO (2003) *Quality Improvement for Mental Health.* World Health Organization, Geneva.

WHO (2006) *Quality of care.* World health Organization, Paris.

WHO (2008) *Policies and practices in mental health in Europe.* World Health Organization, Copenhagen.

WHO (2011) *Mental Health Atlas 2011.* World Health Organization, Geneva.

WHO (2012) World Suicide Death Rate Rankings. Retrieved 21 September 2015, from: http://apps.who.int/gho/data/node.main.MHSUICIDE?lang=en.

WHO Europe, SEE Mental Health Network. (2008) *Approaching Mental Health Care Reform Regionally: The Mental Health Project for Southeast Europe.* (WHO Europe, Sarajevo).

World Bank (2014) *Databank.* From http://www.worldbank.org/.

CHAPTER 8

The Way Forward: Improving Mental Health Systems in Central and Eastern Europe

Richard M. Scheffler[*], Grayson Dimick[†], and Ivan Duškov[‡]

[*]School of Public Health and Goldman School of Public Policy, University of California, Berkeley, California

[†]Georgetown University Law Center, Washington, USA

[‡]Institute for Language and Preparatory Studies, Charles University, Prague, Czech Republic

In the quarter century since the fall of communist rule, the countries of Central and Eastern Europe (CEE) have made respectable progress in reforming their mental health care systems. However, this progress is far from complete. Mental health care in the region remains outdated and ineffective compared to international standards. Future reform is a crucial task: CEE has one of the highest proportions of disease burden due to mental and substance use disorders in the world (Krupchanka and Winkler, 2016, p. 96), among the highest rates of suicide worldwide (WHO, 2018), and extremely high—and rising—levels of alcohol consumption (Krupchanka and Winkler, 2016, p. 96).

The following section will first compare and contrast the challenges facing the individual countries of CEE. Second, we look at the way forward for mental health care reform in CEE, by providing seven areas of action that the region must focus on.

8.1 Overview of the Challenges Facing Central and Eastern European Countries

All 6 countries share a need for further deinstitutionalization of the mental health care system and to provide more community-based care as they move forward with reform. Community-based care is chronically underfunded and underdeveloped in all countries, and its improvement will allow for better quality of life, independence, and health outcomes. By supporting deinstitutionalization and improving the accessibility of mainstream services, more people will have the opportunity for social inclusion and the ability to contribute to their communities' social and economic growth. In developing these community-based systems, all 6 countries must work on developing resources that are more evenly distributed across geographic regions to resolve issues of access as well as to resolve issues of lack of communication between different levels of the medical system, such as general practitioners and psychiatrists. The not-for-profit sector has built expertise and resources that could be used to expand and strengthen community services.

Beyond deinstitutionalization and developing community-based care, the 6 countries share different challenges and priorities based on their specific histories and developments. For Serbia, beyond the need for the mental health services to be reorganized in better alignment with the needs of the population, being in better alignment with international standards for mental health care is a top priority, which will require more allocation of resources to mental health and development of new distribution systems. Serbia also notes the need for access to improved information and communications technology, better inter-sectorial cooperation, as well as enhanced public representation and advocacy. In achieving this, Serbia notes that its primary challenges are insufficient cooperation between sectors and mental health associations, insufficient financial support, inadequate work conditions, and the need for more professional staff development. Like Serbia, Moldova also shares a reform priority of meeting international standards. Future reform efforts will build upon the country's recent achievements in advancing respect for fundamental human rights and the ratification of the Convention on the Rights of Persons with Disabilities (CRPD). Moldova's desire for European integration should help to promote a constructive dialogue between national authorities that is needed to adequately address issues related to the rights of persons with disabilities, although this dialogue must include broader engagement in civil society as well as greater participation by social partners and representatives from organizations representing persons with disabilities.

In Romania, priorities include addressing the massive migration of psychiatrists and nurses, the lack of data on mental health, and the low level of financing for mental health services. Resolving institution-based care in Romania has a unique component in which many of the psychiatric hospitals are remotely located in old buildings; they are costly to maintain and even costlier to upgrade. For Albania, a key challenge is coordination with primary care physicians, due to the lack of health services in most of the county. Meanwhile, in Bulgaria unique challenges include the split of responsibilities for mental health care between the Ministry of Health and NHIF, which causes regulatory problems that are manifest in lack of access and underfinancing of the mental health system. Cost is also a major factor that must be addressed moving forward in Bulgaria, as a lack of insurance coverage for many types of mental health care persists. However, the fact that the political system has given some priority to mental health care and has adopted several pieces of new legislation and strategies may be a promising sign for reform in the years to come. In contrast, the Czech Republic's largest problem in implementing future reforms is a lack of political will. The lack of clear political support for mental health is a persistent problem in the Czech Republic and has been perhaps the primary obstacle to achieving much needed system reform. Improving mental health care requires long-ranging policy changes whose results, and potential political benefits, will require 5–10 years to be realized, while the standard election cycle is 4 years. Relatively, there is a lack of user associations and NGOs promoting the interests of service users and their families in the Czech Republic; this leads to insufficient lobbying with political decision makers who then feel little pressure and demand for change.

8.2 Looking Forward: Seven Areas of Action for Continued Progress

There are 7 areas of action that each CEE country must consider to ensure the continued progress of their mental health systems: (1) improve the integration of care, (2) strengthen mental health legislation and policies, (3) increase and integrate mental health financing, (4) develop and maintain a diverse mental health workforce, (5) increase utilization of technology, (6) reduce stigma, and (7) strengthen information. Each of these 7 components has its separate role, but also builds on the others—a mental health system is only as good as the weakest link in the component systems.

8.2.1 *Improve the integration of care*

Due to the legacies of the Semashko model, the health systems of CEE overwhelmingly lack integrated care. As the previous chapters illustrate, there is little to no coordination between primary care doctors and psychiatrists. Primary care doctors do not receive sufficient mental health training to be able to identify mental illness. Neither doctors nor psychiatrists are well connected with community resources. Thus, a critical improvement must be the integration of mental health into primary care. This includes empowering primary care doctors to deal with common mental disorders (i.e. depression, anxiety)—an essential step to ease burdens on the impacted mental health systems and allow patients to receive care in a more accessible setting. Increased integration of care will help identify mental health problems earlier.

Integration of mental health into the primary care setting is essential because individuals with mental health problems face much higher levels of premature mortality. This life expectancy gap exists partly due to suicide, but also because people with mental health problems tend to lead poorer, more disadvantaged lives, experience more physical health problems, and receive worse treatment for their physical health problems.

Integrated care can help ensure these individuals receive care that meets their multifaceted needs.

Furthermore, while the integration of primary care and mental health is fundamental, there are other areas of integration that CEE countries should consider. It is important to integrate mental health systems with community services and school-based programs, as well as public and private health care systems. As mentioned above, individuals with severe mental illness often face higher levels of poverty and unemployment, and have been among the first to lose their jobs in times of economic transition, and the most affected by national budget cuts (Winkler *et al.*, 2017, p. 639). These individuals would benefit greatly from easier access to both mental health services and social services. Thus, an expanded and fully integrated system is likely to produce the best mental health outcomes and best effective use of the resources available in each country.

8.2.2 *Strengthen mental health legislation and policies*

The incorporation of mental health into the global development agenda has been instrumental in advancing mental health care in CEE. WHO's mh-GAP program and comprehensive Mental Health Action Plan 2013–2020, as well as EU agreements, have provided the region's countries with frameworks for reforms. CEE countries have adopted many of these frameworks, and compliance with these and other regional and international agreements will be an important vehicle for the implementation of continual improvements (Winkler *et al.*, 2017, p. 641).

However, because much of the mental health current legislation in CEE was adopted from international requirements, policies are often not tailored to local needs nor "owned" by local leaders. New legislation should be tailored to individual countries' needs and fill gaps in current policy. Furthermore, throughout the region, reforms and policies are often lacking any real sort of implementation (Dlouhy, 2014). Future reforms must include incentives and enforcement mechanisms to ensure that goals are met, as this is frequently lacking in current policies. There must also be incentives for politicians to care about mental health reform. International pressures have been successful in producing action at times. For example, Bulgarian and Romanian mental health policies have benefited from EU membership, because mental health and human rights were important issues raised during the accession process (Dlouhy, 2014). While other CEE countries may benefit from the pressure to reform that accompanies EU accession in the future, in the short term, mental health policies should be framed as an investment for the country's economic benefit (i.e. leading to fuller participation in the workforce, etc.) in order to incentivize politicians to act.

In addition, it is crucial that CEE countries provide ways for stakeholders to be involved in the crafting of mental health legislation and policies. A 2016 study found that there was not a single country in the region with full participation of users in policy-making, in contrast to 53.5% of EU15[1] countries (Krupchanka and Winkler, 2016, p. 96).

8.2.3 *Increase and integrate mental health financing*

There is little doubt that a key element of successful reform and implementation of the mental health system depends acutely on adequate and sustainable financing. CEE countries consistently devote less funding for mental health as a percentage of GDP compared to most of their western European counterparts (Knapp and McDaid, 2007, p. 76), and this must be improved. Beyond improving the levels of funding, there must also be changes in the usage of these funds. Fundamentally, resources must be shifted from institutional care, as hospitals close, toward community care (Knapp and McDaid, 2007, p. 94).

The structure of mental health financing is also important to the region's future. As the previous chapters illustrate, in each country, there is a mixture of both public/government financing and private financing, including out-of-pocket payments. Public financing, usually paid for by some sort of government insurance program, is the fundamental

---

[1] "EU15" refers to the EU member countries prior to the accession of 10 candidate countries on 1 May 2004. The EU15 is comprised of the following 15 countries: Austria, Belgium, Denmark, Finland, France, Germany, Greece, Ireland, Italy, Luxembourg, Netherlands, Portugal, Spain, Sweden, and United Kingdom. https://stats.oecd.org/glossary/detail.asp?ID=6805.

underpinning of the financing of a mental health system. Typically, there are 2 types of government financing: some countries have separate financial budgets for mental health services, while others have financing of mental health services integrated into budgeting for the overall health care system. Both types of financing schemes have advantages and disadvantages. Having a separate mental health budget identifies the resources required to be spent on mental health. These resources typically cover payments and financing for inpatient hospital services, as well as some outpatient clinics. As attractive as individual budgets are, they create issues with coordination with the other areas of the health care system, creating a barrier to more integrated care. When mental health budgets are a subset of the overall budget of the health care system and are controlled by a central authority, this allows for the better coordination of funding. Thus, given the importance of integrating mental health services into the general health care systems in CEE, the integration of mental and general health care budgets is preferable for the region's future. Countries must also be mindful of the need to integrate mental health funding not only with the broader health system, but also with social services (Knapp and McDaid, 2007, pp. 76–77).

In terms of private financing, many countries are now developing private hospitals and private clinics to treat mental health problems. These private institutions are a useful addition, but do raise issues of equity, as they are beyond the budgets of most of the population. Beyond treatment in inpatient or outpatient settings, the financing and payment for pharmaceuticals is another key component of the mental health system. Pharmaceuticals are often paid for by public funding, but can often include copayments for certain drugs. It is important for countries to have policies in place that waive or lower copayments on drugs for lower income populations.

Thus, a balance between public and private financing and payments is a characteristic of the mental health system in CEE. It is likely this structure will continue into the future. Looking toward the future, beyond an obvious need to increase funding for mental health services—especially community services—a close and continued monitoring of the financial integration of these systems should receive the highest priority.

8.2.4 Develop and maintain a diverse mental health workforce

The fundamental underpinning of the mental health care system in any country is an adequate and well-trained workforce, yet, as the previous chapters illustrate, the countries of CEE face shortages of mental health care providers.

Critical shortage of mental health providers results from a combination of factors. One of them is clearly the inadequate resources being devoted to the training of these providers. An additional driver of this shortage is low salaries and poor working conditions. Given the ability to move within the EU, many well-trained health care providers are leaving CEE for better paying jobs and positions. It is clear that if countries want to retain their providers, specific policies including higher wages need to be developed. Finally, stigma poses a barrier, disincentivizing many from entering the mental health care field in the first place.

Typically, in CEE, the mental health workforce has primarily been psychiatrists. The training of psychiatrists is long and quite expensive, and the overall numbers are relatively small. This causes bottlenecks in the efficient functioning of mental health systems. Furthermore, countries must more adequately respond to the rising demands for specialist psychiatric services, such as child and adolescent, geriatric, forensic, and substance abuse, through more specialized training of psychiatrists (Tomov et al., 2007, p. 416). Many countries have expanded training of psychologists, particularly for outpatient treatment, and this has proven to be quite successful. Further training of mental health care providers is an important priority.

Community and primary health care workers can be trained and supervised to perform a variety of roles including identifying and referring cases, delivering psycho-social therapies, and supporting medication adherence. A top priority should be the expanded training of clinical social workers, who can treat many mental health problems in a cost effective and high quality manner. They are quite useful in outpatient settings, particularly in community settings, and can also be used effectively to treat elderly patients who need supportive care. Furthermore, countries must build non-specialist capacity, such as peer-to-peer counselors.

8.2.5 Increase utilization of technology

Increased use of technology can help address many long-standing obstacles in mental health delivery that are illustrated in the country case studies, such as transportation barriers, stigma associated with visiting mental health clinics, clinician shortages, and high costs of treatment. For example, in CEE, where community resources are primarily concentrated only in the largest cities, technology can help connect those outside the countries' largest urban centers to mental health resources via telemedicine appointments, mobile screening tools, or SMS reminders to encourage medication adherence (Naslund *et al.*, 2017). Furthermore, technology can extend workforce capacity and reach by enabling mental health specialists based in urban areas to supervise non-specialist workers and coordinate care (Naslund *et al.*, 2017). Thus, the adoption of technology into the mental health care system should be a priority.

8.2.6 Reduce stigma

It is essential that CEE regions tackle the pervasive stigma that surrounds mental health in the region. The region's high levels of public stigma, and in turn, societal unwillingness to accept those with severe mental health disorders as members of the community, has significant consequences. Stigma influences mental health policy and funding, as well as the willingness of individuals to seek help, service quality, and quality of life for people with these disorders (Winkler *et al.*, 2017, p. 635). Human rights abuses of those with mental illness, especially in institutional settings, still persists across the region (Knapp *et al.*, 2007, p. 8).

Thus, addressing stigma is a crucial component of mental health reform. However, no single easy solution exists for policymakers. Studies have found that long-term interventions such as intervention in schools to raise awareness of mental health and engagement with the media to dissuade sensationalist and inaccurate portrayals of mental health that perpetuate stereotypes appear to be effective (Knapp *et al.*, 2007, p. 9). An essential component of addressing stigma in CEE is to increase the visibility of mental health. People with mental illness were hidden from the public during the Soviet era, thus, the more the public sees and hears of mental health, the more normalized and understandable it will become. As the case studies detail, NGOs and organizations of service users have been instrumental in these efforts, and their continued work should be supported. While primarily supported financially by international NGOs and the EU (for those in EU member countries), their activities should also be encouraged and welcomed by CEE governments. Furthermore, anti-stigmatization efforts must go beyond the general public. Efforts must address stigma among family members of those with mental illness and medical professionals—2 groups that are critical in providing care and support to those with mental illness, yet who are still prone to stigmatization (Winkler et al., 2017, p. 636).

8.2.7 Strengthen information

Transparency and data-based decision-making are important components in all health care systems. Yet, as the case studies illustrate, routine information systems and clinical standards/indicators for mental health data collection are largely rudimentary or absent in CEE, making it difficult to understand the needs of local populations and to plan accordingly (Tomov et al., 2007, pp. 411–412). Thus, moving forward, CEE countries must prioritize the collection of data specific to mental health. Data that is publically available on the mental health system needs to be accurate and available in a timely manner so planners and governments can use them in a timely way to both identify and address the mental health problems in each of the countries. Reliable, systematic, and credible mental health data are needed in each of these countries, and should receive the highest order of priority by each government.

Furthermore, a crucial goal must to be to continue, promote, and expand mental health research in CEE. A lack of mental health research in the region has been widespread, with CEE countries having the lowest publication rate per person in Europe in both public mental health research and stigma-related research (Winkler et al., 2017, p. 634). A key component of the National Institutes of Health (NIH) Fogarty[2] program, upon which this book is built, is the understanding that mental health services

---

[2] For more information about the NIH Fogarty program, see https://www.fic.nih.gov.

research training needs to expand dramatically in each case study country—and all countries in CEE. The purpose of the Fogarty program is to train the future faculty in these countries, of which we have trained more than 100 with our grant. Moving forward, more faculty members must be trained so mental health services research can flourish in CEE. There must also be incentives for researchers and practitioners to engage in this research. In-country research by those who understand the problems, have access to the data, and understand the history, culture, laws, and regulations are necessary for the future development and improvement of the mental health systems in eastern and central Europe.

Thus, looking forward, improvements in data collection and expansion of research will better allow CEE policymakers to make sound, evidence-based decisions regarding the mental health care policy.

8.3 Conclusion

The countries of CEE must continue to improve their mental health systems. While much remains for improvement, the above 7 areas of action provide a conceptual framework for sorting and grouping future efforts. Each area of action is complex, containing a plethora of policy potentials. However, through undertaking action in each area, CEE countries will be closer to realizing a mental health system that effectively provides the best promotion of mental well-being, prevention of mental disorders, protection of human rights, and care and quality of life for those affected by mental illness.

References

Dlouhy, M. (2014) Mental health policy in Eastern Europe: A comparative analysis of seven mental health systems. *BMC Health Services Research* **14** (42). https://doi.org/10.1186/1472-6963-14-42.

Knapp, M. and McDaid, D. (2007) Financing and Funding Mental Healthcare Services. In Knapp, M. *et al.* (eds.) *Mental Health Policy and Practice across Europe: The Future Direction of Mental Health Care* (Open University Press/ World Health Organization), pp. 60–99.

Knapp, M., McDaid, D., Mossialos, E. and Thornicroft, G. (2007) Mental Health Policy and Practice across Europe: An overview. In Knapp, M. *et al.* (eds.)

Mental Health Policy and Practice across Europe: The Future Direction of Mental Health Care. (Open University Press/ World Health Organization), pp. 1–14.

Krupchanka, D. and Winkler, P. (2016) State of mental healthcare systems in Eastern Europe: Do we really understand what is going on? *BJPsych International* **13** (4), 96–99.

Naslund, J. A. *et al.* (2017) Digital technology for treating and preventing mental disorders in low-income and middle-income countries: A narrative review of the literature. *The Lancet Psychiatry* **4** (6), 486–500.

Tomov, T., Van Voren, R., Keukens, R. and Puras, D. (2007) Mental Health Policy in Former Eastern Bloc Countries. In Knapp, M. *et al.* (eds.) *Mental Health Policy and Practice across Europe: The Future Direction of Mental Health Care* (Open University Press/ World Health Organization), pp. 397–425.

WHO (2018) Suicide rate estimates, age-standardized Estimates by country. Global Health Observatory data repository. 17 July 2018. http://apps.who.int/gho/data/node.main.MHSUICIDEASDR?lang=en.

Winkler, P. *et al.* (2017) A blind spot on the global mental health map: A scoping review of 25 years' development of mental health care for people with severe mental illnesses in central and eastern Europe. *The Lancet Psychiatry* **4** (8), 634–642.

Index

A

Access to mental health care, 27–31, 63, 94–95, 126–127, 159–160, 190–194
Adolescents, *see* children and adolescents
Adults, 55, 83, 92, 127, 154, 162
Advocacy, 41–43, 70–72, 105–106, 133–136, 167–170, 206–212
Albania
    access to mental health care, 27–31
    advocacy, 41–43
    challenges, 44, 223
    demographics, 15–16
    financing, 20, 25–26, 35–37
    history of mental health care, 18–20
    mental health workforce, 31–35
    morbidity and mortality, 15–18
    organization of the mental health system, 20, 25–27
    outcomes, *see* quality of care
    policies and legislation, 21–25, 42
    political history, 8–9
    population mental health status, 15–18
    priorities, 44
    quality of care, 37–40
    stigma, 40–44
Alcohol use disorders (*see also* substance use disorders), 16–17, 72, 79–80, 83–84, 119, 158, 221
Ambulatory mental health services, *see* outpatient mental health services
Anti-stigma campaigns, *see* stigma
Anxiety disorders, 16, 81–82, 141–143, 154, 167

B

Bismarckian model, 27, 145
Budget, *see* expenditures and financing

Bulgaria
    access to mental health care, 63
    advocacy, 69–72
    challenges, 73–74, 223
    demographics, 48
    financing, 65–69
    history of mental health care, 47–52
    mental health workforce, 63–65
    organization of the mental health system, 56–63
    outcomes, *see* quality of care
    policies and legislation, 52–56
    political history, 9
    population mental health status, 47–48
    priorities, 74
    quality of care, 73
    stigma, 69–72

C

Central and Eastern Europe (CEE)
    cold war, 3–5
    communism, 1, 5–7
    current conditions, 8–11, 221–231
    history, 1–11
Challenges, 44, 73–74, 108–111, 136–137, 170–171, 212–213, 222–224
Children and adolescents, 20, 25, 63, 79, 91, 119–120, 149–151, 158–159
Communist government, 19–20, 31, 49–51, 84–86, 106, 134, 221
Community-based services, 19, 23, 30, 52, 87–88, 93, 108, 122–123, 135, 179, 222
    see also community mental health centers; outpatient mental health services

Community mental health centers (CMHC), 20, 28, 40, 93, 107–108, 121, 124, 131–132, 149, 155–158
Community residential care, *see* residential care
Czech Republic
    access to mental health care, 94–95
    advocacy, 104–106
    challenges, 108–111, 223
    demographics, 78
    financing, 101–103
    history of mental health care, 84–88
    mental health workforce, 95–100
    morbidity and mortality, 79–80
    organization of the mental health system, 90–93
    outcomes, *see* quality of care
    policies and legislation, 84, 86–90, 106–111
    political history, 9
    population mental health status, 77–84
    priorities, 106–111
    quality of care, 103–104
    stigma, 104–106

D

Data systems, *see* information systems
Day centers, 27, 74, 93, 148, 179, 187
Deinstitutionalization, 20, 23, 51–52, 87, 109, 136–137, 180, 211, 222
Depression, 80, 82, 154, 167, 177, 194, 204–205
    see also mood disorders
Developmental disability, 79, 119, 124

Disability, 21, 42, 52–54, 81, 118, 133–135, 182, 192
Disability Adjusted Life Years (DALYs), 16, 81, 205
Discrimination, *see* stigma
Disparities
    geographic, 74, 94, 97, 126, 158–160
    vulnerable groups, 94–95, 159–160, 193–194
Drugs, *see* medications and substance use disorders

E

Eastern Europe, *see* Central and Eastern Europe
Education and training, 32–33, 64, 97–99, 128–129, 154, 161–162, 194–195, 228
Elderly, *see* geriatric population
Emergency mental health services, 62, 93, 124, 127
European Union (EU), 8–11, 63, 81, 117, 168, 226
Expenditures, 35–37, 65–69, 101–103, 130, 146–147, 149, 152–153, 162, 199–201

F

Female, *see* women
Financing, 20, 24–26, 35–37, 65–69, 101–103, 126, 129–130, 152–153, 162–164, 196–201, 205, 226–227
Fogarty International Center, 2, 230

G

General hospitals, *see* hospitals
General practitioners (GPs), 31, 88, 123, 143–144, 154, 180, 186, 195
Geography, 73–74, 94, 96–97, 126, 159–160
Geriatric population, 158, 176, 228
Guardianship, 21, 55–56, 118, 204

H

Health insurance, 25–30, 53, 58, 65, 67, 84, 90–91, 94, 101–103, 126, 145–146, 162–163, 191, 197–198, 205
Health system, 1, 4, 7, 19, 57–58, 68, 86, 145–146, 164, 178, 185, 192, 197, 224, 227
History of mental health care, 18–20, 47–52, 84–88, 120–122, 145–148, 178–180
Homelessness, 95, 194
Hospitals
    general, 91–92, 156–157, 186–187
    psychiatric, 49–50, 92, 120–121, 147, 156–157, 178–179, 186–187
    see also inpatient mental health services
Human resources, *see* mental health workforce

I

Information systems, 78, 119, 188–189, 230
Inpatient mental health services, 20, 49, 60, 85, 88, 91–92, 120–121, 125, 131, 156–157, 164, 187
    see also hospitals
Insurance, *see* health insurance
Integration of care, 26–27, 122, 189–190, 224–225, 229

236

Index

Intellectual disability, *see* developmental disability
Involuntary treatment, 21, 72, 134, 182, 189–190

L

Laws, *see* policies and legislation
Legislation, *see* policies and legislation
Length of stay, 51, 79, 92

M

Male, *see* men
Media, 40, 70, 103–105, 167
Medications, 40, 62, 73, 94, 102, 125–127, 154, 165, 189, 192, 227
Men, 31, 79, 92, 144, 176
Mental health expenditures, *see* expenditures
Mental health care provider perspectives, 34, 61, 66, 196
Mental health system organization, 20, 25–27, 56–63, 90–93, 123–126, 154–159, 185–190
Mental health workforce
    compensation, 69, 95, 125, 163, 228
    composition, 31–32, 63–64, 95–98, 128, 194–195
    education and training, 32–35, 64, 97–100, 128–129, 154, 161, 194–195, 228
    professional organizations, 50–51, 60, 91, 106–107, 209, 214
    shortages, 31–33, 63–64, 95–98, 100, 126–128, 148, 160–161, 170, 192, 195, 228

Mental retardation, *see* developmental disability
Ministry of Health
    Albania, 21–23, 25–26
    Bulgaria, 53, 57–58, 69, 72
    Czech Republic, 90
    Moldova, 122–123, 135
    Romania, 146, 149
    Serbia, 185
Moldova
    access to mental health care, 126–127
    advocacy, 133–136
    challenges, 136–137, 223
    demographics, 118
    financing, 126, 129–130
    history of mental health care, 120–122
    mental health workforce, 126–129
    morbidity and mortality, 118–120
    organization of the mental health system, 123–126
    outcomes, *see* quality of care
    policies and legislation, 121–123, 134–136
    political history, 10
    population mental health status, 118–120
    priorities, 136–137
    quality of care, 130–133
    stigma, 133–136
Mood disorders, 80, 142–143
    see also depression
Morbidity and mortality, 16–18, 78–84, 119–120, 141–144, 175–178

N

North Atlantic Treaty Organization (NATO), 8–11
Non-governmental organizations, 42–43, 70, 72, 74, 90–91, 93, 105–107, 169–170, 188, 206–209, 230
Nurses, 31–32, 64, 95–96, 100, 122, 128–129, 154, 162, 195

O

Organisation for Economic Co-operation and Development, 8–9
Out-of-pocket payments, 36, 67–68, 127, 160, 198–199
Outcomes, *see* quality of care
Outpatient mental health services, 27, 40, 50, 54, 59–62, 79, 92–93, 108, 124, 143, 146–147, 155–156, 163, 187, 201

P

Patient perspectives, 43, 71–72, 166–167, 207–208, 210–211
Patient rights, 22, 50, 55, 70, 72, 88, 91, 106, 109, 133–136, 168, 182, 204, 206–209,
Physicians, 31, 63–64, 95–96, 122, 168
  see also psychiatrists
Policies and legislation, 21–25, 42, 51–56, 84, 86–90, 106–111, 121–123, 134–136, 145, 148–154, 180–185, 225–226
Policymaker perspectives, 24, 28–29, 150–151, 183–184
Political history, 8–11

Population mental health status, 15–18, 47–48, 77–84, 117–120, 141–144, 175–178
Prevention, 20, 55, 70, 89, 108–109, 188, 213
Primary health care, 26–27, 59, 122, 146, 154, 182, 186, 224–225
Priorities, 44, 74, 106–111, 136–137, 171, 212–213
Professional organizations, 51, 60, 91, 106–107, 209, 213
Psychiatric hospitals, *see* hospitals
Psychiatric drugs, *see* medications
Psychiatrists, 31–32, 64, 95–100, 128–129, 154–155, 160–161, 163, 186, 194–195, 228
Psychologists, 65, 94–100, 128, 188, 195, 228
Psychotherapy, 56, 59, 73, 97, 162, 192

Q

Quality of care, 37–40, 73, 104, 130–132, 165, 201–205
Quality of life, 74, 108–109, 204–205

R

Referral processes, 87, 122–123, 189–190
Recovery, 5, 131, 209
Reform, 20–22, 41–44, 51, 84, 87, 107–111, 121–122, 134, 145–146, 148, 170, 178–180, 195, 212–213, 221–229
Rehabilitation, 40, 53, 121, 125, 131, 188

Research, 35, 44, 85, 108, 167, 230–231
Residential care, 52, 126, 135, 189
Roma, 95, 160, 194
Romania
    access to mental health care, 159–160
    advocacy, 167–170
    challenges, 170–171, 223
    demographics, 142
    financing, 152–153, 162–164
    history of mental health care, 145–148
    mental health workforce, 148, 154, 160–162, 170–171
    morbidity and mortality, 141–144
    organization of the mental health system, 154–159
    outcomes, *see* quality of care
    policies and legislation, 145, 148–154
    political history, 10–11
    population mental health status, 141–144
    priorities, 152, 170–171
    quality of care, 164–165
    stigma, 167–170
Russia, 4, 9–10
    see also USSR, Soviet influence

S

Semashko system, 19, 85, 145, 224
Schizophrenia, 79, 104–105, 119, 127, 167–168, 204
Serbia
    access to mental health care, 190–194
    advocacy, 206–212
    challenges, 212–213, 222
    demographics, 176
    financing, 196–201, 205
    history of mental health care, 178–180
    mental health workforce, 194–195
    morbidity and mortality, 176–178
    organization of the mental health system, 185–190
    outcomes, *see* quality of care
    policies and legislation, 180–185
    political history, 11
    population mental health status, 175–178
    priorities, 212–214
    quality of care, 201–205
    stigma, 206–212
Smoking, *see* tobacco use
Social care, 50, 52, 65, 93, 179
Social workers, 65, 95–100, 128, 195, 228
Soviet influence, 51, 134, 229
Soviet Union, *see* Union of Soviet Socialist Republics
Stakeholder perspectives
    mental health care providers, 34, 61, 66, 196
    patients, 43, 71–72, 166–167, 207–208, 210–211
    policymakers, 24, 28–29, 150–151, 183–184
Stigma
    anti-stigma campaigns, 41, 105–106, 167–168, 206–209, 229–230
    prevalence, 40–41, 69–70, 103–105, 166, 206, 229

Substance use disorders (*see also* alcohol use disorders), 16, 58, 72, 78, 83–84, 90, 105, 152, 158, 221
Suicide, 18, 81–82, 105, 119–120, 144, 178, 194, 221

T
Technology, 229
Tobacco use, 83

U
Union of Soviet Socialist Republics (USSR), 1, 3, 5, 51, 124, 145, 185
   see also Russia, Soviet influence
United Nations (UN), 11, 90, 117, 133

W
Women, 31, 79–84, 98, 119, 143–144, 176, 178
Workforce, *see* mental health workforce
World Health Organization (WHO), 41, 78, 87, 89–90, 160, 225
World Mental Health Survey Initiative (WMSHI), 141–143

Y
Yugoslavia, 6–7, 11, 179, 185

World Scientific Series in Global Health Economics and Public Policy

(Continued from page ii)

Forthcoming:

Social Capital and Health
    Dov Chernichovsky (Ben Gurion University of the Negev, Israel) and
    Chen Sharony (Ben Gurion University of the Negev, Israel)

Aging and Long Term Care: Global Policy and Organization
    Audrey Laporte (University of Toronto, Canada)

Healthcare Financing
    Winnie Chi-man Yip (Harvard)

The World Scientific Casebook Reference on Healthcare Reforms
    Peter Berman (The University of British Columbia, Canada &
    Harvard University, USA)

Tracking Resources for Primary Health Care: A Framework and Practices in Low- and Middle-Income Countries
    Hong Wang (Bill & Melinda Gates Foundation, USA & University of
    Washington, USA) and Peter Berman (The University of British Columbia,
    Canada & Harvard University, USA)

International Oral Healthcare Systems: Policy, Organization, Financing, Delivery
    Carlos Quinonez (University of Toronto, Canada)

Global Health Expenditures: Growth and Evolution
    Thomas Getzen (Temple University, USA)

Cancer Health Services Research: Improving Health Outcomes and Innovation
    Maarten J Ijzerman (University of Twente, The Netherlands)

Lectures in Financing and Delivery of Healthcare in Developing Countries
    Peter Berman (The University of British Columbia, Canada &
    Harvard University, USA)

CPSIA information can be obtained
at www.ICGtesting.com
Printed in the USA
LVHW041047210220
647558LV00003B/13

9 789811 205637